D0909438

8436240

758

My Sister, My Spouse

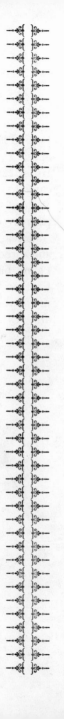

H. F. PETERS was born in Germany and educated in England and at the University of Munich. He left Germany in protest when Hitler came to power, lived and taught in England, and in 1940 came to the United States. He began his American teaching career at Reed College, and is at present professor of German and comparative literature at Portland State University. The founder of the American Institute at the University of Munich, and the founder and director of the *Deutsche Sommerschule am Pazifik*, Professor Peters has been honored by the Goethe Institute and the West German Government for distinguished service in furthering international culture. He is a frequent contributor to scholarly journals and is also the author of *Rainer Maria Rilke: Masks and the Man*.

H. F. Peters

My Sister, My Spouse

A Biography of
Lou Andreas-Salomé

With a Preface by Anaïs Nin

The Norton Library
W·W·NORTON & COMPANY·INC·
NEW YORK

PT
2601
N4
2 75
1974

To Helga—who has borne the
brunt of my long search for Lou

Books That Live
The Norton imprint on a book means that in the publisher's
estimation it is a book not for a single season but for the years.
W. W. Norton & Company, Inc.

Copyright © 1962 by H. F. Peters
Preface to the Norton Library edition copyright © 1974 by Anaïs Nin

ALL RIGHTS RESERVED
Published simultaneously in Canada
by George J. McLeod Limited, Toronto

Book design by James J. Harvin

Library of Congress Cataloging in Publication Data
Peters, Heinz Frederick.
    My sister, my spouse.
    (Norton library)
    "The writings of Lou Andreas-Salomé": p.
    1. Andreas-Salomé, Lou, 1861–1937—Biography.
I. Title.
PT2601.N4Z75   1974   838'.8'09 [B]   74-14679
ISBN 0-393-00748-0

Printed in the United States of America
1 2 3 4 5 6 7 8 9 0

3 3001 00576 1159

Contents

281841

Illustrations between pages *152* and *153*

Preface to the Norton Library Edition

It is thanks to H. F. Peters that I was introduced to Lou Andreas-Salomé and this preface to the republication of his book is an act of gratitude. He presented a full portrait of her even though not all information about her was available. He was handicapped by her own destruction of many of her letters. But through his sensitivity, understanding and empathy we acquire an intimate knowledge of a woman whose importance to the history of the development of woman is immeasurable. Peters has done a loving portrait which communicates her talent and her courage.

The lack of complete knowledge of Lou's life forces our imagination to interpret her in the light of woman's struggle for independence. We can accept the mysteries, ambivalences and contradictions because they are analogous to the state of our knowledge of woman today. There is much to be filled in about the inner motives and reactions, the subconscious drives of women. History and biography have to be rewritten. We do not possess yet a feminine point of view in evaluating woman because of so many years of taboos on revelations. Women were usually punished by society and by the critics for such revelations as they did attempt. The double standard in biographies of women was absolute. Peters makes no such judgments. He gives us all the facts we need to interpret her in the light of new evaluations.

Lou Andreas-Salomé symbolizes the struggle to transcend conventions and traditions in ideas and in living. How can an intelligent, creative, original woman relate to men of genius without being submerged by them? The conflict of the woman's wish to merge with the loved one but to maintain a separate identity is the struggle of modern woman. Lou lived out all the phases and evolutions of love, from giving to withholding, from expansion to contraction. She married and led a non-married life, she loved both older and younger men. She was attracted to talent but did not want to serve merely as a disciple or a muse. Nietzsche admitted writing *Zarathustra* under her inspiration; he said that she understood his work as no one else did.

For many years she suffered the fate of brilliant women associated with brilliant men: she was known only as the friend of Nietzsche, Rilke, Freud, even though the publication of her correspondence with Freud showed with what equality he treated her and how he sought her opinion with respect. She made the first feminist study of Ibsen's women and a study of Nietzsche's work. But her books are not in print.

If she inspired Rilke, she also rebelled against his dependency and his depressions. Her love of life was weighed down, and finally after six years, she broke with him because as she said: "I cannot be faithful to others, only to myself." She had her own work to do, and her faithfulness was to her expansive nature, her passion for life and her work. She awakened others' talents, but maintained a space for her own. She behaved as did all the strong personalities of her time whose romantic attachments we all admired *when they were men*. She had a talent for friendship and love but she was not consumed by the passions of the romantics which made them prefer death to the loss of love. Yet she inspired romantic passions. She was in attitude, thought and work, way ahead of her time. All this Peters conveys, suggests, confirms.

It was natural that Lou should fascinate me, haunt me. But I wondered what Lou would mean to a young woman, a creative and modern young woman. That is when I decided to discuss Lou with Barbara Kraft who writes in a study of Lou: "During the span of Salomé's life (1861–1937) she witnessed the close of the romantic tradition and became a part of the evolution of modern thought which came to fruition in the twentieth century. Salomé was the first 'modern woman.' The nature of her talks with

Nietzsche and Rilke anticipated the philosophical position of existentialism. And through her work with Freud she figured prominently in the early development and practice of psycho-analytical theory. I began to see her as a heroine—as a person worthy of hero worship in its most positive aspects. Women today suffer tremendously from a lack of identification with a heroic feminine figure."

Barbara felt that the feminine heroic figures hardly existed because their biographies were usually written by men. As women we sought women who would give us strength, inspire and encourage us. This is what Peters' portrait of Lou does.

We discussed why she moved from one relationship to another. We could see that as a very young woman she feared the domination of Nietzsche who was seeking a disciple, one who would perpetuate *his* work. After reading her letters to Rilke, we could understand why after six years she felt she had fulfilled her relationship to Rilke and had to move on. She showed remarkable persistence in maintaining her identity. Gently and wisely she expressed feminine insights in her discussions with Freud and he came to respect her judgment. She preserved her autonomy while surrounded by powerful, even overpowering men. Because she was a beautiful woman their interest often shifted from admiration to passion; when she did not respond she was termed frigid. Her freedom consisted in acting out her deep unconscious needs. She saw independence as the only way to achieve movement. And for her movement was constant growth and evolution.

She took her pattern of life from men but she was not a masculine woman. She demanded the freedom to change, to evolve, to grow. She asserted her integrity against the sentimentality and hypo-critical definitions of loyalties and duties. She is unique in the history of her time. She was not a feminist at all, but struggling against the feminine side of herself in order to maintain her integrity as an individual.

H. F. Peters, who fully understood Lou, quotes her own summa-tion: "Human life—indeed all life—is poetry. We live it uncon-sciously, day by day, piece by piece, but in its inviolable wholeness it lives us."

Anaïs Nin

Preface

In 1937 a remarkable woman died in the German university town of Göttingen. She was seventy-six years old and the widow of Professor Andreas, but she was much better known by her maiden name—Lou Salomé. The house in which she died is perched precariously on the steep slopes of the Hainberg, high above the town. From the balcony of her study Lou had a magnificent view over the broad valley of the Leine River below and the wooded hills on the western and southern horizon. For more than thirty years she had shared this house—but not her bed—with her husband, and for more than thirty years she had looked down upon Göttingen—"famous for its university and its sausages" —with cordial indifference. Resenting her aloofness and not quite sure what to think of a faculty wife who took no part in the social life of the town or the university, the good burghers of Göttingen spread all sorts of rumors about her. Their wives, who knew that in her younger years Lou was often seen traveling in the company of men other than her husband, called her "the Witch of the Hainberg."

They paid little attention, and were probably not much surprised, when a few days after Lou's death a police truck, led by a Gestapo official, rumbled up the Herzberger Landstrasse, stopped in front of the recently vacated house, carted away Lou's library, and dumped it in the basement of the city hall. The witch was dead. But the witch hunt was on.

The reason given by the Gestapo officials for this confiscatory

act was that Lou had been a psychoanalyst, a practitioner of
what the Nazis called "Jewish Science," that she had been a
collaborator and close personal friend of Sigmund Freud and
that her library had been stacked with books by Jewish authors.
All these charges were true. Almost from the beginning of the
psychoanalytic movement Lou had been a member of it. With
her customary élan she had participated in its congresses and
meetings, had written articles for Freud's journal *Imago,* and had
become one of the first practicing women psychotherapists. Two
years before Hitler's rise to power she had publicly acknowledged
her admiration for the work and the person of the founder of
psychoanalysis in a slim volume entitled *My Gratitude to Freud.*

These activities had not endeared her to the powers of Nazi
Germany. But she was left unmolested while she was alive,
probably because they felt she was too old and too ill to merit
serious attention. If she had been younger she would hardly have
fared so well. For the young Lou was a rebel against all established authority, an unrepentant individualist, an iconoclast and
one of the most controversial figures of her time. Her friendship
with Nietzsche in the eighteen-eighties had given rise to a
scandal that reverberated all the way from Rome to St. Petersburg, climaxing in suggestions that she be expelled from Germany and sent back to her native Russia by the police. Like
many other episodes in her long life, Lou weathered this one
with complete equanimity. She refused to be intimidated, either
by the threats of her enemies or by the entreaties of her friends.
For she was determined to live her life according to her own
standards, regardless of what people thought of her and contemptuous of all conventional forms of behavior.

She was a writer; her books on Nietzsche and Ibsen, her
novels, stories and essays made her famous. In the eighteen-
nineties her name appeared with those of such well-known German women writers as Ricarda Huch and Marie von Ebner-
Eschenbach. But she never considered writing her primary mode
of expression. A female Faust, she was not interested in rummag-
ing in empty words. She wanted to "detect the inmost force that
binds the world and guides its course," she wanted to know it,
to experience it, to live it.

She enjoyed the company of brilliant men and had an unerring instinct for seeking them out. She knew Wagner and Tolstoy, Buber and Hauptmann, Strindberg and Wedekind, Rilke and Freud. Her detractors said that she collected famous men, as others collect paintings, to hang up in her private gallery. But since her detractors were, for the most part, women who feared her as a rival, this criticism was perhaps unjust. Most of Lou's friendships were based on mutual attraction, for in addition to being a very intelligent woman she was also a beautiful one. She was tall and slender and had such radiantly blue eyes that Helene Klingenberg said: "The sun rose when Lou entered a room." Her silver-blond hair, her little snub nose, but above all her soft, willful mouth, so articulate and so inviting, fascinated all who met her. So great was her personal charm that her presence aroused powerful creative forces in the men who were in love with her. As one of her admirers put it: "Lou would form a passionate attachment to a man and nine months later the man gave birth to a book."

Like the great hetaerae of old, she knew that there is far more to the art of love than the physical act. An intimate rapport has to be established between mind and spirit before the body can come into play. Only then, only after reaching the most intense spiritual affinity, can two people enter into the fullness of love. She took the German word "Hochzeit," for wedding, literally, as the hightide which sweeps two people, even against their will, into a culminating embrace during which all their faculties are intensified. Time and again she entered into such relationships and time and again she discovered that her love partners longed to give permanence to a state which to her seemed transitory by its very nature, like the ebb and flow of the tides. Her refusal to carry on an affair once the high tide of passion was spent came as a great shock to the men who loved her. Some broke under it, others transmuted it into works of art.

"Wherever Lou went," one of her critics wrote, "she caused whirlpools and currents of spirit and feeling, untroubled like a cataract whether its course would bring blessing or desolation. A mighty, unbroken force of nature, daemonic, primordial, without any feminine or indeed human weaknesses—a virago in the sense of the ancients, but lacking in genuine *humanitas,* a being from prehistoric times."

Lou's friends would take violent issue with such a description. They saw in her a very warm-hearted, very human and entirely unpretentious woman, whose laughter was infectious and whose wit disarming. Thus, when the inquisitive wife of one of her husband's colleagues wondered why Lou left Göttingen every spring, she replied: "Yes, Frau Professor, you are quite right, it is spring fever, that special feeling we get. Alas, I get it all the year round!" It was precisely her humanity that appealed to her friends, her selfless devotion to her work, her vitality, her joy of life. Helene Klingenberg wrote: "She walks through life, her head slightly bent, as if listening, listening to all things that throw a bright splendor on her face which her eyes reflect like two promising stars of happiness."

"I am at home in happiness." This is how Lou herself summed up her life. And in the same breath: "Why is it that my most spontaneous actions have caused so much unhappiness?" But she did not brood over this question. No matter what, life was magnificent and death a return to the roots. To find those roots was her lifelong quest. She carried it on radiant, self-absorbed and entirely unconcerned by the passions she aroused. Right up to the threshold of death, while her body was gradually succumbing to the diseases of old age, her mind worked with undiminished vigor. She was almost a recluse when she died in 1937, but she still possessed that bewitching quality of the spirit that proved such a fatal fascination to the men and women she met in her long life.

Lou's autobiography, *Lebensrückblick*, was published in Germany in 1951. It did not attract much attention for it is a hard book to read. I found it intriguing, not so much because of what she said—that she was an extraordinary woman I had long suspected, having noted her influence on Nietzsche and Rilke—but because of what she failed to say. It is a book that must be read between the lines. This intentional mystification, or so it seemed, aroused my curiosity. I wrote to the editor of *Lebensrückblick*, Ernst Pfeiffer in Göttingen, and asked him if he knew of a biography of Lou Andreas-Salomé. He replied that there was none, and added that there was no need for one since Lou had said all there was to say about herself in her autobiography.

Not satisfied with this answer I entered into a long correspondence with Pfeiffer. I reminded him that an autobiography was one thing, a biography something else again and that there was surely room for a more objective presentation of Lou's life than she had given herself. Since he was, I gathered, in possession of Lou's entire literary estate, including her unpublished manuscripts, letters and diaries, I suggested that he undertake to write her life. He did not rise to this suggestion. He stressed that he was Lou's friend; he would edit some of her correspondence and manuscripts, but he was not interested in becoming her biographer. In that case, I informed him, rather rashly perhaps, I would undertake the job myself.

At first everything went well. Since Lou had been a writer I set out to become familiar with all her work: some twenty books and more than a hundred essays, articles and reviews. It was a rewarding task, for in her fiction as well as in her articles and reviews Lou made frequent use of personal experiences that provided a considerable amount of biographical information. Her unpublished manuscripts, letters and diaries posed a more difficult problem. Most of them (though, as I discovered, not all) were in Pfeiffer's possession, and he was reluctant to let me see them. I could only read them in Göttingen in his presence and under his supervision; any notes I took would have to be submitted to his inspection. I went to Göttingen in September 1958, provided with a travel grant from the American Council of Learned Societies, which is here gratefully acknowledged, and spent several months there working in the library of the university and in Pfeiffer's study.

Pfeiffer seemed genuinely interested in what I was trying to do and yet I could not help feeling that he looked upon me as a rather dangerous intruder in his private domain. He himself had published three important volumes: in 1951 Lou's autobiography, in 1952 her correspondence with Rilke, and in 1958 the diary she kept during her work with Freud. He felt that he was the only legitimate interpreter of Lou's thoughts, her life and her work. Hence his reluctance to open her private papers to public inspection. Rather than do that, he told me, he would destroy them.

Nevertheless I worked with Pfeiffer in his Göttingen study for the best part of a month. I listened to the stories he told me, looked at the documents he permitted me to see, and learned a great deal from him—more perhaps than he realized. But I could not have written this book if I had had to rely entirely on Pfeiffer's cooperation. Fortunately, a number of people are still alive who have known Lou even more intimately, and over a longer period of time, than Pfeiffer. Whenever possible I went to see them; and they were without exception willing to put their knowledge at my disposal. Here I wish to record my gratitude to them. I have tried to be faithful to the accounts they gave me, but of course I accept sole responsibility for the form in which they appear. It would be difficult, if not impossible, to express the particular debt I owe to each of them, or to mention that phase in Lou's life they helped to clarify. I must content myself, therefore, with mentioning their names: Martin Buber and Lea Goldberg in Jerusalem; Professor Poul Bjerre in Stockholm; Josef Meidl in Vienna; Sylvia Koller and her brother in Lower Austria; Professor Karl Schlechta and Tilly Wedekind in Munich; Ellen Delp in Reichenau; Professor H. Lommel in Prien; Professor Victor von Gebsattel in Bamberg; Professors Ewig, König and Kühnel and Mrs. Klein in Göttingen; Professor W. Lentz in Hamburg; Anna Freud and E. M. Butler in London; and Franz Schönberner in New York.

I am particularly indebted to Sylvia Koller for putting at my disposal a number of unpublished letters Lou wrote to her mother; as well as to her and her brother's account of the role Dr. Friedrich Pineles played in Lou's life. Here is an instance where both Lou in her autobiography and Pfeiffer in his commentaries are guilty of the sin of omission. After learning by accident that Dr. Pineles had been a very close friend of Lou's for years, I questioned Pfeiffer and met first with stony silence and later with lengthy letters in which he tried to belittle Dr. Pineles and to suggest that I omit any mention of him. He made the same suggestion concerning Poul Bjerre, the famous Swedish psychotherapist, who introduced Lou to Freud and who had also been an intimate friend of hers. But I was fortunate enough to meet and talk with this wise old gentleman. His intellectual honesty and human candor offered a welcome relief from the frustrations I suffered in Göttingen.

The rule I adopted before making use of confidential information given me by word of mouth was that it had to be corroborated by at least two independent sources. I hope that this method exonerates me from the charge of having too recklessly listened to gossip. Some aspects of Lou's life—such as her interrupted pregnancy—are hard to document. When I first saw it mentioned, in Miss Butler's book on Rilke, I was inclined to dismiss it as unproven. Even after discussing it with Miss Butler personally in London and examining the evidence which Professor Eudo C. Mason submitted from Edinburgh, I remained unconvinced. But when four witnesses came forward, mentioning the man in question and the approximate time it happened, I felt I could no longer disregard it. Even if the account I give is not accurate in all details, and necessarily incomplete—I have left open the question whether Lou's pregnancy was interrupted intentionally or unintentionally—I am convinced that it comes very close to the truth.

Truth, alas, what is truth? "Human life, indeed all life, is poetry," said Lou. Her own life, lived with such inner intensity, poses special problems to the biographer. For he often looks in vain for the outer equivalents, the day by day incidents, that shed light on the inner event. In his effort to draw a clear and convincing portrait he runs the risk of oversimplification. In trying to guard against this risk he must take to heart an Eastern proverb. "The moon," say the Orientals, "has many faces." Lou Salomé, too, had many faces. Her image appears in a bewildering variety of shapes and colors. Reflected in the distorting mirrors of love and hate, exaltation and despair, it often seems like a caricature of reality. One thing is certain, she cannot be contained in a single frame.

Here then is the record of her long and turbulent life, a gallery of pictures which extend from her birth in Czarist Russia to her death in Nazi Germany. An unusual life, whatever judgement we pass on it. *"Voilà un homme,"* said Napoleon when he met Goethe. By way of introducing Lou Salomé I can only say, *Voilà une femme.*

A Brief Acknowledgment

In writing this book on Lou Andreas-Salomé I found two previous studies helpful: Hans Jürgen Bab's unpublished dissertation *Lou Andreas-Salomé: Dichtung und Persön-lichkeit,* Freie Universität Berlin, 1955; and Ilonka Schmidt Mackey's brief biography written in French, *Lou Salomé,* Librairie A. G. Nizet, Paris, 1956. The other, not too numerous, biographical source material is acknowledged in the notes.

Here I wish to record once more my gratitude to the people whose names I have mentioned in the preface. Their help and encouragement were invaluable. There are of course many others both in this country and abroad to whom I am indebted: friends, colleagues, librarians. I wish it were possible to mention them all. Perhaps a book of this nature should carry a plaque with the inscription: "To the author's friends." One or two I must mention, however: my sister Kate (Mrs. John Cheney), who helped with the first rough draft of the manuscript; Mrs. Annilou Stavely, who saw it through the second phase; and my editor, Mr. Burton L. Beals of W. W. Norton & Company, whose monumental patience has been a source of constant wonder to me.

My Sister, My Spouse

How fair is thy love, my sister, my spouse!
How much better is thy love than wine!

Song of Solomon 4:10

PART I

A Childhood in Russia
1861-1880

I

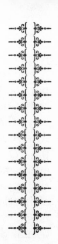

The Salomés of
St. Petersburg

SALOMÉ: THE NAME CONJURES UP CONFLICTING IMAGES OF PASSION and piety. It brings to mind Princess Salomé whose dance of the seven veils so aroused King Herod's passion that he promised to give her anything her heart desired, "unto the half of his kingdom." She asked for the head of John the Baptist. "And the king was exceedingly sorry, yet for his oath's sake he would not reject her." Less well known is another Salomé who was present at the Crucifixion and who, together with Mary Magdalene and Mary, the mother of James, went to Christ's sepulchre to anoint Him. There they discovered the empty tomb. "And they went out quickly, and fled from the sepulchre; for they trembled and were amazed."

The root of the name Salomé is the Hebrew word *shalom* which means "peace"—ironically, it would seem, for the lives of the two Biblical Salomés were anything but peaceful. That of their modern namesake, Lou Salomé, reads like a projection in time of those contradictory qualities which the name evokes. *Nomen est omen.* Lou Salomé, too, aroused destructive passions in the hearts of men. She, too, suffered the shock of the "empty tomb," when she lost faith in God as a living presence. Like an incandescent arc the brightness of her spirit illuminated many lives, but it also darkened many, for she turned it on and off at will. Self-centered and self-absorbed she passed through life almost unaware of her fateful influence on the lives of others: a *femme fatale* despite herself.

Lou, or Louise as she was christened, was born in St. Petersburg on the twelfth of February, 1861. Her birth coincided almost
to the day with one of the major events in modern Russian history: the emancipation of the serfs. There was great rejoicing.
After decades of struggle the Russian peasant had finally broken
the yoke of bondage. Everywhere freedom bells were ringing,
everywhere the traditional division of society into masters and
slaves was being challenged. Lou was born under the rising star
of freedom. And the poet says: "You will remain as you began,
no matter how great the perils and the powers, for most is determined by birth."

Lou's father, Gustav von Salomé, was a Russian general. Long
and loyal service to the Romanovs had carried him to the top of
his profession. At the time of Lou's birth the Salomés occupied an
official residence in the huge, crescent-shaped building of the
General Staff, opposite the Winter Palace. There, surrounded by
the pomp and circumstance of Imperial Russia, Lou entered the
world.

Her arrival had given rise to more than the usual speculation
about whether to expect a boy or a girl. Since five brothers had
preceded her, the bets were heavily in favor of yet another son
for the General. Even the General's wife seems to have thought,
and indeed hoped, that she would give birth to a son once more.
She was a precise and meticulous woman. The idea of being the
mother of half a dozen sons appealed to her. A daughter at this
stage would interrupt the male progression, to say nothing of the
confusion a girl child was bound to cause in a solidly masculine
household. As it turned out, the *Generalscha* was right in her
forebodings. Her only daughter proved to be far more difficult to
bring up than all the rest of her family. The General, on the
other hand, had wanted a daughter for a long time, but being a
discreet and polite man, he had never voiced such hopes openly,
and perhaps by now he had given them up. He was fifty-seven
years old. The thought that his wife was about to present him
with yet another baby filled his heart with joy. Boy or girl, he
would love it.

When the suspense was over and word came that Madame
von Salomé had been delivered of a healthy daughter, laughter

and rejoicing filled the high-ceilinged halls and corridors of the General Staff Building. Congratulations poured in from all sides. Even the Czar sent a message, and the event was duly reported in the Russian and German papers of the capital.

The German papers announced it because General Salomé, like many high-ranking officers in the Imperial Russian Army, was of German descent, or rather his family had lived for generations in the German-speaking borderlands of Russia, the Baltic States. As the name implies, however, the Salomés were not originally Germans. They were French Huguenots who had been exiled from France during the religious persecutions of the sixteenth century. Tradition has it that their ancestral home was Avignon and that they had belonged to the lower French nobility. According to an unverified statement which Rilke, that assiduous pursuer of noble lineage, made later in a letter to Lou, the Salomés were "sons and grandsons of the notary, André Salomé, who wrote his memoirs under the first Governor de Manville."

During the first stage of their exile the Salomés had settled in Strasbourg before joining the trek east and taking service, as many of their coreligionists did, with the King of Prussia. They had become firm supporters of the Prussian ideals of duty and discipline and helped administer the large estates of East Elbean Junkers, while still adhering to many of their French traditions. Lou writes that there was much talk in her childhood of the "little Versailles" in Mitau and Windau. From there, at the beginning of the nineteenth century, her father's family moved to St. Petersburg. This move, too, followed a general pattern. In their efforts to Westernize their country the rulers of Russia sought the help of foreigners. Germans and Frenchmen were particularly welcome. They were given high positions in the civil and military administration of the Empire and occupied a privileged status in Russian society. This caused resentment among native-born Russians, especially the intelligentsia, whose anti-Western and Slavophile sentiments began more and more to dominate Russian life. Writers like Dostoevsky and Tolstoy extolled the virtues of Russian folkways and created a *mystique* of the mujik, the simple-minded but generous-hearted Russian peasant. They felt the future of Russia belonged to him, illiterate and primitive though he was, rather than to the sophisticated foreigners whom the

Czar favored. A groundswell of discontent swirled around the
cosmopolitan island of St. Petersburg during Lou's childhood.
She did not, of course, understand its meaning at first, but she
sensed that something was wrong from the air of anxiety in the
eyes of her beloved father.

Gustav von Salomé had been six years old when in 1810 his
family moved to St. Petersburg, hoping to rebuild their fortunes
that had been shattered by Prussia's defeat at the hands of
Napoleon three years earlier. It was a badly timed move, for no
sooner had the Salomés settled in the Russian capital than
Napoleon invaded Russia. He vowed to teach a lesson to that
"Byzantine Greek," as he called Alexander I, for refusing to participate in the "Continental system." While the rest of Europe
watched the irresistible advance of the *Grande Armée*, the
Russian people braced themselves for the defense of their homeland. Even the foreigners among them were stirred by their spirit
of patriotism. None more so than young Salomé. Tense with
excitement, he read the daily communiqués in a language he had
quickly mastered, listened to the heroic tales of the battle for
Moscow and identified himself completely with the fate of "Holy
Mother Russia." It was his country. He would serve it and if
necessary he would die for it. When the tide turned and the little
Russian flags on the map of Europe moved farther and farther
to the west until they reached Paris, young Salomé's mind was
made up. He decided to enter Russian service. Being an unusually
bright youth, he rose rapidly. At the age of twenty-five he was
already a colonel. He distinguished himself during the Polish
insurrection of 1830 and was decorated for valor in the storming
of Warsaw. His military prowess attracted the attention of Czar
Nicholas I, whose favorite he became, and who made him a
member of the hereditary nobility. In the course of his brilliant
career General von Salomé was called to the General Staff, made
a State Councilor and, under Alexander II, an Inspector of the
Army.

His rise to prominence was not, however, due solely to the
accident of his birth. Lou's father would have made his way in
any society. He was a brave and chivalrous man, endowed with
a strong will and a militant Lutheran faith. But he was not a
stolid man by any means. Traces of the Gallic temperament of

his forebears often broke through his calm surface. Like his daughter he was noted for his quick temper, and again like his daughter he enjoyed the company of brilliant men. Lou says he counted among his friends the poets Lermontov and Pushkin.

He was tall and handsome, upright in his bearing, a warm-hearted autocrat who lived the motto: *noblesse oblige.* When he wore the gala uniform of a Russian Guards officer with his sword and row of medals, he was an impressive sight, irresistible to the ladies. But he was no "ladies' man." An inborn sense of dignity and decorum kept him from amorous adventures in his youth. After his late marriage in 1844 he lived only for his family. His love for his young wife—he was nineteen years her senior—was proverbial; whenever she entered a room he would rise. This chivalrous gesture made a deep impression on the minds of his children. They, too, rose when their mother appeared and abruptly stopped whatever childish pranks they were engaged in. Being high-spirited children—*Emigrantenblut,* as Lou says—this sudden change from playful insouciance to solemn courtesy had a startling effect on their playmates. One never knew what the Salomés were up to. When the General had to think of a name for his daughter, the last born and best loved of his children, the only one he deemed good enough was Louise, because that was his wife's name.

Louise von Salomé, née Wilm, was the daughter of a wealthy sugar manufacturer of North German and Danish descent. Born in St. Petersburg in 1823, she had been educated both there and abroad in the style befitting a young lady of her circumstances. She was a petite, blond and blue-eyed girl, meticulous in dress and manners, who became a resolute young woman. Like many girls of her generation she kept a diary to which she confided her most private thoughts. It contains reflections on life and death, religious meditations and aphorisms. Written in German, French and Russian in an extraordinarily neat hand, it is noteworthy less for the thoughts expressed than for the precision of the expression. It shows that Louise Wilm was a thoughtful and exact young girl who pondered the problems of life in a matter-of-fact and un-sentimental way.

She lost both her parents at an early age and was taken care of by her grandmother. When the latter also died, Louise, not yet twenty, was left in sole charge of a large household. Despite her youth she proved herself a very competent manager. It was this trait that first attracted General von Salomé to her. He was a great admirer of managerial competence, a talent notoriously lacking in Russian society. At last he had found the woman who shared his ideals.

Louise Wilm was twenty-one years old when she married the General. She loved him. But more pronounced than love was the feeling of devotion and respect she had for her distinguished husband. On her wedding day she wrote in her diary that henceforth she would dedicate her life to the service of her husband, her family and her God—in that order. And she kept this vow to the end of her long life.

Madame von Salomé was not blind to the shortcomings of the society into which she was born. Like her husband, she felt the revolutionary tremors in the body politic of Czarist Russia, but her deeply ingrained sense of order and duty kept her revolutionary sympathies in check. Throughout the ninety years of her life she remained convinced that there are certain fundamental truths ordained by God which man must not challenge. One of them was her conviction that the proper place of a woman is the home. She could not understand why so many women of her daughter's generation clamored to be emancipated and were prepared to forgo their natural rights to be wives and mothers for the dubious privilege of competing with men in professional pursuits. She did not deny that women had a right to be free. She merely questioned the wisdom of demanding a freedom which to her was meaningless.

When she noticed that the freedom fever of the age infected even her own children, she shook her head sadly, pretending not to understand and yet always ready to defend her children against any criticism. However much she privately disapproved of their ideas, she never expressed her disapproval publicly. Right or wrong: they were her children. Her motherly love protected them all, particularly her stubborn young daughter whose rebellious temperament caused her a great deal of secret sorrow. The very fact that Lou was a daughter, when she had wanted a son, seemed to her an act of defiance. But she saw to it that no outsider noticed the tension that existed between her and Lou, or "Ljola" as she called her, using the Russian form. Outwardly, at least, the peace of the Salomé household remained undisturbed.

No such undercurrent of tension existed between the General and his young daughter. On the contrary, a secret bond of tenderness, unknown to the rest of the family, marked their relationship. They were particularly careful not to display it in front of the Generalscha, who was opposed to any outward show of emotion. But when the General was away on one of his numerous trips of inspection he would regularly end his letters to his wife with the phrases: "Kiss my little girl for me," and "I wonder whether she still thinks of her old papa now and again?" Something of this tenderness can be seen in an old photograph which shows Lou sitting on a banister with her father standing behind her. The General, wearing a frock coat and a black cravat, holds his young daughter very gently with an air of quiet happiness on his handsomely mustached face. He was in his early sixties when the picture was taken, Lou was about three, a beautiful child with the face of a quizzical angel. She obviously enjoyed having her picture taken with her old papa. They are holding hands, and one can sense the pleasure they derive from their closeness.

The General, who was a great believer in authority when anybody else was concerned, was very lenient with Lou in this respect. Much to the chagrin of his wife, he tended to take Lou's side in every domestic dispute. When she once complained about having to study Russian in school, which she found difficult because at home they spoke German or French, he permitted her to drop the subject. With a twinkle in his eyes he said: "Louise does not need compulsory schooling." And he was right, she did not. She was a born autodidact.

Lou, in turn, did all she could to please her father. The idea that she might hurt him, even involuntarily, horrified her. Once as a schoolgirl, when she was about eight or nine years old, she was bitten by their little family dog, Jimka, on her way to school. She thought nothing of it and did not tell anybody because she loved the dog and wanted to spare it punishment. Imagine her horror when she was told on her return home that Jimka had also bitten one of their servants and had to be destroyed because he showed all the symptoms of rabies. Their family doctor, who attended the servant, said that it was too late to do anything now.

They had to wait and see if the disease had been transmitted. "How does it show?" Lou asked anxiously. The doctor explained that one of the symptoms was fear of water, the other that the patient would start foaming at the mouth and try to bite his best friend. Lou's heart stopped. "I remember the horrified thought, the most terrible thing that could happen," she wrote in her memoirs years later, "I would bite Papa!"

She had no such compunctions about hurting her mother. Once during her earliest childhood she accompanied her mother to the seashore and watching her swim, cried out: "Darling, Mushka, please drown!"

Her mother replied with amazement, "But child, I would be quite dead then."

"*Nitschewó!*" roared Lou: "It makes no difference."

There is no doubt, Lou was her father's child. She experienced the greatest joy of her young life when she could walk arm in arm with him along the broad boulevards and public parks of St. Petersburg. Her mother disliked walking but the General was very fond of it and often invited his young daughter to accompany him. Gallantly he offered her his arm which she took, fairly bursting with pride. She tried to keep up with his grave steady steps by long wobbling strides of her own. As she noticed the respectful glances that met them on all sides her heart beat faster and she listened attentively to her father's earnest conversation. He did not talk down to her. He treated her in the same chivalrous manner as he treated his wife.

Once during a walk they were accosted by a beggar. The General had just given Lou a silver ten-kopeck piece to teach her the value of money. Impulsively, as was her wont, she wanted to give it to the beggar. But her father stopped her. This was not the proper division of wealth, he told her. She needed to give the beggar only half of her money; the other half she could keep. But both halves must be exactly equal. Copper coins would not do. Gravely, he exchanged her ten-kopeck piece for two equally shiny five-kopeck ones. Just as gravely she gave one of them to the beggar, who watched the episode with awed amusement.

The happiness Lou felt in her father's company turned to bliss when he picked her up and carried her in his arms. He used to do this when she was sick and she sometimes simulated sickness merely to have him carry her. When he noticed the deception he pretended to be very angry, put her down, lifted up her frock and went through the motions of chastising her with a birch rod. At such moments her love was intense. With tears in her eyes she begged him to go on punishing her; later at night she implored God not to be angry with her father because he really had not hurt her much. And there was no doubt in her mind that God understood.

The course of Lou's life was profoundly influenced by her youthful attachment to her father. The picture of this kind old man whose love enfolded her during the most formative years of her life merged imperceptibly in her mind with the picture of a kind and paternal God. She could always turn to him for comfort and help. He never wanted anything from her, but he was always there when she needed him. Thus, the male image imprinted on Lou's subconscious was primarily that of the protector. It colored all her relationships with men.

But if her father was the ruling deity in the heaven of Lou's childhood, it must be remembered that she spent the most impressionable years of her life in the company of her brothers. Originally there had been five but two had died young. The other three always treated her as their "little sister" whose whims had to be understood and forgiven. They were all high-spirited children, especially Lou, who refused to be treated as a "little girl" and insisted on taking part in their most vigorous games. The solemn rooms of the General's official residence often rang with loud shrieks and laughter. A favorite game of theirs was "sleigh-rides" on the polished parquet floors. Lou, of course, was the horse. Wildly she galloped around the room, accompanied by shouts of "*hus*" and "*hos*," as her brothers encouraged her to go faster. She felt very proud when they complimented her on being the fastest little troika horse in Russia.

There were times, however, when her brothers disapproved of her tomboy behavior. Much to her annoyance they made her curtsy when they watched the Czar ride past their summer residence in the Peterhof. And on one occasion Lou was so incensed at her brother Eugene's unsolicited advice to be a little more ladylike that she threw a glass of hot milk at him. Eugene ducked and the milk spilled all over Lou, burning her arms and face. "You see," he said calmly, "that's what I mean; that's what happens when you do things wrongly." A scream of pain and anger was Lou's answer. With flashing eyes she rushed at her much taller brother and started pommeling him with her little fists. Eugene warded off her blows good-naturedly and the quarrel ended as suddenly as it had begun.

Such scenes were not infrequent because all four of the Salomé children were hot-tempered and not afraid to fight for their rights. The only person to whom they deferred without a murmur was the General. His word was law; he presided over his family like a patriarch. When the question arose what careers his sons should follow, it was the General who made the decisions.

Lou's eldest brother Alexander, called "Sascha," a kind-hearted but energetic man like her father, became the official head of the family when the General died in 1879. Lou says he had the most contagious laughter she ever heard. He took care of her needs for years, supplied her with money and gave her advice which, more often than not, she disregarded. But she knew that whenever she was in trouble Sascha would help her. Hence her stunned shock when the telegram of his sudden death reached her. She was already in her fifties then, living in Germany and cut off from her family by the first World War. But her immediate reaction was: "Now I am really alone and unprotected." Only death could sever her strong family ties.

Her second brother, Robert von Salomé, "the most accomplished Mazurka dancer at our annual houseballs," was a sensitive youth. He loved uniforms and wanted to become a soldier like his father. But the General vetoed the idea. Deeply disillusioned with the vacillating policies of Alexander II, he did not want his sons to follow in his footsteps. Robert took up engineering instead, a profession in which he distinguished himself. Like Sascha he married his childhood sweetheart, settled in St. Petersburg and raised a large family. He was the only one of Lou's brothers who survived the Great War. But like most members of his class he lost everything he possessed in the Bolshevik Revolution; everything, except love for his native land. Left entirely destitute he found shelter with his wife and children in the attic of his country house which now belonged to a former servant who took pity on them. Lou had tears in her eyes when she read in a letter Robert wrote her in the midst of the revolution that the humanity of this illiterate peasant was so much truer to his nature than his Marxist creed. She thought so too and believed to the end of her life in the eventual awakening of the Russian people from their communist nightmare.

An air of mystery surrounded Lou's third brother Eugene, a tall thin youth who, although not at all good-looking, "aroused the maddest passions in women." Unlike his brothers he never married. A puckish sense of humor was in his make-up. Lou remembers that on one occasion he took her place at one of their houseballs by dressing up as a woman, wearing a wig and a corset, and dancing the night through with amorous young officers who did not realize that the belle of the ball was a man. Highly amused at the time, Lou understood later in her life that her brother's eccentric behavior on that and other occasions was not just innocent fun. A daemonic streak in his nature seemed to drive him to do what he did. Her fondness for him—he was her favorite brother—is perhaps a sign that she felt such a streak in herself. Eugene wanted to enter the diplomatic service, for which he was very well suited, but his father would not permit it. He decreed that his youngest son was to become a doctor. Obedient to the General's wishes Eugene studied medicine and became a well-known pediatrician in the Russian capital. Lou says that when he died of tuberculosis at the age of forty "a duchess wept on his grave."

In her memoirs Lou mentions her brothers only briefly. They were all older than she, and while she remembers them vividly as a little girl, they faded out of her life as she grew older. But not out of her mind. The universe to which her youthful mind was conditioned consisted of men: her father and her brothers. All her life she cherished the memory of the years she spent in their company.

This inner circle, close-knit and self-sufficient, over which the General presided with undisputed authority, was surrounded by a retinue of officers and servants from all parts of the Empire. There were Tartar coachmen renowned for their sobriety, pretty Estonian maids, Swabian peasants in colorful costumes who took care of the Salomé summer home, and a host of Russian footmen and gardeners. There were members of the Greek and Russian

Orthodox Church, Mohammedans, and Protestants of all denominations—a kaleidoscope of faiths and faces, as colorful as
an Oriental bazaar, but hierarchically ordered with everybody
knowing his place and function.

As far as Lou was concerned the most important member of
this army of servants was her *njanka,* her Russian nurse, who
loved her as if she had been her own mother. "She was a gentle,
pretty woman who later, after she had made a pilgrimage to
Jerusalem on foot was declared 'a little saint' which made me very
proud of her and my brothers roar with laughter." It was her
nurse, Lou says, from whom she inherited her abiding love for
Russia and the Russian people. Much less important was her
French governess, obligatory for young girls of her class, who
tried to teach her deportment, not too successfully, and provided
her with a working knowledge of French which stood her in good
stead later on. Other than that, Mademoiselle left no traces on
Lou's development. The rest of the servants, the cooks and maids
who took their orders from her mother, and the footmen and
gardeners who reported to the General, formed the human background of Lou's childhood.

It was a fairytale childhood, spent amid what was perhaps the
most brilliant society in the world at the time. While the rest of
Europe was rapidly becoming ugly and industrialized, with the
bourgeoisie entrenched in all positions of power, a glow of feudal
glory lingered on in Russia. It was as though Europe's aristocratic
past had found refuge in the capital of the Czars. Its broad
boulevards on the left bank of the Neva, bordered by magnificent
palaces, churches and public buildings, whose heavily columnated
fronts stand out with Grecian splendor against the northern sky,
were the thoroughfares of the most elegant and sophisticated
society in Europe. In winter, during the social season, St. Petersburg's fashionable main street, the Nevsky Prospekt, was crowded
with troikas and reindeer sleds carrying bejeweled ladies in sable
and ermine and officers in gala uniforms from one round of
pleasure to the next. Music and laughter rang through the ornate
halls and corridors of the marble mansions, and on high church
festivals the granitic splendor of St. Isaac Cathedral reverberated
with the passion of the Orthodox rites.

Like the little princess in the fairytale Lou lived in an enchanted world. She was unaware that, lurking behind the splendid surface of life in St. Petersburg, were the spectres of poverty, disease, ignorance, superstition and the distant rumbling of revolt. Protected by the loving care of her father she busied herself with her own universe. It kept her so occupied that she hardly noticed the passage of time. She escaped those harsh confrontations with reality that are the lot of most children. As far as she knew, life was a perennial spring and the world a garden for children to play in. The sense of loss she felt when she was finally forced out of it stayed with her all her life. Her passionate quest for what she called "the roots of life" was her longing to re-enter the lost paradise of her childhood.

2

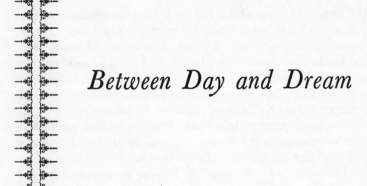

Between Day and Dream

THE SALOMÉ TOWN RESIDENCE IN THE EAST WING OF THE GENERAL
Staff Building lay in the very heart of official Russia. Situated
between Mosakaya Boulevard and Moika, one of the four great
canals of St. Petersburg, it bordered the Palace Square alongside
the Treasury and the Foreign Office, with the Hermitage. the
Winter Palace and the Imperial Archives opposite, and the Ad-
miralty to the west. It was also the diplomatic quarter—the
French, Italian and German Embassies were close by—and the
quarter of exclusive clubs, such as the Imperial Yacht Club, of
museums, theatres and libraries. Wherever the eye turned impressive sights greeted it, magnificent gardens, bronze statues on
polished granite pillars, sweeping stairways: an eloquent picture
of the grandeur of the Czars combining Byzantine luxury with
Western pomp.

In keeping with this outer splendor, the interior of Lou's home
was equally magnificent. Long corridors with parquet floors led
to spacious rooms and to the great hall at the end, resplendent
with high ceilings, white and gold wallpaper, a grand piano and
heavy brown plush furniture. Here her parents received their
guests.

On such occasions Lou was rarely present. For in spite of the
glitter and excitement of her surroundings she was a dreamy,
introverted child, living in a world of her own into which the
great world outside hardly intruded. She was not fond of parties

and stayed away from official functions whenever she could. She enjoyed nothing better than to slide silently on her ballet shoes over the polished parquet floor of the great hall. "In my memory," she writes, "I see myself most easily in that motion which was as though you were alone in the world."

Actually she was not alone. Her inner world was crowded with people of all sorts and conditions, figments of her vivid imagination. From a very early age she got into the habit of making up stories, of imagining strange and wonderful adventures in which she participated so intensely that they were more real to her than the world and the people around her. She could spend hours in a state of dreamlike enchantment, indifferent to the passage of time and completely absorbed in her own universe. This intense self-sufficiency, which at times threatened to divorce her entirely from reality, became a permanent part of her personality. All her life she found it hard to distinguish between her own imaginary world and the world in which other people lived. As a result she was often accused of not telling the truth when by her own standards she did. She writes that once as a young child she went for a walk with a somewhat older relative of hers. Upon coming home they were asked by her parents to describe what they had seen. Much to the surprise of her friend, Lou told a wonderful, dramatic story made up on the spur of the moment. This was too much for the older girl: "Disturbed in her childish honesty and truthfulness she stared at me disconcertedly and finally blurted out with a loud and terrible voice: 'But you are lying!'" In her later life these words were often thrown into Lou's face.

By far the most important figure in the imaginary world of her childhood was God. Since she grew up in a very pious household it is not surprising that the idea of God entered early into her thinking and occupied her deeply. It was a very personal kind of God who in many respects resembled her father. He was kind and understanding. He listened to the stories she told Him with infinite patience and He never called her a liar, nor did He ever scold or reprimand her. He was simply there waiting for her to come to Him. Every night, before she went to sleep, she talked with Him. Snuggling close to Him in the darkness of her room she told Him how badly one of her dolls had behaved, how cute her little dog was, and the trouble she had with her brothers. And

God listened. He never interrupted her and He seemed to nod quietly in the dark when she started every story with the words, "As you know." She had no doubt that He did know.

During their regular prayer meetings at home, when her whole family was present, God was not nearly as close to Lou as when she was alone. Consequently she did not pay much attention to what went on during these meetings, and she remembers that on one occasion, when her father suddenly asked her to recite the Lord's Prayer, she was startled out of her daydreams and started to sing a folk song which she had learned in kindergarten. She was quite hurt when her father raised his eyebrows in surprise and her brothers began to giggle. Was not God in her song?

Losing her faith in God was the first major shock that Lou suffered. It happened quite accidentally. One of the servants who looked after their house in the country, and once a week came into town to deliver a basket of eggs, told her one day that he had found an old couple standing in front of the miniature summerhouse that belonged to Lou. They had asked to be let in but he had refused because they were not the kind of people who could be invited into her house. She was troubled when she heard this and when the servant returned the next time she asked him eagerly what had happened to the old couple. She was afraid they might have frozen or starved to death. He told her that they had become thinner and thinner until one morning he had found nothing but the black buttons from the woman's white dress and the old man's battered hat. And the ground had been covered with frozen tears.

The servant's tale shocked Lou. He was obviously making fun of her and the old couple were merely snowmen who had melted in the spring sun. And yet she worried. She asked herself how something that unquestionably existed could disappear so completely, melt away, as the servant said. Where did it go? That night in bed she turned to God and asked Him for an answer. She had always talked to Him and He had listened. Now she wanted Him to speak and reassure her. She only wanted Him to say the words: Mr. and Mrs. Snow. Just those, for she knew that God was far too busy to enter into long explanations. But she waited in vain. There was no answer. The more she begged God to speak the deeper His silence, and there was something terrifying about God's silence. The darkness of her room, so comfortable in God's warm presence, became menacing. At first she cried because she thought God was angry with her and wanted to punish her. But gradually a horrible thought entered her mind: What if God did not answer because He did not exist? All of a sudden a curtain was torn aside and a godless universe appeared before her terrified eyes. What should she do now? Obviously she could not go on telling stories to God; she had to get used to living in a world without Him.

That night Lou lost faith in God as a personal presence, the sense of shelter and protection He gave her. It left a wound that never healed. All through her life she tried to find Him again, the God of her childhood. Her first book, written in her early twenties, was titled *A Struggle for God,* and when she was seventy years old she told Freud that the problem of faith still occupied her.

Lou kept her loss a secret. She still attended the family prayer meetings but when she heard her parents speak of God she felt sorry for them. What a disappointment it would be to them if they, too, discovered there was no God. Something had to be done to protect them. She decided not to annoy them unnecessarily and to be a good little girl from then on.

That was not at all easy for her because she had inherited her father's quick temper and was constantly provoked by the way her brothers treated her. They always wanted her to behave better than they themselves did, merely because she was a girl and girls were supposed to behave better than boys. Why, she wanted to know? Why should boys have greater freedom than girls? She was determined to find her own answer to that question.

Her chance of meeting other girls came when she went to school. But the girls she met there did not impress her. They were like magpies, always chattering and never saying anything. She had much more fun in her own company or with her brothers. School in fact was not an important chapter in Lou's life. She went first to a private English prep school where she mingled with children of all nationalities and then to the Protestant Petre Gymnasium where she learned nothing. No, she was not suited for public instruction. What she learned, she learned at home or by herself and later from the men she loved.

Her earliest love, when she was about eight, was the young

and handsome Baron Frederiks, an adjutant of Czar Alexander II.
The Baron also resided in the General Staff Building and Lou
caught frequent sight of him. But she never tried to talk to him,
she adored him from afar. One day when she saw her idol
approaching she got so excited that she slipped and fell on the
icy steps. Gallantly rushing to her aid, the Baron also slipped and
sat down hard beside her on the ice.

"We stared at each other nonplused. Then he laughed heartily.
I kept quiet but felt in the Seventh Heaven."

The incident is typical of the dreamworld in which Lou spent
much of her childhood. Only by accident did other people enter
into it. She did not really need them. She was happiest when they
continued to play the parts she had assigned to them in her
imagination. This trait caused a great deal of confusion later in
her life. For she persisted in assigning parts to the people she
met and was startled when they failed to live up to them. An
invisible wall separated Lou's world from the world around her.
But she felt so much at home there that she hardly noticed how
much it isolated her.

Since she grew up on a cosmopolitan island Lou was also isolated from the mainstream of Russian life. Only distant echoes
reached her of the great social ferment in Russia which had begun
with the emancipation of the serfs at the year of her birth and
had been growing steadily since. She noticed of course her parents'
increasing anxiety: her father's worry about Alexander's policies,
her mother's disapproval of the younger generation who were
imbued with the spirit of revolt against the established order. But
she took no active part in it. And yet, as she says herself, "It was
hardly possible to be young and vital without being affected by
what went on around me." Consciously or unconsciously, Lou
shared the revolutionary excitement that filled the air of Russia
during her adolescence. She sensed the fanaticism, the missionary
zeal that animated so many young Russians who called themselves
nihilists and who devoted their lives to improving the lot of the
Russian peasant.

She heard of the *narodniki* who went among the people like the
first apostles of Christianity preaching a new gospel of brotherhood. She also heard that because the freedom-loving youth of
Russia felt betrayed by the volte-face of the Czar liberator, the

socially-minded *narodniki* were being replaced more and more by revolutionary committees advocating terror. And it is quite likely that she was secretly thrilled by the acts of terrorism committed in the name of "Holy Mother Russia." In fact, hidden in her desk drawer, she kept a picture of the revolutionary heroine Vera Sassulitsch, who in January, 1878, made an attempt on the life of the hated Governor of St. Petersburg.

By temperament Lou was a rebel herself. Early in life she chose as her guiding principle the motto:

> Life will treat you badly,
> Don't mistake it;
> Hence, if you want your life:
> Go—take it.

She was irked by the pomp and pretense of court life and wanted no part in it. Everything about it was false and unreal. The whole of St. Petersburg was a mirage. Unlike Moscow it had no roots in the soil of Russia. "Have you ever seen St. Petersburg in a 'White Night'? In June, for example, when it remains bright as daylight. Then there is something strange about the town. It looks unreal. Everything is light and colorless. Everything seems to float. Are you made of granite, one says to St. Isaac Cathedral, are you not light as if made of grey paper, one says . . . and everything is like that. Everything exciting and not at all orderly. A dream. Yes, you have to be an official in St. Petersburg if you don't want to go mad."

There was no danger of Lou's going mad. Life was opening up for her and she enjoyed every minute of it. Undistracted now by the presence of her brothers, who were away in school, she watched the coming and going of people in the big city. She loved roaming the streets and talking with laborers, coachmen and peasant women. She found them much more interesting than the diplomats and officers she met at home. This was another source of friction between her and her mother. Madame von Salomé wanted Lou to make friends with the daughters of families of her own class. She arranged parties and afternoon teas to which she invited half a dozen or so young ladies of St. Petersburg society. Dutifully, Lou put on the party dress her mother laid out for her, tied a ribbon around her blond hair and tried to be civil to her guests. But it was no good. They had nothing in common to talk about. All the others were interested in was clothes and parties, while she wanted to talk about life, that mysterious force she felt pulsating in her youthful body. To be alive: that was the miracle. To walk barefoot over a spring meadow early in the morning was far more to her taste than dancing the night through with empty-headed young officers. She was not a bit interested in acquiring those social graces which her mother insisted she needed as a future hostess, for the simple reason that she did not intend to be a future hostess. Much to Madame von Salomé's chagrin she made no bones about her contempt for the society into which she was born. She laughed at the idea that she would soon marry and settle down like the rest of them.

Like all teen-age girls Lou did, of course, ponder the problem of marriage, but her major concern was the effect it would have on her freedom and her right to develop her own personality. She was much intrigued when she heard rumors of "fictitious marriages" that were current among the Russian intelligentsia—marriages in name only, platonic unions concluded between a man and a woman for the purpose of their mutual improvement, a sort of co-operation among comrades. "Others regarded it as a fine chance to show their contempt for an institution blessed by the Church and sanctioned by the State, a way of placing themselves above society while obeying its laws." It was a theme often used by Russian novelists. In one of Tschernikofsky's novels a married couple lived side by side like brother and sister, quite happily and without taking advantage of their marital rights. When the husband realized that his wife was having an affair with his best friend, he discreetly withdrew so as not to embarrass the lovers. Such ideas were grist to the mill of a young rebel like Lou. Most of them she would try out herself.

She still enjoyed the company of her father most of all. But the General, now in his seventies, was showing signs of his age. He was obviously worried about the future, the future of Russia and the future of his beloved daughter. Lou noticed that when he talked about the *narod*, the common people, there was a tone of reverence in his voice. He was critical of their ignorance and their superstition and yet he loved them. It was her father who made Lou see the puzzling paradoxes that Russia presents to the

Western mind. In many respects it was a backward country, crude and uncivilized by Western standards; its people were more ready to pray than to work. At the same time it was a country where many modern ideas—that of women's right to equality in education, for example—were advocated and practiced long before they became the battle cries of Western suffragettes.

"What other country," asked a contemporary Western observer, "has seen young men of good family, university students, cast off the garb and habits of their class, put away books and pen to labor like workmen in factories, so as to be in a position enabling them to better understand 'the people' and initiate them to their own doctrines? In what other country do we see young ladies, well-bred and well-informed, on their return home from foreign countries rejoice at having obtained the position of cook in the family of a superintendent, so as to get nearer to 'the people' and personally study the labor question?"

Lou was thrilled by such accounts. In long bull sessions with her brothers, when they were home on vacation, she discussed the pros and cons of the reform movement. Sitting huddled together in her room around the steaming samovar like a group of conspirators, the children of General von Salomé talked about the ills of Russia. She learned from her brothers that many girls of her class gave up a life of leisure to study medicine because they wanted to help the sick and poor in Russia's villages. Others trained as nurses and midwives or became schoolteachers and social workers. Lou admired the spirit of revolutionary idealism that animated her Russian contemporaries. There was something noble in their eagerness to get a university education. It made perfect sense to her that men and women students frequently studied and lived together. Unlike her parents she saw nothing wrong in that. And perhaps there was not, although a French critic noted that "this frequent cohabitation, even though unprejudicial to the morals, helped to increase the exultation of young people of both sexes who mutually excited and, so to speak, wound each other up."

In the cloistered solemnity of the General Staff Building, Lou felt the revolutionary excitement of the times. Her longing for personal freedom, her unorthodox ideas concerning the relationship of the sexes, her desire to get a university education, were all influenced by her Russian environment, notwithstanding the fact that she was kept isolated from it by her family and that these ideas were diametrically opposed to everything her family stood for. This was particularly true of her ideas concerning love and marriage. Her parents' example showed that love and marriage were not mutually exclusive, as she thought, but while she loved her parents, especially her father, she felt that in such a relationship one partner, usually the woman, had to sacrifice her intellectual growth and subordinate her own personality to that of the husband. No matter how much her mother insisted that such subordination was a woman's duty, Lou was violently opposed to it. If she got married at all she would insist on true equality, on a feeling of brotherhood, on respect for the sanctity of the other person, on altruism and mutual sympathy.

"Why is it," she asks in her book *Rodinka*, subtitled "Russian Reminiscences," "that we know nothing better than to be cavaliers, lovers or lords? Have we forgotten that we are brothers?"

Brotherhood and Russia—to her these words were synonymous. She became rhapsodic when she used them. She loved Russia and the Russian people because, unlike the people in the West, they were simple and childlike and had not lost the sense of brotherliness of all the creature world. They had not yet been divorced from the great rhythm of life. They were not afraid to show their feelings, their piety, their humility, yes, even their ferocity; quite in contrast to the polished hypocrites of the Petersburg society. She loved the earthen warmth of their *isbas*, those primitive peasant huts that seem to grow out of the ground. She loved the little round Russian churches with their golden cupolas, but above all she loved the wide and calm expanse of the Volga with its mixture of intimacy and distance. All this, she felt, was akin to her because it was more than a people, more than a landscape: it was a force, elemental like water, wind and rain. Its strength flowed from the depth of the Russian soul. Bitterly she complained before she died that Europe had lost that force: "Europe has no mysteries any more, no depth left, it is really dead."

But this insight she gained only gradually. She had to travel far into the West, had to become steeped in Western thought and ideas, before she could discover Russia and herself. First she had to tear herself away from the dreamworld of her childhood. She had to submit to a rigorous intellectual discipline, to a severe training in Western philosophy. All this she had to do, and did, because the man she loved with all the passion of her adolescent heart willed it so. He was a man of the West who despised Russia and everything Russian. His name was Hendrik Gillot and he was the minister of the Dutch Reformed Church in St. Petersburg.

3

God and Gillot

ADOLESCENCE IS A TIME OF TURMOIL, A SECOND BIRTH. WITH LOU IT was particularly turbulent because the revolutionary ferment around her stimulated her own rebellious nature. Her Russian contemporaries, despairing of peaceful reforms, steadily increased their terrorist activities. Shots were aimed at the Czar and a bomb exploded in the Winter Palace. Change was in the air; and Lou's life too was changing. A self-centered child she became a strong-willed, obstinate young girl.

She was rather tall for her age, and slender. Like many girls who grow up in northern climates she was slow in developing those feminine characteristics which are in full bloom with southern girls by the time they are twelve or fourteen. At that age Lou was flat-chested and had a rather boyish figure, small hips and long legs. Her clear blue eyes looked at the world fearlessly, and yet she often had an air of dreaminess that softened her otherwise clear-cut and almost masculine features. Soft blond hair with a reddish sheen crowned her high forehead. She had a small nose and a gently rounded chin, but the most remarkable feature of her face was her mouth, a soft, feminine mouth with a full and sensuous lower lip.

The turning point in Lou's life came when she was seventeen years old. It coincided with the political turmoil into which Russia was plunged in the wake of the Russo-Turkish War. It had been a very popular war. The revolutionary youth of Russia, imbued

with pan-Slavic ideals, considered it a "holy war." They wanted
to liberate their Slavic brothers in the Balkans from the heathen
Turks. Even among non-Russians patriotic sentiment ran high.
"In our German home," Lou remembers, "I sat with others and
did needlework, or helped mother in the women's organization
send packages to the front." Russia had won the war but felt
cheated of her victory by the terms of the Berlin peace settlement
over which Bismarck presided. Germany was widely blamed for
Russia's defeat at the conference table and there was a sharp
increase in anti-German feeling among the Russian people, the
intelligentsia and the army. From his sickbed General von
Salomé watched this new unrest with alarm. He had been ailing
for some time and it was impossible to tell how much longer he
would live. Madame von Salomé looked after her husband with
quiet efficiency but could not dispell the gloom that settled over
her family. Lou especially was disconsolate. The idea that she
might lose her beloved father was beyond her comprehension.
She spent hours sitting by his bedside, reading to him or trying
to cheer him up with light conversation.

It was not easy for her, for she was just then in the throes of a
serious crisis of conscience. She was getting religious instruction
in preparation for her confirmation. Like her brothers she was to
be confirmed by Pastor Dalton of the Reformed Evangelical
Church. It was her father's church. The General had been in-
strumental in its establishment by personally obtaining the Czar's
permission to found a Lutheran church in the Russian capital.
This was one reason why Lou took her instruction very seriously.
The other was, of course, that it dealt with problems that had
troubled her as a child. Although she had long since lost her
childish faith, she felt she had to come to the defense of the God
of her childhood, as she listened to the learned theological arguments Pastor Dalton advanced to prove His existence. Her piety
revolted against the need of such proofs and on one occasion,
when Dalton talked about God's omnipresence, concluding with
the categorical statement that there was no place where God was
not, she interrupted him quickly by saying: "Oh, yes, there was—
Hell!"

Taken aback, Pastor Dalton considered it from then on his
special duty to impress upon General von Salomé's young daugh-

ter the traditional truths of the Protestant faith. But the more
dogmatic he became the less willing Lou was to accept them. An
impasse was reached when she finally refused to be confirmed at
all and talked of leaving the Church. Dalton was outraged. Never
before had he come across such obstinacy, and in a girl too. He
felt it was a personal affront for the daughter of one of the most
devout families in his congregation to voice such sentiments. But
Lou was adamant. The only point she was willing to concede was
to take a second year of instruction. She did not want to bring
the matter to a head while her father was ill. In her heart, however, she was determined not to go through with an act in which
she no longer believed. She was, of course, troubled about the
effect an open break with the Church would have on the rest of
her family. Her father, she hoped, would understand and forgive
her. But she knew it would greatly offend her mother and
suspected it would scandalize her family's friends. However,
fear of scandal did not stop her then—or at any time in her life—
from doing what she felt she had to do.

She was still struggling with Pastor Dalton's fuzzy theological
arguments without getting anywhere when an event occurred
that changed her life. She met Hendrik Gillot. He, too, was a
minister but a very different kind of minister and a very different
kind of man from Dalton. While Dalton was a typical example of
the learned but pedestrian Lutheran clergyman, Gillot was a man
of the world, a fascinating *causeur* and a brilliant orator. Of Dutch
descent he was widely traveled, had acquired the manners of a
grand seigneur and the *Weltanschauung* of an eighteenth-century
rationalist, despite the fact that he was an ordained minister of the
Dutch Reformed Church. He was thirty-seven years old when, in
1873, he arrived in St. Petersburg to take up his duties as Pastor
at the Dutch Embassy.

Gillot was a man of considerable willpower. He had such
penetrating eyes that one felt naked in front of him. His liberal
views caused much resentment among his more orthodox fellow
theologians who thought that he was somewhat of a charlatan.
They were envious of his popularity and resented the air of con-
descension with which he treated them. One of his bitterest
enemies was Pastor Dalton.

The little church were Gillot preached was located in the most fashionable section of St. Peterbsurg, on the Nevsky Prospekt opposite the magnificent baroque Straganov Palace. Soon after his arrival Gillot was appointed tutor to the children of the Czar, a signal honor which showed the respect he enjoyed among the aristocracy. He was a handsome man with the face of an actor and the gestures and force of expression of a prophet. No wonder he was adored by the feminine members of his flock. He, in turn, was not insensitive to feminine charm although he was married and the father of two teen-age daughters. His sermons, preached in German or Dutch, became social events of the first order in the Russian capital.

Every Sunday, Gillot's church was crowded with elegantly dressed men and women of all denominations and all nationalities. They stood in the aisle, on the stairs and even outside the door. When he ascended the pulpit the heart of many a great lady beat faster. There was something about his bearing, his manner and his looks that stirred more than pious sentiments. And then there was Gillot's voice, that beautifully modulated voice that seemed like an aural caress. It kept his listeners spellbound.

The secret of Gillot's success as a preacher was that he appealed both to the emotions and to reason. He did not insist on blind faith or on an unconditional submission to Church dogma. By the cogency of his reasoning he tried to move his listeners to appreciate the miracle of life and the power of God, often basing his texts on scientific or philosophic arguments rather than on the Bible. Science and faith, he insisted, were not contradictory, they complemented each other. Man had been endowed by his Creator with a mind as well as a soul. To cultivate both was his duty. Ignorance, blindness and superstition were the real enemies of God. The deeper man penetrated into the mysteries of nature the closer he came to Him. For God had said: "Let there be light."

Presented, as they were, with an almost Faustian ardor, such arguments had a tremendous effect on the Russian intelligentsia, who were prone to skepticism and were often militant atheists. Here, they felt, was a way that led back to God without offending man's reason.

It was only a few blocks from the Salomé residence to Gillot's church, and yet for five years Lou made no effort to hear him, although she must surely have heard what a powerful preacher he was. Perhaps her curiosity was aroused when she was told that Gillot also had come into conflict with Pastor Dalton's unbending dogmatism. She certainly needed support in her struggle to free herself from the power of the Lutheran faith.

When she agreed to accompany a relative of hers to Gillot's church she was in a state of expectancy. Her father's illness made life at home somber and uncertain. Change was in the air. The world of her childhood, the private world of her dreams and fantasies, in which she had lived so happily under her father's protective love, was drawing to a close. An outer, alien world made demands on her. Not a friendly world. For the first time in her life Lou felt like an outsider in her own country, a hated foreigner. She was forced to accept responsibilities and was continually reminded of her duties as a Christian adult. This, Pastor Dalton told her, was the meaning of the confirmation vow. And her mother heartily agreed. Lou would have to take it, to stand up and be counted. By publicly embracing the Lutheran faith she would also serve notice that she was a member of the German community. That was very important just then. Lou knew that by rejecting her Church she cut the closest ties she had with any group in Russia. She would really become an outcast. But that was not the worst. The worst was that it would break her mother's heart. However, taking a vow which she did not believe would mean violating her own integrity. Could she live with herself after that? It was a terrible dilemma. If only she could have confided in her father. But her poor father could not help her any more. He was close to death.

The moment Lou saw Gillot ascend the pulpit she felt that she had at last found the man who could and would help her. "Now my solitude is over," she said to herself with deep gratitude. "This is what I have been seeking." She meant the man. "What he said was unimportant." There and then she decided that she must get to know him. She found out where he lived and wrote him a letter asking if she might see him, "but not because of any religious scruples."

"A living being entered into my dreamworld," she writes in her memoirs, "not aside from it but becoming part of it and yet the epitome of reality. The shock he caused can only be expressed by the one word which to my mind describes the most unusual, most unlikely event as well as that which is most familiar and always hoped-for: 'A Man!'"

Gillot no doubt received many similar letters from his feminine admirers. His curiosity may have been aroused by the candor of Lou's note. She did not cloak her desire to see him by pretending she needed religious guidance. She said frankly that she wanted to see the man, not the pastor. Even a less vain man than Gillot would have been flattered by such spontaneity. He received her with open arms.

Impatiently Lou waited for the appointed day of their meeting. She did not tell anybody about it. With a fiercely beating heart she walked to Gillot's house, was led into his study and told to wait. The next few minutes seemed like an eternity. With her hands pressed tightly over her heart she waited for the door to open. When it finally did, Gillot, standing in the doorway, exclaimed: "Have you come to me?" and opened his arms wide. Lou rushed into them, tears flowing, like a child seeking refuge.

From then on over a period of months she visited Gillot regularly but without telling her family. The clandestine nature of these visits added much to their excitement. In the privacy of Gillot's study they found each other: the girl transported in his presence into a state of ecstasy—there were moments when she felt she loved him as Santa Teresa loved the Lord Jesus—and the man overwhelmed by an adoration no other woman had ever shown him. Her fervor moved and alarmed him. Unless she learned to control it she would get badly hurt some day. Her overactive imagination needed restraints. In talking with her Gillot also saw that Lou had an excellent mind which, if properly trained, would act as a brake on the flights of her fancy. Quite methodically he set about to train her mind by feeding it an intellectual fare so rich it seems incredible that a seventeen-year-old girl could have digested it. But Lou did, although at the expense of her health.

The numerous blue notebooks she kept in a handwriting as neat as her mother's give an idea of the scope and intensity of her work with Gillot. One shows that she studied the history of religion, comparing Christianity with Buddhism, Hinduism and Mohammedanism; she considered the problems of superstition in primitive societies, the symbolism of their rites and rituals, and pondered the basic concepts of the phenomenology of religion. Another notebook deals with philosophy, logic and metaphysics and with the theory of cognition. A third with dogmatism and such questions as the messianic idea in the Old Testament and the doctrine of the Trinity. A fourth, written in French, contains notes on the French theatre before Corneille, on the classical age in French Literature, on Descartes, Port Royal and Pascal. A fifth has German essays on Schiller's *Maria Stuart* and on *Krimhild* and *Gudrun*. Gillot made her read Kant and Kierkegaard, Rousseau, Voltaire, Leibnitz, Fichte and Schopenhauer. He was amazed at her mind which, like a sponge, absorbed in a few months a great part of the cultural heritage of the West.

It was a violent process, a rude awakening from the dreamworld of her childhood, but it provided her with an intellectual armor that stood her in good stead for the rest of her life. Even her interest in writing was aroused at this time, for Gillot permitted her to compose some of his Sunday sermons for him. It was a valuable practice and gave her a chance to observe the effect of her words on a large audience. Alas, it came to an end when instead of using a text from the Bible she wrote a powerful sermon on the well-known words from Goethe's *Faust:* "Name is sound and fury." Preaching it exactly as Lou had written it, Gillot was reprimanded by the Dutch Ambassador, who was present, and who admonished him to stick to the Bible in future. "Slightly ill-humored," Lou remembers, "Gillot passed on this reprimand to me."

But valuable though this forced intellectual training was, it had one serious drawback: it cut Lou off from her roots and set her adrift. It was a kind of shock therapy. By activating Lou's intellect Gillot tore down the invisible wall behind which she had spent much of her childhood. He turned her around, away from herself, her home and her country, and made her face the world. She submitted to this violent process because she loved him, and all her life she felt indebted to Gillot for having liberated her. However, by a strange twist of fate Gillot soon discovered that liberating Lou also meant losing her.

During the months of Lou's secret association with Gillot, in the winter and spring of 1878–79, three events occurred which finally severed her bonds with her past. Her father's death, her break with the Church, and her frank admission to her mother that she had been seeing Gillot. Of the three, her father's death was by far the most important. He had been more than a father to her; he had been the center of her universe. Now he was gone and with him the world of her childhood. As long as he was alive she remained in the Church. She left it only after his death. To be sure, she says that her father would have understood her action, even while deploring her loss of faith, but the fact is she waited until he was dead before she openly broke with the Church by refusing to be confirmed. It was a bold, an unheard-of step and caused a great deal of suffering to her mother who confided to a relative:

"I am surprised that this completely unexpected shock passed without my falling sick. I have had to call upon my entire moral strength to get over it. And during these days I have again felt, as so often in my life, that God supports the weak. I know my simple faith is no longer fashionable but I feel very fortunate that I still have it. You say that Ljola suffers for me but I do not believe it. If she did she would have acted differently. You ask me to be kind and understanding toward her but how can I with such a stubborn girl who always and in everything insists on having her own way? . . . Ljola says it would be hypocritical and a crime to be confirmed by Dalton but I know that on other occasions she has not had such scruples."

There was widespread sympathy with Madame von Salomé who, having just lost her husband, now had lost her daughter as well. The Church was the guardian of morality. By rejecting it openly Lou gave public notice, or so people thought, that she was going to live an unchristian life.

This impression was confirmed when one day she told her mother in the presence of friends that she had just come from Gillot whom she had been seeing secretly for some time. Madame von Salomé was outraged. Gillot's reputation did not inspire confidence and his feud with Dalton was common knowledge. Suddenly the thought struck her that her daughter's rejection of the Lutheran Church had been abetted by this dangerous man. Sternly she told Lou to go up to her room and stay there. Then she called Gillot. In a scene worthy of the grand tradition she accused the minister of having committed a serious crime against her daughter and said that she would hold him responsible for it. Gillot denied everything. Far from wanting to shirk his responsibilities toward Lou, he proudly proclaimed that he accepted them. He explained in detail what they had been doing; he told Madame von Salomé that her daughter was a genius and asked her to let him continue to supervise her education. Lou, listening in her room to the, at times, heated interchange, heard Gillot gradually persuade her mother that no harm had been done and that it would be a pity if she refused Lou permission to go on with her studies. Somewhat reluctantly Madame von Salomé finally gave in to Gillot's persuasive arguments. Lou was overjoyed. Another battle in her fight for freedom had been won.

In the course of the following months the relationship between Lou and Gillot, which had been close before, became closer. But the emotional exultation Lou felt in Gillot's presence, the rigorous intellectual discipline to which he subjected her, proved too much for her. She began having fainting spells. Once she fainted while sitting on Gillot's lap. She insists that "to do anything wrong was impossible." But her insistence is unconvincing. An eighteen-year-old girl on the lap of a man whom she adores and who is obviously fascinated by her is asking for trouble. However innocent Lou was and however pure her emotions, Gillot was no saint, even though she had cast him in that role. The situation was fraught with danger. Like mute witnesses, the shades of Héloïse and Abelard hovered over them and it did not take long before the minister's intense involvement in the life of his pupil turned into love. One day, as they were working in his study, he suddenly embraced her passionately, told her that he was in love with her and asked her to become his wife. Without Lou's knowledge he had already made preparations for their marriage.

Lou was dumbfounded. Again a world had collapsed, the world of reason and spirit. Another god had tumbled. Or was the man who kissed her a god? Unbelieving, she looked at him. He was the same man still, the man she loved, and yet he was not the same. Everything was different now. The innocence of her love had gone. Something terrifying had happened. She had heard the distant roar of the ancient river-god of the blood and she knew instinctively that, if she gave way to it, she would be overwhelmed. Everything would be lost. With a supreme effort of will she got up and left Gillot. She said she would always be his child, would always love him, but now she had to leave him before his image was broken.

There were, of course, other reasons for her refusal to become Gillot's wife. One was the difference in age. Gillot was forty-three; Lou was only eighteen. Then, too, the fact that he was married and had two daughters of her own age troubled her, although in her memoirs she says that, since it is an attribute of God to be related to all men—and to her Gillot was a substitute for God— his relationship to his family would not have prevented her from accepting his proposal. The main reason for rejecting him was simply that she was not ready for marriage. "My persistent child-likeness, a result of the Nordic late development of my body, forced him [Gillot] to conceal from me at first that he had already made all the necessary preparations for our union." The poignancy of her love for Gillot was that she loved as a child. He stirred but failed to rouse the woman in her. Being an experienced man of the world Gillot suspected that, hence the secrecy of his approach. It must have come as a rude shock to him when his well-laid plan met with such an adamant refusal. "How he must suffer from the contradictory feelings that rage within him!"

Many years later, in her novel *Ruth,* Lou tried to re-create the story of her first love. As in all her books autobiographical and fictional elements are fused in *Ruth,* but the former predominate. The heroine, Ruth Delorme, is clearly a self-portrait; Erik, her teacher and the main protagonist in the story, is modeled after Gillot. The novel tells how they meet, work together, and fall in love. It abounds in psychological observations about the various forms of love: the aggressiveness of the male, the female's longing for surrender, the adoration of the child. To the modern reader its surcharged atmosphere, its emotional exultation, is rather trying, but Lou's contemporaries found *Ruth* very moving. In the imagination of adolescent girls no subject is of greater interest than that which treats a love affair between a teacher and his pupil. Lou's feminine readers at any rate took the book to their hearts and wrote passionate fan mail to its author. Some of them even came to see her and became lifelong and devoted friends. The Gillot episode thus had repercussions in Lou's life that went far beyond its immediate impact.

The setting in *Ruth* is a country house in Russia not far from Moscow. The heroine is pictured as a high-spirited schoolgirl, carefree and fanciful. Often behaving like a tomboy, she is fiercely individualistic. She wears her ash-blond hair loose so that it falls softly over her shoulders. Her Russian peasant blouse and her simple grey-blue frock are unpretentious and quite unlike the richly embroidered costumes of her playmates. She is a born storyteller and finds it difficult to distinguish between the world of her fancy and the real world around her. Her teacher Erik notices her unusual gift but is afraid that, unless it is directed into constructive channels, Ruth may exhaust herself in her dreamworld.

The moment she meets Erik, Ruth knows that a turning point in her life has come. Impulsively she goes to him and begs him to accept her as his private pupil. She is bored with school; she needs a greater challenge. Erik consents to teach her. Ruth is to become his pedagogic masterpiece. He tells her that he hopes she will turn out to be a strange and beautiful flower in his garden. Her happiness is complete. She spends night after night in Erik's study totally absorbed in the world he opens for her. "As they sat together in the silent night with the world around them asleep, they both seemed saturated with life and a kindred expression lay on both their faces, kindred beyond age and sex, desirous of life, demanding life."

Gradually Erik notices that his love for his pupil is turning into love for the woman. At first he resists it. Even after his invalid wife, who is aware of what is going on but knows she cannot stop it, tells him that he is free, if he wants to be free, even then he resists it. Under some pretext he sends Ruth away to a friend in Germany. But when she unexpectedly returns and finds him alone in his study, his resistance collapses. He takes her into his arms, kisses her passionately and asks her to become his wife. But now he discovers with shocked dismay that he has completely misunderstood the girl's feelings:

Slowly Ruth got up, an expression of utter surprise appeared on her face. Doubt, disbelief, even horror were mirrored in it. She felt as though she should call a distant friend, Erik, to come to her aid against this unknown assailant. But then she realized that it was he, it was Erik, who stood before her.

Quietly she tells him that she must leave him now because she wants to remain his child. She does not want him to step down from the pedestal upon which her love has placed him. Her refusal to submit to him does not mean she is afraid for herself:

What did she matter? But he had to stay up there where she had placed him, his life had to remain what it had always been. Everything depended on him. Otherwise was he still Erik?

She realizes, of course, that she is not being realistic, that she closes her eyes to life as it actually is and that some day she will have to face it. But not now, not yet. For the present she prefers to remain in the world of her childhood.

In the novel, as in the Gillot episode, the character of the heroine appears as a strange mixture of innocence and experience. When she met Gillot, Lou was emotionally still a child, in some respects more immature than most of her friends. But intellectually she was far advanced, the equal of men twice her age. Her mind had forged far ahead into regions where none of her playmates dared to go. It was her mind and the spontaneity of her being that first attracted Gillot and kindled his passion for her. She was so much alive, so vibrantly responsive to all his ideas, that he quite naturally assumed she would also respond to his love. And Gillot was but the first in a long line of men who made the same mistake. They all felt that this brilliant and vivacious girl who seemed to anticipate their every thought was ready for love and could easily be won. But they were mistaken because, paradoxically, the mind of this passionate woman was encased in the body of a child.

Lou herself was aware of the ambiguity of the feelings she aroused in men. There is a dream sequence in her novel *Ruth* which depicts Erik seeing his beloved in two different dreams: once he sees Ruth as a withered old maid who mutely accuses him of having failed her; in his second dream she appears as "a voluptuous harlot whose white body is shamelessly ravaged by strange men, a white body that was not hers, a seductive face that was not hers, and yet he knew: it was Ruth."

We can only guess what Gillot felt when his beloved pupil turned him down. He was a proud man. It was a terrible blow to his ego to realize that he had misjudged Lou so completely. There was nothing to do but try to find solace in his work and content himself with the role of father confessor into which Lou had cast him.

The weeks following this emotional crisis were also painful for Lou. She would have liked to go on working with Gillot for he had aroused her intellectual curiosity and there was so much more she wanted to know. But that was not possible now. She knew that she could not see him any more, but she knew, too, that as long as she lived in St. Petersburg she had to see him. The best solution was to leave Russia and pursue her studies abroad. Her choice was the university of Zurich. In the eighteen-eighties Zurich was one of the main centers of higher learning in Europe that admitted women. It was no secret that many young Russians who were in revolt against parental authority and imbued with all sorts of revolutionary ideas congregated there. A contemporary observer noted that: "Zürich in Switzerland has lately seen numerous specimens of these [Russian] girl students who strive to eradicate in themselves all the qualities natural to their sex in order to establish their right to the pursuits of the other sex—of these, as Shakespeare says, unsexed girls who, the better to rise to the level of men, work hard to cease being women."

Lou, of course, had heard these reports. But she did not want to go to Zurich to find sexual freedom. Nor was she inspired by the *narodniki* ideals of her compatriots who studied in Zurich to prepare themselves for missionary work among the Russian people. She wanted to go there for reasons of her own, chiefly because she wished to work with Alois Biedermann, one of the leading Protestant theologians at the time. Still, the fact that she chose Zurich, the center of Russia's revolutionary elite, proves that she was not uninfluenced by her Russian evironment and that Gillot's efforts to de-Russify her had not been entirely successful.

Gillot was shocked at first when Lou told him of her plans. Perhaps he hoped that as long as she lived near him he might yet win her. But he knew how strong-willed she was and that nothing could deter her from a course of action she had decided upon. Willy-nilly he resigned himself to the inevitable. Much more formidable was the opposition of Lou's family. The whole idea of her daughter studying—let alone studying abroad—was repugnant to Madame von Salomé. She would not hear of it. Since her father's death had deprived Lou of her strongest supporter she was forced to meet her mother head on. For weeks a bitter contest of will raged between them, with her brothers counseling moderation, and there were times when Lou despaired of the outcome. But in the end Madame von Salomé gave in. She had heard of Gillot's proposal and was deeply offended by it. It was perhaps just as well to remove Lou from the influence of that dangerous man.

But when everything seemed settled, an unforeseen difficulty arose which put the whole plan in jeopardy again. The Russian government refused to issue Lou a passport because she had not been confirmed. According to the subtle reasoning of the Czarist officials, a person whose existence had not been confirmed by the Church did not exist, and hence did not need a passport. In the halcyon days of the nineteenth century, passports were not as important as they are nowadays and few countries, apart from Russia, required them. It was therefore totally unexpected when Lou was told that she could not travel without a passport and that she could not get a passport unless she was confirmed.

In this predicament she once again turned to Gillot. He suggested that she and her mother come to Holland with him where he would confirm her in the church of a friend. This suggestion was accepted. In May of 1880 a strange ceremony was held in a small Dutch village church. On a Sunday after the regular service when the local peasants had left, Lou knelt before the altar and vowed to become a faithful member of the Christian Church. In view of her previous refusal to take this oath and her strong convictions against taking it, this act smacks of opportunism. However it was Gillot who administered it. It was to him rather than to any Church doctrine that she swore allegiance. Apart from Gillot the only witness at Lou's confirmation was her mother. But since the service was conducted in Dutch, Madame von Salomé could not follow it—fortunately, Lou thought, for it was almost a marriage ceremony.

"Fear not: For I have redeemed thee, I have called thee by thy name: Thou art mine." She shuddered as she heard these words with which Gillot blessed her. In a flash of intuition she understood that no matter how far away from him she would go he would always be part of her life.

A minute later, when he called her by her name, the spell was broken. She knew that Gillot had difficulty pronouncing her actual name—Lolja. To her surprise he did not use the Russian form, nor the German either. He called her Lou. Henceforth this would be her name because Gillot had thus christened her. Together with her childhood she left her name behind. As she watched Gillot in his difficult dual role as minister and friend, realizing that with this act of consecration her separation from him began, a wave of gratitude filled Lou's heart. She owed him much. He had helped her cross the threshold from childhood to adolescence, had trained her mind and made her face the world. He had made her feel that deep down a woman was asleep waiting to be awakened. And he had set her free. With the blessing of the Church he had given her a passport to freedom.

Gillot, too, had mixed feelings. Here she was, his beloved, leaving him for good after having forced him to accept the role of divine counselor when all he wanted to be was her husband. He hated the thought that he would have to return to St. Petersburg without her, to a post which now seemed empty and meaningless. Once more, as he saw her kneeling in front of him, all the love he bore her welled up in his heart. Sheer willpower and the presence of Madame von Salomé kept him from interrupting the ceremony and taking her into his arms. He knew that he could never forget her, no matter how long he lived. There would always be an irreparable sense of loss. Perhaps he felt at this moment what most men did who fell in love with Lou: that love and hate spring from the same root and that a disappointed heart becomes bitter and resentful. In any event, while Gillot the minister blessed and forgave Lou, the man could not.

4

From St. Petersburg to
Rome via Zurich

IN SEPTEMBER, 1880, THE WIDOW OF GENERAL VON SALOMÉ AND her nineteen-year-old daughter arrived in Zurich. It was not their first visit. While the General was alive the family had often spent their vacations in Switzerland. Lately, good friends of theirs from St. Petersburg had bought a house in Ries near Zurich. They helped the two women get settled.

Zurich was then, as even now in some respects, an oversize Swiss village which had grown into a busy commercial center and took pride in being called "the most cosmopolitan *Kleinstadt* in the world." It owes its size and fame not only to the undoubted industry of its citizens but to its magnificent Alpine setting on the north shore of the lake that bears its name. Surrounded by wooded hillsides to the east and west, it is framed on the southern horizon by the snow-capped chain of the Swiss Alps. A group of ancient churches and monasteries on both banks of the Limmat River, that traverses the city, forms its inner core and reminds the passing stranger of the powerful Christian tradition of its inhabitants. *Ora et labora*—pray and work—has always been the motto of the people of Zurich, with perhaps a greater emphasis on the word "work."

Much to their chagrin these hard-working, frugal and God-fearing burghers have time and again seen their home town invaded by a host of transitory visitors. Kings and emperors, grand dukes and duchesses, artists, writers, political exiles and revolutionaries have sought relaxation or refuge within its walls, often behaving in a very eccentric manner. The ruling head of the Romanovs spent some time in Zurich and so did Lenin while he was plotting the final phases of the Russian revolution. There is a house in the old part of town which has a tablet with the inscription: Here lived Joseph II, Czar Alexander I, Frederick William IV, Louis Philippe, Louis Napoleon, Gustav IV, Alexander Dumas, Mozart, Volta, Goethe, Madame de Staël, Schlegel, Fichte, Ludwig Uhland, Victor Hugo, Carl Maria von Weber, Liszt, Brahms. . . . Others display such names as Richard Wagner, James Joyce, Thomas Mann. A veritable stream of celebrities has passed through Zurich without, however, affecting its basically Swiss character.

It has remained, despite its cosmopolitan clientele, a sober town, over which the stern moralistic commandments of its great son, the reformer Zwingli, cast a long shadow. It displays none of the gaiety that is found in German university towns and has none of the frivolous night spots that Vienna and Paris boast of. Long ago, the city fathers of Zurich, refusing to have the morals of their citizens polluted by the often loose-living strangers among them, decreed that midnight is bedtime for every good Christian man or woman. Whoever wants to plot a revolution in Zurich after midnight must do so in the privacy of his own home.

Madame von Salomé found Swiss sobriety very much to her liking. It appealed to her own sense of Protestant morality and put a reassuring brake on the activities of those young hotheads —French atheists, Italian anarchists and Russian nihilists—who congregated in Zurich. She also liked the air of cleanliness that permeated every aspect of life in the town, its well-kept gardens, neat houses and clean streets. If her daughter had to go through with her rash scheme of attending a university—and she still saw little point in it—thank God it was Zurich and not Vienna or Paris. But the university apart, she did not mind being in Zurich at all.

Lou, to be sure, would have preferred to come alone, but in this instance her wishes had not prevailed. Madame von Salomé refused categorically to let her daughter travel unaccompanied. As long as no other chaperon was in sight she would go with her. Reluctantly Lou had agreed to what seemed to her an unnecessary concession to conventional propriety. She felt that she had shown by the way in which she had handled herself with Gillot—she was quite frank about the affair and told her mother what had happened—that she was perfectly capable of looking after herself. However, it was precisely the Gillot affair that caused her mother to feel concern for her daughter's future. She was willing to believe that nothing improper had happened that time, but she was not going to risk a similar episode. She wanted Lou to get married and the sooner the better.

Lou gave her no encouragement on that score. On the contrary, she dismissed the idea of marriage as slightly ridiculous, a time-honored but old-fashioned method of preventing women from being free by transferring parental authority to the husband. She reminded her mother that if she had wanted to get married she could have married Gillot. He had asked her. Such arguments infuriated Madame von Salomé. Gillot had had no right to ask her. He was a married man and had a family. As for his getting a divorce, it was shocking that Lou even mentioned such a possibility. There was no divorce in a Christian marriage. It was scandalous for a minister to suggest it. Lou should stop boasting of the affair.

Lou said she did not want to boast about it, but since it had been the great passion of her life she was entitled to feel proud of the fortitude she had shown in turning down such a flattering proposal. Many prominent women in St. Petersburg would have been glad to marry Gillot. Madame von Salomé was indignant. What was the world coming to? The modern generation seemed to have no shame left. In Zurich she heard hair-raising tales of women students of good families advocating free love. She suspected that moral irresponsibility was the force behind the clamor to get women emancipated, and she was determined not to relax her guard.

Another reason for Madame von Salomé's worried watchfulness was the political intrigue of many young Russians who said they were students but acted more like conspirators. She did not want her daughter to become involved with them. She felt they were abusing the hospitality of the Swiss who, indeed, looked askance at the conspiratorial airs of the large Slavic contingent that had invaded their peaceful city. Madame von Salomé thought that it was a sign of shockingly bad manners when soon after their arrival Russian students carried on noisy street demonstrations and a torchlight parade to celebrate the assassination of Czar Alexander II. Thank God she was present to prevent her daughter from joining them.

Actually there was no cause for alarm in Lou's case. Lou had come to Zurich to study, and study she did to the exclusion of everything else. She took courses in comparative religion, theology, philosophy and the history of art. Her teachers agreed that she was a brilliant student, and there were famous men among them, like the theologian Biedermann, the art historian Kinkel and the historian Baumgartner. She impressed them all with her seriousness and determination.

A photograph taken while she was a student bears out this impression. It shows a tall and slender girl in an austerely cut black dress, buttoned up to the neck and bare of all frills except for white lace trimmings on cuffs and collar. Her little nun's dress, she called it. She said it was the preferred garment worn by the women students at Zurich. It was certainly a far cry from the bustle-and-pompon creations of her more conventional contemporaries. Her face was even more striking than her costume. A prominent forehead, bordered by blond hair severely combed back, deeply set blue eyes looking straight into the camera, a soft rather sensuous mouth and a well-shaped chin. Not, perhaps, a beautiful face—her high boyish forehead somehow belied her sex—but a memorable one.

The best description we have of her from that time is by Professor Biedermann, then at the end of a great academic career. He got to know Lou well and took great personal interest in her. As a token of his esteem he gave her a copy of his book *Christian Dogmatism* with the handwritten inscription: "The spirit searcheth all things, yea the deep things of God." And in a letter to Lou's mother he wrote:

"Your daughter is a very unusual woman: she has a childlike purity and integrity of character and, at the same time, a quite unchildlike, almost unfeminine, direction of her mind and independence of will. She is a diamond. I hesitate to use this word because it sounds like a compliment and I do not pay compliments to those I respect, least of all to a girl in whose well-being I take

a genuine interest. I would be afraid to harm her by paying her
compliments. Nor do I want to compliment the mother on her
daughter's character for I know very well that it imposes on her
painful privations of that kind of happiness a mother is entitled
to expect from her daughter. Nevertheless, in her innermost
being, Louise is a diamond."

Professor Biedermann was not the only one who was struck
by Lou's strength of will. Her intellectual honesty and energy,
the severity of the routine with which she pursued her studies,
were noticed by all with whom she came into contact. She was
admired and feared. There were many who felt that she was far
too independent for a girl of her age, that she lacked feminine
interests, that she was too self-centered and too unconcerned
about the feelings she aroused in others. Her vitality was too
cerebral, her will too masculine. Besides, it was soon obvious
that she was studying far too hard and was overtaxing her
strength.

Signs of mental strain and physical illness had appeared before
Lou went to Zurich. She had had fainting spells when she worked
with Gillot. Now they became more frequent. She complained
of fatigue. Her face looked drawn and pallid and, most alarming
of all, she started to cough blood. Scarcely a year after they had
arrived in Switzerland her mother realized that Lou was seriously
sick. She took her to a number of watering places, put her on a
diet, and made her rest. But nothing seemed to help. While Lou's
mind was as active as ever, her body became visibly weaker. In
the end Madame von Salomé was told that the only hope for her
daughter's recovery was in a complete change of climate. She
must not stay in Switzerland in the winter. She must go south.
Italy was the obvious answer. Hence, in January, 1882, Madame
von Salomé and her ailing daughter arrived in Rome. They decided to live in Italy for a while, and there Lou was swept into a
whirlpool of events that neither she nor her mother could have
foreseen.

It started with a poem. Like many adolescents, Lou was in the
habit of writing poetry when the spirit moved her. It was really
the spirit in her case, not a momentary mood of sentimental
exultation. She wrote poetry because she wanted to express ideas,
grand and universal ideas, such as the meaning of pain and the

glory of life. A few of her poems she showed to old Professor
Kinkel who taught her art history in Zurich. Kinkel, one of the
leading German revolutionaries of 1848, and now a venerable old
man, was a poet himself. He liked Lou's verse. He was particularly
impressed with her poem "A Prayer to Life," which opens with
the grandiloquent statement:

> Assuredly, a friend thus loves his friend
> As I love you, O Life, mysterious Life;
> Laughter or tears, no matter what you send,
> Fortune and happiness, or grief and strife,
> I love you dearly, even love your pain.

Kinkel knew that Lou was dangerously ill and that she might
not live much longer. This knowledge added poignancy to the
poem. That this young and talented girl, standing at the door of
death, did not give way to morbid self-pity was, he thought, a
sign of great moral fortitude. When Kinkel heard that, to improve
her health, Lou was going to Rome, he gave her a warm letter
of introduction to an old and dear friend of his, Malwida von
Meysenbug. He asked Malwida to look after this brilliant young
Russian who was so fond of life and yet so dangerously close to
the end of it.

Malwida von Meysenbug, the grand old lady of the German
feminist movement, was then in her late sixties. A woman of
quality, she had sacrificed a life of ease and comfort to which
she was entitled by birth and had joined the social revolutionaries
of 1848 in defiance of her family. She was an idealist, a champion
of women's right to education, and an ardent advocate of social
justice.

Her warm-hearted temperament, her sympathy for the under
dog, and her concern for personal and political freedom had
brought her, the daughter of a German nobleman, in close contact
with the leaders of the 1848 revolution. When it failed she was
forced, like the rest of them, to leave her fatherland and go into
exile. For years she had struggled to support herself in England
first by giving private lessons to the spoiled offspring of the rich
and later by supervising the education of Olga Herzen, the
youngest daughter of the famed Russian writer and social critic
Alexander Herzen.

She had become one of the most indefatigable workers in the

:ause of human freedom. Wherever it was threatened she raised
1er voice, wrote articles, made speeches and promulgated prac-
ical schemes for the improvement of the lot of the under-
privileged. Her selfless efforts had gained her the love and
idmiration of Europe's revolutionary elite. She knew them all:
5churz and Kinkel, Froebel, Garibaldi, Herzen, Kossuth, Mazzini,
Wagner. In France, in England, even in America, she had devoted friends and admirers. Her personal contacts and her vast
:orrespondence with the most progressive minds of the nine-
eenth century gave her insights into the shape of things to come
vhich sound prophetic, as when she wrote: "Russia and the
geographically similar America, with their broader contours,
vere perhaps chosen to realize those socialistic tendencies which
1overed before all our eyes as the ideal of the future, for whose
ulfillment we had fought and whose downfall we were now
mourning."

Richard Wagner was a particularly close friend of hers. She
'elt that his music presaged the dawn of a new age. She had be-
:ome one of the earliest and most ardent Wagnerians and had
lone everything in her power to help the struggling genius dur-
ng his lean years in Paris. She had followed his career closely
ind was in Bayreuth at the historic moment in 1872 when
Wagner, in the presence of his friends, laid the foundation stone
of the Festival Theatre. On that occasion Malwida had met the
orilliant, young Friedrich Nietzsche, who was then the master's
most devoted disciple. She had quickly learned to like the young
professor with the serious mien whose recently published essay
on tragedy was causing a good deal of comment. But what had
eally moved her was to hear Nietzsche improvise on the piano.
5he had sensed then that an artist was lost in the scholar and
igreed with Wagner that a man endowed with so much musical
nspiration had no business being a professor.

Later, when she had settled in Italy, Malwida heard that
Nietzsche was a very sick man, that he suffered from terrible
migraine headaches and might be forced to give up his pro-
ession. Her motherly instincts were aroused and she invited
Nietzsche to come to Italy so that under her care he could recover
1is health. Nietzsche gladly accepted the invitation and asked
f he might bring two friends, equally in need of rest and care—

a law student and a young philosopher named Paul Rée. Malwida readily agreed and during the winter of 1876 she and her three scholars lived together in a beautiful villa in Sorrento, overlooking the Bay of Naples.

It was an ideal existence. In the mornings they each worked on their own projects, Nietzsche on *Human, All Too Human,* Rée on the *Origin of Morals.* In the afternoons they went for walks or drives through the glorious surroundings of Naples, and in the evenings they read aloud or talked. Whether on certain nights Nietzsche received clandestine visits from a young Neapolitan peasant girl, as Rée says, is of course not verifiable. Malwida seems not to have noticed anything unusual, but then she lived in an ideal world of her own. One of her pet projects was the establishment of an academy where young men and women could get a thorough education in the arts and sciences. She was a great believer in higher education for women. In the "Mission School" which she wanted to found, women would have a chance to compete with men on equal terms in the quest for knowledge. They would share the best teachers, they would have leisure to read, write and think, and would be able to prove that, intellectually, women are not inferior to men. At the same time Malwida did not want women to forget that they were women. In their struggle for equality they must not lose sight of their feminine heritage.

Nietzsche and Rée at first seemed to be wholeheartedly in favor of Malwida's pedagogical ideals and even offered their services as teachers. But there was a good deal of tongue-in-cheek in their offers, for in the books which both were writing at the time there was no place for any such idealistic enterprise. In his aphorisms on morals, Rée, following in the footsteps of his admired teachers, the French moralists and La Rochefoucauld in particular, insisted that the basic motivation of all human actions was vanity. And Nietzsche, then an admirer of Voltaire, directed bitter barbs against the "intellectual" woman.

Even Malwida realized in the end that there was not much chance of getting support for her school from her two skeptical protégés. But her disappointment did not lessen her friendly feelings for them. While she deplored their ideas, she remained genuinely fond of them personally. This was especially true of

Paul Rée, whom she treated almost like a son.

When, after many years of wandering, Malwida finally made her home in Rome, "the only town that is a living poem and satisfies the aesthetic needs of the soul," her drawing room on the top floor of a house in the Via della Polveriera, next to the Colosseum and overlooking the Albanian hills and the Aventine, became a meeting place of writers, musicians, artists and politicians from all parts of the world. They came to pay homage to one of the noblest souls of the age, whose major work, *Memoirs of an Idealist,* shows to what heights the human spirit can rise when it obeys the dictates of conscience.

Among Malwida's visitors was the French writer Romain Rolland, who describes her as "a little woman, simple in dress and bearing, her eyes wide and their texture more vigorous than her frail person; in the protruding globe, the iris was clear blue. . . . There was nothing pinched about her face. A rather heavy nose, a large mouth, a firm bone structure for cheeks and chin. . . . The most striking thing about her face was the virile crease at the corners of her lips.

"Her drawing room in Rome boasted a white bust of Wagner against a purple background, and anemones in a silver vase.

"Their texture was not more delicate and transparent than was the little old lady with greyish-blue eyes and white hair drawn tightly back under a black neckerchief who, smiling and silent, calm and quick, came toward me with noiseless steps, took my hand, and pierced me with that limpid look of hers which washed one's soul of its impurities without seeing them and then went on to its depths. . . .

"She had passed a whole lifetime with the heroes and monsters of the spirit, their sorrows and their contaminations; all had confided in her, and nothing had altered the crystal of her thought."

Lou could hardly wait to meet this extraordinary woman. She had read Malwida's memoirs with great emotion. Here was a woman very much like herself in background and upbringing who had dared to defy the whole world in order to be able to live her life according to her own ideals. Like herself, Malwida had been forced to struggle against the prejudices of her family and her class, like herself she had left the Church, and, again like herself, she had experienced the joys and sorrows of a great love.

There were passages in Malwida's book that startled Lou because she felt she could have written them herself. The one, for example, where Malwida speaks of the unity of being went straight to her heart. Again and again she read it: "The atom of carbon which today is part of the mechanism of immortal thoughts in a poet's brain and tomorrow blooms forth as a flower or, in the throat of a lark high in the eternal ether, sings a hymn of joy to light, seemed to me to be the profound proof of unity of being." Or another one, where Malwida deplores the educational system of her time which keeps people, especially women, "away from the great liberalizing influences, from association with elemental forces, from everything primitive, and thus destroys all originality in them. To be able to give oneself up to great impressions with real zest is what makes people strong and good. To seek intercourse with stars on bright, lonely nights, to step boldly into the most difficult labyrinth of thought, to harden one's body by struggling with storms and waves, to look death fearlessly in the face and bear its pain with understanding . . ." Such passages thrilled and excited Lou, for the thoughts they expressed were her own thoughts and she was determined to live them even as Malwida had.

Soon after her arrival in Rome she made her way to the Via della Polveriera. There she was received with the utmost kindness. Malwida took her in as if she had been her own daughter. In many heart-to-heart talks they got to know each other: the little old lady with the stormy past and the young girl standing on the threshold of life—or death. For Malwida had heard from Kinkel how ill Lou was and how badly in need of rest and peace. She knew what this meant because she was of delicate health herself and had passed through similar crises more than once in her life. Her sympathy deeply aroused, she did all in her power to make Lou's stay in Rome pleasant and agreeable. The better she got to know her, the more she was struck—just as Lou had been after reading Malwida's book—by the similarity of their interests and ideals. "It is long since I have felt such a warm tenderness for a young girl," she wrote Lou. "When I first met you I felt as though my own youth was re-arising."

As it turned out, Malwida was mistaken. She did not understand, nor did Lou at the time, that a wide gulf separated their
personalities and their aims and objectives in life. Lou was by
nature self-centered. She was determined to live her life regardless of the consequences to herself or to others. Malwida was an
altruistic idealist. She was bent on following her own conscience,
but only if in doing so she did not hurt others. She gave up her
plan to emigrate to America when she heard it would break her
mother's heart. No such consideration would have stopped Lou
from doing what she wanted to do.

The event that cast the first shadow over the relationship between Lou and Malwida occurred when Paul Rée came to Rome
to visit his former patroness. "It happened in Rome one evening
in March, 1882," Lou writes. "A few friends were sitting in
Malwida von Meysenbug's salon when the bell rang and Malwida's faithful servant Trina came rushing in. She whispered something into her mistress's ear, whereupon Malwida stepped quickly
over to her bureau, took out some money and left the room. She
laughed when she returned but the fine silken kerchief on her
head fluttered from excitement. At her side stood young Paul
Rée, an old friend of hers, whom she loved like a son. He had
just come, head over heels, from Monte Carlo, and was in a hurry
to return the fare he had borrowed from a waiter after he had
gambled away everything he possessed, literally everything."

Lou was much amused by Rée's dramatic entrance. It made
him appear like a real daredevil, a bold adventurer who had
suddenly stepped into her life out of a Roman night.

"Paolo," as Malwida affectionately called him, was the son of
a wealthy Prussian landowner. He was thirty-two years old. He
was interested in philosophy but, bowing to his father's wishes,
he had studied law. However, the Franco-Prussian War, in
which he was wounded, had cut short his law career and after
his return home he had decided to take up the subject of his
choice after all. He had studied philosophy at Halle and had
published, anonymously, a small book of aphorisms entitled
Psychological Observations which had led to his friendship with
Nietzsche, who called him "a very thoughtful and talented person, a follower of Schopenhauer."

All who came in contact with Rée stressed his kindness and

generosity. He was unassuming and possessed a gently ironic sense of humor. His appearance was not distinguished. His rather soft, roundish face, in which the nose was the most prominent feature, made him look pudgy and squat, an impression that was heightened by his thick neck and stout body. An aura of sadness surrounded him even at the times when he seemed cheerful and relaxed. He was Jewish and suffered from an intense, almost pathological, self-hatred. Lou, who got to know him well, writes that it was almost frightening to see how Rée disintegrated when the stigma of his origin was mentioned.

"I have often observed half-Jews who suffer from their mixed birth, but their suffering can hardly be called pathological. It is almost normal, like the limping of a man who has a long and a short leg. But to see someone with two healthy legs limp as Rée did is horrible beyond description."

As a philosopher Rée started by being a follower of Schopenhauer but he went far beyond the latter's pessimism. Nietzsche called him "the boldest and coldest thinker" he knew. Rée's concern was with the problem of ethics. He subjected the moral universe to a rigorous scientific analysis and reached the conclusion that it did not exist. "Our ideas of good and evil are products of culture, not nature," he wrote. There is no innate moral sense. God is an illusion and the Heavenly Kingdom a mirrored image of man and earth. But man and earth, too, are illusions. They are products of the mind. The object does not exist. Every "objective something" turns out to be something subjective. Kant and Berkeley were right: "Our body is nothing but a complexion of such qualities or ideas as have no existence distinct from being perceived by a mind." But they were wrong in assuming that there must be something, a "thing in itself," or a "God" behind the phenomenal world. They lacked the courage to think their thoughts to the end. They dared not face up to the void, the nothingness of existence. Rée had that courage, but he paid a terrible price for it: he reached the conclusion that life was meaningless, and murder a lesser crime than creation. His own tragic life—he fell to his death (or did he jump?) in the mountains of the Upper Engadine—epitomizes his philosophy and illustrates Lou's point that all philosophical systems reflect the personal lives of philosophers.

As Rée, led by his motherly friend, entered Malwida's drawing room on that historic night in March, he was pleasantly surprised to see a new face among the dignified countenances of Malwida's visitors. A young face, pale but with the interesting pallor of a high-strung, intellectually active temperament. He and Lou were introduced and spent the rest of the evening talking. When Lou left to go back to the pension where she and her mother were staying, Rée asked to accompany her. Lou accepted without hesitation. But Malwida paused before bidding them good-by. She wondered whether it was proper for Lou to accept in such a nonchalant fashion the company of a young man she hardly knew. Malwida was troubled by the behavior of many emancipated women. She deplored their defiant attitudes and strident gestures. Dignity and decorum, she insisted, were as important in a truly civilized society as intellectual brilliance. There must not be the shadow of a suspicion that the emancipation of women meant a relaxation of feminine morals. On that point Malwida was adamant.

And yet, as she watched them leaving together now, Lou and her dear Paolo, a wave of expectancy rose in Malwida. She had long been worrying about Paul. His ideas seemed to her all wrong. His solitary brooding led him to quite inhuman conclusions. She felt he should get married. He needed someone to look after him and cheer him up. Perhaps Providence had come to the rescue and had sent the right girl at last. She would in any case do all in her power to help Providence, even if it meant closing her eyes to some slight irregularities. It was certainly irregular for a young girl to be out at night unchaperoned with a young man. But then, times were changing and in any case it was not very far from her place in Via della Polveriera to Madame von Salomé's hotel.

However, after they had left Malwida's, Paul and Lou discovered that they still had much to talk about, far too much for a short walk. It was a beautiful, starlit night with spring in the air and it seemed a pity to go straight home. They decided to keep on walking, across the Square San Pietro in Vincoli and by the monastery of the Monks of Lebanon. They strolled past Forum and Colosseum and watched the moon in the distance silhouetting the Aqua Paola on the Janiculum. And they talked, they talked incessantly, each trying to outtalk the other.

The range of their interests was very similar; they were both philosophers. Lou told Rée of her studies in Zurich, what she had learned from Biedermann, and why she was interested in metaphysical speculations. She also told him of her break with the Church and her search for God. That was a topic always on her mind. Since Rée considered God an illusion, there was perhaps an amused smile on his face as he listened to Lou's impassioned arguments. It was not so much what she said, as the way she said it, that intrigued him. Her face, her whole body, seemed filled with speech. It was evident that she was very much in earnest, that these problems really troubled her. What a pity that he had to disillusion her. He told her that many sensitive young people who believe in God are shocked when they discover that He does not exist. But such shocks are a necessary part of growing up. Our childish faith is like an umbilical cord which gives us a sense of security when our minds are immature and the world around us too vast for our comprehension. God belongs to the world of children, like legends and fairytales. There is no room for Him in the world of adults. The growth of reason inevitably leads to a decline of faith.

It is unlikely that Lou was impressed by such arguments. She had read Kant, she knew that there were limits to reason. Reason could not explain the mystery of life; that was why man needed faith. She challenged Rée to explain the phenomenon of the *homo religiosus,* the man who believes in God because he has experienced Him. Reason cannot deny the reality of such experiences. This provided Rée with an opening to expound his theories on how to investigate the phenomenon of religion. He believed it could only be done by probing man's inner self. A new science was needed—psychology. He told Lou that he himself had done some work on it and that he had written a book on the origin of morals.

Lou wanted to read it. She was always eager to explore new roads that promised to lead closer to the central mystery of life. Rée volunteered to explain his psychological observations on subsequent walks. He found the company of this intelligent young girl fascinating and exciting. As for Lou, she certainly enjoyed walking and talking with Rée far more than sitting among elderly ladies in Malwida's drawing room. She proposed they meet again the following night. Realizing that both Malwida and Madame von Salomé were bound to object to unchaperoned walks, they decided not to tell them.

One walk followed another, and in the course of these clandestine nightly excursions several things happened. Lou saw many aspects of Roman life that no young lady of her class would normally see. So this was the night life of a big city: elegance and squalor, virtue and vice, magnified under the cloak of darkness. Street vendors and streetwalkers, revelers in evening dress, middle-class matrons accompanied by their stout husbands, bohemians of both sexes, drunken soldiers, couples on park benches making love, and everywhere ancient monuments proclaiming the glories of Imperial Rome, *Roma aeterna:* the center of Christendom. Or Roma—read backward—Amor, the city of love.

Soon Lou noticed that her escort's feigned indifference, his cultivated scientific detachment, began to change. Rée was obviously falling in love with her. Not that she encouraged him other than by being with him at this hour of the night. She told him in unmistakable terms that the chapter of love was closed in her life. Gillot had been her great and only love. He and God. There was no room for any mortal lover. All the same, she felt flattered by Rée's increasingly more tender attentions. If she felt sorry for the turmoil she was causing him, she does not say.

It was not long before Rée reached the point where he could not bear to be so close to Lou and yet not close enough. Since, as she said, love was out of the question, he had to leave her. That was the only honorable course for him to take. In his distress Rée turned to Malwida and, much to Lou's horror, told her everything. Malwida, of course, spoke to Madame von Salomé. Now the fat was really in the fire. Madame von Salomé was outraged when she heard what had been going on and threatened to take her daughter straight back to Russia. Malwida, too, was shocked. It seemed to her incomprehensible that a girl of Lou's intelligence should voluntarily place herself in such a compromising position.

"Imagine my pained surprise," she wrote to Lou, "when Rée came to me extremely upset and said he had to leave Rome at once for your sake and his. I talked to him quite sternly and asked him not to spoil a pleasant and happily innocent friendship in this manner. And I succeeded in calming him. When I talked with you the first time, before I knew of these nightly excursions, you seemed so unembarrassed that I was quite reassured. But then came your very embarrassed admission of these excursions which really looked as if you wanted to keep something secret. I knew that the reputations of several young girls had been damaged by similar indiscretions and I thought of your mother and of myself. Once before I have suffered great embarrassment because of the behavior of a girl in whom I had put my trust. Rée knows of that affair and it hurt me that in his selfishness he did not think of it. Then he came to me a second time in even greater agitation, said again that he would leave the following day, and asked me to tell his mother that he was sick. I declined, of course, and told him finally that if his flight was absolutely necessary, he should go.

"But you will understand, dear child, that I was very sad when I saw that once again the attempt to establish an innocent, intellectual friendship had failed because the will was not kept within bounds. It seemed strange to me that you should act like this, you who are so level-headed and who, according to your own confession, have experienced something so painful in this respect. Surely, you must have known that this is not the way that leads to the goal we both desire. And you did know it, too, my dear, otherwise you would not have said that nobody need know about these nightly excursions. Had an acquaintance seen you in the middle of the night you surely could not have blamed him if he had thought it very strange. And what would Rée have done if an officer or somebody else had offended you? Fought a duel? The more proudly we want to preserve our independence, the more careful we must be not to provide the rest of the world with weapons against us by our thoughtless acts."

Admonitions of this kind annoyed Lou. She did not see anything wrong in what she had done. Was it her fault that Rée had fallen in love with her? She had certainly not encouraged him. She wanted Rée to be her friend. She did not want to get married to him or to anybody else. She wanted to remain free. These were familiar arguments to Madame von Salomé but to Rée they were

new and he did not know what to make of them. He was in love
with Lou. How could he be her friend? As far as he could see
there was only one course of action for him—flight. He had to
get away from her, far away. When Lou heard of Rée's plan, she
got very angry and called him a coward. What was wrong with
men? Were they incapable of friendship with women? Could
they only be lovers or husbands?

Then she told Rée of a dream she often had. She dreamt
that she was sharing a large apartment with two friends. There
was a study and library in the center, filled with books and
flowers, and bedrooms on either side. They were all three living
and working together in perfect harmony and it made no difference at all that they were men and she was a woman.

It was a remarkable dream which she later attributed to the
prolonged naïveté of her adolescence but which should be attributed to the strongly masculine component of her character.
For if dreams are wish fulfillments Lou subconsciously wished
to be a man. The trouble arose that by confusing her dream wish
with reality her "brotherhood ideal" seemed to be a thinly veiled
proposition for a *mariage à trois*.

It was this kind of arrangement which she now proposed
to Rée, who did not trust his ears when he first heard it. For a
young girl to suggest cohabitation with two men was fantastic.
Surely Lou could not be serious. But she certainly was. She
insisted that this was one of the dreams she wanted to come true.
Rée was by then far too infatuated to be able to dismiss the
proposal with his customary ironic shrug. He gave it serious
consideration. In the end he thought it might be realized, provided the third member of such an unusual household—Lou, of
course, would be the first, he the second—was a mature man,
or better still a mature woman like Malwida. But the latter would
not hear of it. She was rapidly becoming disillusioned with Lou.
And Madame von Salomé was obviously in no mood to participate in such a wild scheme. She had just about made up her
mind to call on one of her sons for help, "in order to drag her
daughter back home, dead or alive." Tempers flared and emotions
were tense while all around them the Roman spring unfolded its
glory.

In this predicament Rée thought of his old friend, Friedrich Nietzsche, whom he had recently visited in Genoa. As a former university professor, Nietzsche would add respectability to their scheme, provided of course, that he was willing to participate in it. As it turned out, Nietzsche was more than willing.

PART II

Eagle and Serpent
1882-1883

5

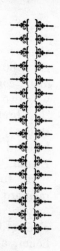

Sowing the Wind

NIETZSCHE—THE VERY NAME HAS AN OMINOUS RING. NO MODERN thinker, with the exception of Karl Marx, has had such a fateful influence on the course of world history as this gentle professor turned Antichrist who proclaimed that God was dead, Christianity a disease, and democracy a sham. Nietzsche, the philosopher with the hammer who glorified war, ridiculed mercy and exhorted his readers to "live dangerously." These thoughts, perverted to be sure and taken out of context, have served as the intellectual armor for all the *condottieri* and would-be supermen of our time. Nietzsche himself was convinced that his ideas were "dynamite" and prophesied that there would be wars the like of which the world had never seen. We know now how right he was, but when he said these things in the peaceful eighteen-eighties, nobody listened; nobody took him seriously, least of all his friends. They considered him a harmless eccentric driven to despair by his solitude and his suffering, and they followed his erratic course with compassion or dismay, as the case might be.

Nietzsche, the retired university professor and solitary thinker —this was Rée's impression of his friend when, in March, 1882, he turned to him for help. At this time Nietzsche was thirty-eight years old and about to enter the final phase of his meteoric career.

He was born in 1844, the only son of a Protestant pastor, and displayed early in his youth those studious habits that are characteristic of the future scholar. He was a solemn and serious lad who deserved his nickname "The Little Pastor." His playmate, confidante and closest friend was his sister Elizabeth, who was two years younger and who adored him. In her eyes, her "big brother Fritz" could do no wrong. Even when he was a student, Nietzsche confided his most intimate thoughts to his beloved sister Lisbeth, affectionately calling her his "Faithful Llama."

He fulfilled his scholarly promise. At a time when most men are still students Nietzsche was already a professor. He was only twenty-four when the Swiss appointed him to the vacant chair of Classics at the University of Basel. It was an unheard-of honor, almost as if an army sergeant had been promoted to general. No wonder Nietzsche had a high opinion of himself and a correspondingly low one of most of his contemporaries.

In his personal life, however, he was far less fortunate. He was of delicate health, prone to painful digestive upsets, stomach cramps and fierce migraine headaches. There were many days he was forced to spend prostrate in a darkened room, unable to eat, unable to sleep, desperately hoping for some sort of salvation from this living hell. His repeated efforts to find someone who would share his lonely life had been unsuccessful. The women he wanted to marry had declined. The only one he could always rely on was still his sister Elizabeth, also unmarried, who kept house for him at Basel and accompanied him on many of his travels. To all intents and purposes brother Fritz and sister Lisbeth were as inseparable as a married couple. Even their frequent quarrels followed by tearful reconciliations exhibited a conjugal pattern.

The great change in Nietzsche's life came in 1879 when, after only ten years of teaching at Basel, he was forced to give up his job. His health had deteriorated so rapidly, especially his eyesight, that he could no longer carry out his duties. Provided with a small pension by the Swiss, he left Basel and became a solitary wanderer from one dingy boardinghouse to another in Sils Maria, Nice, Genoa, Rome, Turin, always on the lookout for a climate that would make life bearable and for a companion in his solitude. And finding neither, he would go up "into the small, narrow, modest, coldly furnished *chambre garnie*, where innumerable notes, pages, writings and proofs are piled up on the table, but no flowers, no decoration, scarcely a book and rarely a letter. Back in a corner, a heavy and graceless wooden trunk, his only possession, with the two shirts and the other worn suit. Otherwise, only books and manuscripts, and on a tray innumerable bottles and jars and potions: against the migraines, which often render him all but senseless for hours, against his stomach cramps, against spasmodic vomiting, against the slothful intestines, and above all the dreadful sedatives against his insomnia, chloral hydrate and Veronal. A frightful arsenal of poisons and drugs, yet the only helpers in the empty silence of this hostile room in which he never rests except in brief and artificially conquered sleep. Wrapped in his overcoat and a woolen scarf (for the wretched stove smokes only and does not give warmth), his fingers freezing, his double glasses pressed close to the paper, his hurried hand writes for hours—words the dim eyes can hardly decipher. For hours he sits like this and writes until his eyes burn."

The thoughts, ideas, insights, the conjectures and prophecies that then poured forth from Nietzsche's feverish brain established his reputation as one of the most fascinating and provocative thinkers the world has ever seen, but not until his mind had ceased functioning. Not until he was plunged into total mental darkness as the result of a paralytic stroke he suffered in January, 1889, did people take any notice of him or his writings. During the most creative phase of his life which began in 1882, the year he met Lou, and lasted until his breakdown in 1889, he was totally neglected. He lingered on for ten more years, a harmless lunatic, cared for by his mother and sister, equally oblivious of his growing fame and of the thousands of disciples who now embraced his teaching and proclaimed his cult of the superman.

The books Nietzsche wrote while he was a professor in Basel had been received with acclaim by his friends, if not by his colleagues. No lesser man than Richard Wagner, whose devoted friend Nietzsche then was, had hailed the young professor's book *The Birth of Tragedy* as a work of genius. And Malwida von Meysenbug had found much to praise in *Thoughts out of Season*. But with every succeeding book, Nietzsche alienated those who loved him. Wagner felt personally affronted by *Human, All Too Human* and crossed its author off the list of his friends. Even

Malwida, although she was much more charitable than Wagner, shook her head sadly when she read his later books. Poor Nietzsche! He was obviously sick.

Rée, however, was enthusiastic about *Human, All Too Human.* He had fond memories of those happy months six years ago which they had spent together, Nietzsche and he, in Sorrento under Malwida's loving care. Nietzsche had written the book in his presence and Rée felt that it reflected the cold and clear air of the kind of critical analysis that he cherished. He gladly accepted Nietzsche's invitation that he acknowledge paternity for the book. It was indeed a work of "Réealism," as Nietzsche punned. Only lately had Rée begun to wonder about his friend's mind. There was something uncanny about the manner in which Nietzsche had told him, during their recent meeting in Genoa, that he was about to finish a new book which contained some of the deepest mysteries of life. In a low voice, trembling with emotion, he initiated Rée into his doctrine of "eternal recurrence." Rée did not know what to make of it. He found it hard to keep a straight face. Did Nietzsche really believe such nonsense or was he pulling his leg? Hurriedly Rée left Genoa and went to Monte Carlo where he tried his luck at the roulette tables. And just as hurriedly he left Monte Carlo and sought refuge with Malwida in Rome.

A few days after his arrival there, he wrote Nietzsche. He told his friend where he was and mentioned that he had made the acquaintance of a fascinating young Russian girl. We do not know what he said about Lou, but we have Nietzsche's reply from Genoa dated March 21, 1882. It says in part: "Greet this young Russian from me if you think it does any good. I am greedy for her kind of souls. In the near future I am going to rape one. Marriage is a different matter altogether. At the most, I could agree to a two-year marriage, and even that only because of what I have to do in the next ten years."

Rée, who was deeply in love with Lou by the time he received Nietzsche's letter, must have wondered about these lines. Very likely he dismissed them as merely another instance of his friend's eccentricity.

It is also possible, however, that Rée, who had a puckish sense of humor, told Nietzsche that he had met somebody who would make an excellent disciple for him, provided he was willing to marry her because she was a girl. And that Nietzsche, misunderstanding the irony of Rée's suggestion, had taken it seriously. Such misunderstandings were not uncommon between the two. Rée often poked fun at Nietzsche's solemn manner and was amused by the philosopher's constant complaint that he lacked disciples. On the other hand Rée realized that Nietzsche was badly handicapped by his growing blindness and that he needed a pair of eyes to help him. But, in suggesting Lou as a candidate for the dual role of wife and disciple—if that is what he did—Rée could not have been serious; he himself was about to propose marriage to Lou.

In the light of Rée's subsequent action it is more likely that the idea of a two-year trial marriage originated in Nietzsche's own mind. It may seem strange that a philosopher who had such bitter things to say about women and marriage should have contemplated entering this unholy state. But Nietzsche wrote many of his sharpest invectives after his own romantic disappointments. The theme of marriage occurs frequently in his correspondence, particularly in his letters to his sister, and is discussed with the greatest frankness. There is also the case of Mathilde Trampedach, a young Russian like Lou, to whom Nietzsche proposed a few hours after he met her. Hence it is safe to assume that the thought of marrying Lou occurred to Nietzsche the moment he heard of her.

Lou had heard about Nietzsche from Rée in the course of their long talks in Rome. It was pretty obvious, Rée felt, that the young Russian and his friend, the professor, had much in common. They were both preoccupied with the quest for a new faith, they were both unwilling to face the reality of a godless universe. It would be amusing to hear them argue. What Rée said about Nietzsche aroused Lou's curiosity. She wanted to meet him. When Rée suggested that Nietzsche was the right person for their "ménage à trois" Lou was quite agreeable. She insisted, however, that the question would have to be decided soon for her mother was getting impatient and was making preparations for their return to Russia. If Nietzsche was willing to join them there was a chance that her mother would let her stay in Italy. That was her major concern. Rée fully agreed and tried once more to get in touch with Nietzsche in Genoa. But this time he did not get a reply. Nietzsche had left. Where was he?

Rée was not the only one to ask this question. Nietzsche's relatives and friends likewise wondered what had become of him. He had left Genoa suddenly and gone to Sicily. In Genoa he had experienced a mood of intense exaltation. Like Columbus he felt he had sighted a new world. Laughter and tears had shaken him as he had contemplated his fate. There he was in Genoa, alone and unknown, but possessed of a secret that would shake the earth. There he was, *il santo tedesco*, about to depart to the end of the world, to that "rim of the earth" where, according to Homer, happiness dwells. He had felt like dancing in the streets and sometimes, when he had looked at himself in the mirror, his face had twitched and twisted in anticipation of things to come. He laughed and cried and grimaced and felt like shouting from all the rooftops who he was, for if only they knew, those good citizens of Genoa, what dynamite he was carrying in his head, they would fall down on their knees and worship him. But he could wait, his time would come. In five hundred or a thousand years they would erect a monument to mark the spot where he had stood. Columbus : Nietzsche—1481 : 1882. *Liberatores generis humanorum.*

On the spur of the moment he had decided to follow the example of the great Genoese and to embark on a small freighter bound for Messina. To celebrate this event he had written a poem, a copy of which he later gave Lou:

> Spoke Columbus: Trust, my darling,
> Not again a Genoese,
> For the blue sky is his calling
> And his lure the distant seas.
>
> The remotest now I cherish.
> Genoa is gone, is spent:
> Heart stay cold, hand steer or perish,
> Sea in front . . and land? . . and land?

It was a terrible journey; the new Columbus was seasick most of the time. When they finally reached Messina on the first of April, he was more dead than alive and had to be carried ashore on a stretcher. But his spirits revived when he woke up to find himself comfortably installed in an airy, spacious room overlooking the Cathedral Square with palm trees outside his window.

In letters that contain mysterious allusions to his fate, he told his friends where he was. Was he perhaps a king traveling incognito?

"This Messina is made for me, and the people here are so polite and accommodating that the strangest thoughts occur to me. Perhaps somebody is traveling ahead of me, bribing them in my favor?"

Carried away by his euphoria he wrote a number of poems that reflected his gay, almost frivolous mood. He called them *Idylls of Messina* and sent them to his sister to have them published. Some of them are love poems, such as "Pious Beppa," where he mockingly praises God, because even God loves a pretty girl:

> While beauty in my face is
> With piety I'll stand.
> When age has killed my graces
> Let Satan claim my hand.

In a "Declaration of Love" the poet, alas, falls into a pit, and the "Song of a Theocritean Goatherd" is a sad tale of unrequited love:

> Here I lie, sick in my guts,
> Bugs don't give me a chance.
> And over there—music, lights!
> I hear them dance. . . .
>
> She promised to visit me
> Secretly and be mine.
> Here I lie like a dog and see
> Of her no sign.
>
> She promised it on the cross.
> How could she lie?
> Or is she like my goats?
> Can anyone try?
>
> Whence her silken dress?
> Ah, my proud savior,
> Many a he-goat's been blessed
> With your favor.

It poisons the mind to wait
Loving in vain.
Thus grows in sultry night
The toadstool of pain.

Love feeds on me, darling,
Like seven sins,
I don't want to eat anything:
Farewell, onions!

The moon sank into the sea
The stars in a weary sky
Watch the greying day—
I'd gladly die!

A spirit of love and irony speaks out of these poems. When he wrote them Nietzsche was in love, in love with life, in love with his fate—*amor fati*—and, unknown to himself, in love with a girl he had not even met.

"But perhaps," he later told his friend Peter Gast, "you also feel that both as a philosopher and a poet I must have had a certain premonition of Lou? Or should chance? Dear, dear chance!"

He felt that at last the long crisis of his life was over. He had crossed the tropic and his sun was rising while that of his arch-rival, Richard Wagner, was going down. At last the world would see who was the greater of the two. His Mediterranean sun would dissipate the foggy realm of the Nibelungs.

Thus was Nietzsche's mood, when another and more urgent letter from Rée reached him. "Nobody," Rée told him, "was more surprised and chagrined by your sudden decision than the young Russian. She has become so eager to meet you that she planned to return via Genoa, and she is really quite annoyed that you have gone so far away." He added that the reason for Lou's eagerness to meet Nietzsche was "her desire to spend a pleasant year in the company of interesting people. She thinks that you and I and an elderly lady like Miss Meysenbug are necessary for such a project. But Miss Meysenbug does not want to join us." This letter tied a knot around all the complications that were to follow. It refutes Lou's statement in her memoirs that Nietzsche's decision to join them was "unexpected."

This proposal must have aroused memories in Nietzsche's mind of the winter he had spent with Rée and Malwida in

Sorrento. They were pleasant memories, although his present mood was very different from his former skepticism. The idea of spending a year in the company of two young friends appealed to him, especially since one of them was that mysterious Russian. Nietzsche-Columbus and Lou Salomé—somehow these two images became fused in his mind. He had planned to spend the winter in Messina but after a few weeks there he realized that he could not. Sicily was too hot for comfort and when the sirocco started to blow it was impossible. He suffered another fierce attack of nausea which, combined with a severe migraine headache, made his life miserable. Barely three weeks after he had set foot on his "island of happiness" he fled from it in pain and disappointment.

In Rome, meanwhile, Lou and Rée had been trying to overcome the obstacles placed in the path of their joint study project. To Lou the alternative, her return to Russia and a life of captivity in the bosom of her family, was unthinkable. Her desire to be free grew in proportion to her mother's determination to take her back home. In this predicament she once again turned to Gillot. He had helped her before, perhaps he would help her again. She wrote to him, and much to her annoyance he replied that the whole scheme was so fantastic that he advised her to forget it. He told her that she was in no position to judge men like Nietzsche and Rée who were so much older than she and so much more experienced. She must not forget that she was a woman and had certain obligations toward her sex and society. In view of Gillot's own, by no means platonic, intentions toward her, Lou was quite rightly annoyed by his "holier-than-thou" attitude. He sounded exactly like Malwida and her mother.

"What in the devil's name have I done wrong now?" she asked him. "I thought you would be full of praise for me because I am about to prove how well I have learned my lesson from you." As for her not being able to judge Rée and Nietzsche, he was quite mistaken. "What is essential in a man one either knows at once or not at all." She admitted that Malwida, too, was against her plan and she was sorry because she was fond of Malwida. "But I have known that we mean different things even when we agree. She is in the habit of saying: 'this or that we must do, or must not do' and I have not the slightest idea of what this 'we' is, probably some ideal or some philosophic notion—I know only something of myself. I can neither live up to ideals nor serve as a model for anyone else. But I can most certainly live my own life and I shall do it, too, come what may. By doing that I am not representing any principle but something much more wonderful, something that lives in me, something that is quite warm with life, rejoices and wants to break out."

Rée, who by this time was completely captivated by Lou, agreed that it was unthinkable that she return to Russia. A way must be found for them to remain together. Secretly he still hoped that she would marry him. For the time being, however, he pinned his hopes on Nietzsche. If his friend would only come to Rome and talk with Malwida, who respected him greatly, and with Lou's mother, their "holy trinity," as they jokingly called their study plan, might yet be realized. At this stage neither Lou nor Rée seems to have given any thought to what might happen if Nietzsche refused to play his allotted part. They certainly did not take his proposal of a two-year trial marriage seriously, or else they would hardly have invited him. For such a proposal was bound to turn a "holy trinity" into an unholy triangle.

While they waited for Nietzsche's arrival, Rée and Lou continued their joint exploration of the sights of Rome. They spent a good deal of time in St. Peter's. Rée had discovered a quiet corner in one of the side chapels where he could work undisturbed on his new book in which he wanted to prove the nonexistence of God. Lou was highly amused at his choice of a study and often accompanied him there to argue her point of view. One day, when they were thus occupied, Nietzsche suddenly appeared. Malwida had told him where to find them.

He went straight up to Lou, held out his hand and said with a deep bow: "From which stars have we been brought together here?"

Lou, although taken aback by this salutation from the medium-sized, inconspicuously dressed stranger, recovered her wits quickly and said that *she* had come from Zurich. They both laughed, and yet Nietzsche's words struck Lou as just a shade too solemn, even in this solemn environment. Or was he trying to be humorous? If so, he did not succeed for his whole manner belied humor. Lou had the uneasy feeling that Nietzsche believed what he said and that, as far as he was concerned, theirs was not a casual meeting.

She wrote that "the first strong impression Nietzsche made was that of somebody mysterious. He conveyed a sense of hidden solitude." She thought Nietzsche's eyes betrayed him. "They were not the eyes of many shortsighted people, they did not stare or blink at you, or embarrass you by coming too close. They seemed rather like guardians and keepers of his own treasures, mute mysteries upon which no uninitiated glance was permitted to fall. His defective eyesight gave a very special kind of magic to his features by reflecting only that which went on within him instead of changing external impressions."

Lou was attracted and repelled at the same time. There was something forced about Nietzsche's manner, a false pathos that annoyed her. She decided to be on her guard, and how right she was. A few days later, Rée told her that Nietzsche had asked him, Rée, to propose to her for him. He had reasoned that the surest way of obtaining Madame von Salomé's permission to let Lou stay with them was by marrying her. Rée's reaction to that proposal is not hard to imagine. How ludicrous could a situation become? Here he was asked to act as the intermediary for Nietzsche's proposal to the girl he himself loved and wanted to marry. Was it funny, or was it absurd? If it was funny, the joke, as so often in his life, was on him.

It is also not hard to imagine what Lou thought of Nietzsche's proposal. She had only just persuaded her mother that Rée's had been harmless. What would happen now if her mother heard of Nietzsche's? Surely she would think that there was a conspiracy to snatch her daughter away from her. As for Nietzsche's reasons, they made Lou laugh. So he wanted to marry her for appearances' sake? How noble of him and how bourgeois! She had heard that he prided himself on being a free spirit. Well, there was nothing free about this proposal. It sounded all too human to her. Her immediate impulse was to tell Nietzsche to his face what she thought of it.

But Rée counseled caution. There was no need to offend Nietzsche. The matter should be handled diplomatically. He suggested that he tell his friend that Lou could not accept his pro-

posal because, if she married, she would lose her stipend from
the Russian government and, not being wealthy, she would have
to depend on her husband's income. Rée knew that Nietzsche's
income was barely enough for one, and under these circumstances
he had refrained from making a specific proposal. This would
take the sting out of her refusal. He would imply that she had
not really rejected him, she had merely made it plain that, things
being what they were, she could not afford an impecunious husband any more than Nietzsche could afford an impecunious wife.
And that would be the end of it.

He was wrong. It was not the end, it was only the beginning.
Nietzsche was in no mood to give Lou up that easily. Outwardly
he agreed to their joint study plan, but inwardly he was considering ways and means of getting Lou away from Rée. He felt,
and with good reason, that Rée's presence prevented him from
establishing a more intimate relationship with Lou. He wanted
to spend a few weeks alone with her. But, steeped as he was in
the middle-class traditions of his Naumburg upbringing, he
knew that this was only possible if he found a chaperon. He
thought at once of his sister. He would write to Elizabeth and
tell her about Lou but in such a way as not to alarm her. He knew
his sister. If she suspected his real feelings for Lou there would
be trouble. He had to sound casual and unconcerned. In a letter
dated Rome, the end of April, 1882, he began:

MY DEAR SISTER:
Don't faint with surprise. This letter is by me and from Rome. I
have asked Miss von Meysenbug to write the address and, in addition, "private" on it so that the letter really gets into your hands only.
You will understand why. . . .

Elizabeth did understand. She and her brother loved to keep
their old mother in the dark about what they were doing. She
was probably most surprised to hear that he was in Rome. She
thought he was still in Messina. With winning diplomacy
Nietzsche wrote that "her wish had come true." She had always
wanted him to find a young assistant who could help him with his
work. Now Miss von Meysenbug, or rather Dr. Rée, had found
such a person. Alas, it was not a man, it was a young woman. He
had come to Rome to meet her, urged to do so both by Malwida
and Rée. But he was already disappointed, for

. . . up to now I have been able to observe only that the young girl has a good head and learned much from Rée. In order to form a real judgment of her I would have to see her without Rée. He prompts her constantly so much that I have been unable to discover one single thought of her own. Could you not come to Switzerland and invite the young lady? This is Malwida's suggestion.

He went on to say that Lou was twenty-four years old— actually she was only twenty-one—and not pretty. "But, like all plain girls, she has cultivated her mind to become attractive." In a postscript he added:

This letter has been delayed. In the meantime Malwida has told me the young girl has confided to her that she has striven for knowledge from her earliest childhood and has sacrificed everything to that end. I was profoundly moved. Malwida had tears in her eyes when she told me and thinks Miss Salomé is deeply akin to me.

Since the authenticity of this letter, as well as others Nietzsche wrote to his sister, has been questioned, it should be pointed out that while there is no way of knowing if it is genuine in all particulars, its general tone rings true enough. It is a masterpiece of innuendo and studied indifference. And it says as much about Nietzsche's relationship with his sister as it does about Lou. He clearly wrote it for two reasons: to tell Elizabeth about Lou and to disarm any suspicions she might have concerning the sudden appearance of this young Russian.

But if Nietzsche thought he deceived Elizabeth, he was mistaken. She knew him far too well not to see through his doubletalk. Right from the start Elizabeth sensed a rival in Lou and that thought was repugnant to the "Faithful Llama." If there was to be another woman in her brother's life she wanted to have a say in the matter. The aura of secrecy in which the whole affair was shrouded, her brother's sudden trip from Messina to Rome, the letter with Malwida's handwriting on the envelope, the urgent request not to mention any of it to their mother—Elizabeth had ample cause for alarm and suspicion. Who was this girl? She was determined to find out.

Meanwhile, far south under the blue sky of a Roman spring, Lou and her two suitors made plans for the future. They would spend the winter in Paris together, or in Vienna, attending lectures and concerts and enjoying each other's company. As far

as Lou was concerned this was settled. *Honi soit qui mal y pense!*
Once again her mother would have to give in to her wishes.
After all, it was her life and she was determined to live it as she
pleased.

> Assuredly, a friend thus loves his friend
> As I love you, O Life, mysterious life.

So goes her "Prayer to Life" which brought tears to Nietzsche's
eyes when she read it to him, particularly the last verse:

> Millennia to be, to think, to live!
> Hold me in both your arms with might and main!
> If you have no more happiness to give:
> Give me your pain.

6

The Mystery of Monte Sacro

AT THE END OF APRIL IT WAS GETTING HOT IN ROME AND MADAME von Salomé decided to take her daughter back to Russia by way of Switzerland and Germany. Lou's health had improved but she was still far from well and it was not advisable that she continue her studies, at least not in the immediate future. There was thus no point in staying abroad. This was her mother's decision, but Lou had other ideas. She had made up her mind to spend a year in the company of Rée and Nietzsche and the two philosophers were enthusiastically in favor of her plan, each for his own reasons. While Nietzsche had tried to enlist the support of his sister, Rée was not standing idly by. He wrote his mother and arranged a meeting between her and Madame von Salomé in Switzerland. Lou's future was to be settled between the two ladies. Rée hoped that his mother would become Lou's chaperon and Madame von Salomé could return to Russia without her daughter.

This is how matters stood when Lou and her mother left Rome. They agreed that Rée and Nietzsche should leave a day later and join them in Milan and then all four would travel to Switzerland together. They met as arranged, but upon Nietzsche's suggestion they decided to make an excursion to Lake Orta, one of the smallest but most beautiful of the Upper Italian lakes. This slight detour was much to Nietzsche's advantage; he was anxious to spend as much time as possible in

Lou's company. And from his point of view it was an inspired idea.

Madame von Salomé agreed to it and so the party arrived on an early May day in the ancient town of Orta, situated on a peninsula that juts out into the lake from the eastern shore. Opposite it, like an emerging pearl, lies the Island of St. Giulio, and directly behind it, gently rising to a total height of some three hundred feet, a wooded hill, dedicated to the memory of St. Francis and known far and wide as Monte Sacro. Old buildings, churches and monasteries dot the landscape and numerous small hamlets cling to the mountainous rim of the lake.

It is a superb setting, peaceful and majestic, the ideal location for a quiet and contemplative life. For centuries the bells of the ancient basilica on the island have called the faithful to prayer; pilgrims from all over the world have visited Monte Sacro and knelt before the shrine of St. Francis. The very air of Orta seems permeated with piety as if, over the centuries, layers of spiritual energy have been deposited there and become a tangible presence.

The impact of such an environment on sensitive and questing temperaments is profound. It arouses their deepest feelings, confirms their fondest hopes. All their doubts are stilled and their hearts filled to overflowing with exultation and love. It is also a dangerous environment because it bewitches the unwary and carries them into an emotional vortex from which they find it hard to extricate themselves. This is what seems to have happened to Nietzsche and Lou.

When the party arrived in Orta they decided, like most tourists, to start their sightseeing by spending the morning on the island. The crossing took about fifteen minutes in a rowboat; they left the charming Piazza of Orta behind and approached St. Giulio, its ancient square tower of weather-worn, yellow stone reflected in the blue water of the lake. The gently rocking motion of the boat lulled them into a sense of peace and serenity. They disembarked and with hushed voices walked about the old church and stood subdued in front of the magnificent pulpit of black Oira marble, fashioned by a master craftsman of the eleventh century.

The spiritual magic of St. Giulio affected Madame von Salomé

east of all. She had never forsaken her faith and what she experienced on the island merely reaffirmed what she had always
known. With Rée it was different. He could not and did not
want to believe. The force of those irrational sentiments which
he, too, felt irritated him. He wanted to get away from it.
Nietzsche and Lou, on the other hand, were deeply moved.
They were both searching—and this is the secret of the kinship
they felt for each other—for a new faith, a faith that affirmed
the power and glory of life and did not insist on the mortifica-
tion of the flesh. Was this an answer to their quest, this combination of beauty and piety? At any rate, when the party returned
to Orta, Nietzsche and Lou decided to go on exploring. They
wanted to walk up Monte Sacro. Madame von Salomé and Rée
said they had seen enough and would wait for them by the lakeside. Thus Nietzsche's chance had finally come. For the first time
since he met her, he was alone with Lou.

No one knows what happened during that walk because
there were no witnesses. But that something happened we
know from the turmoil that followed in its wake. "It seems," Lou
writes in her memoirs, "that I unintentionally offended my mother
because Nietzsche and I stayed too long on Monte Sacro. Rée,
too," she continues, "who kept her company, was very much
annoyed by that."

A leisurely walk on Monte Sacro should not take more than
an hour at the most. It is unlikely that either Lou's mother or
Rée would have been offended if Lou and Nietzsche had returned within that time. They must therefore have been away
much longer than that. By way of explanation Lou says they
extended their stay because they wanted to see the sunset on
Santa Rosa. The trouble is one cannot see Santa Rosa from the
top of Monte Sacro. Something else must have detained them.
This was the first time they were alone together, and in an
environment that emphasized their kinship. Perhaps they found
they had much to talk about and did not notice the passage of
time. But if this was the only reason they dallied, why did Lou
say in a conversation she had with the friend of her old age,
Ernst Pfeiffer, with a subtle almost embarrassed smile, "Whether
I kissed Nietzsche on Monte Sacro, I do not know now."

And what did Nietzsche mean when he said with respect to

that walk: "I owe to you the most beautiful dream of my life."

And, finally, why did Rée months later write Lou: "I am a little jealous too, that goes without saying. I am wondering what sort of attitude, tone of voice, movements and glances you combined with your words on Monte Sacro." Why did he consider it necessary to "grant her a general pardon"? What had Lou done?

Whatever happened, its impact on Nietzsche's mind was disastrous. In the agonized letters he wrote Lou after their break and in the even more unhinged drafts of letters in his notebooks, the recurring phrase is: "The Lou of Orta was a different being." He complained that he was suffering from "Orta weather" and that the thought of it was driving him mad. The violence of Nietzsche's emotional reaction to the walk on Monte Sacro is surely a sign that he underwent a powerful experience. It is hardly credible that he would have reacted in such a manner if he had merely spent a few pleasant hours in intellectual conversation with Lou. Nor is it likely that he would have behaved as he did when they returned from their walk. He was in a state of jubilant animation. And he remained in this state until Lou disenchanted him.

A few days later the party broke up. Lou, her mother and Rée journeyed to Lucerne, while Nietzsche went to visit his friends, the Overbecks, in Basel. He stayed with them five days still in a jubilant mood. In fact, the Overbecks had never seen him like this. He talked incessantly, mostly about Lou. He told them of his plan to see Lou again in Lucerne, ostensibly to show her Wagner's former home, but actually to propose to her once more, this time personally. Like a man who has caught sight of the promised land, he shared with the Overbecks his high hopes for the future. They were alarmed and wondered what kind of girl Lou was. She seemed to have bewitched Nietzsche.

In Lucerne meanwhile, Lou was already beginning to pay the price for her impetuous behavior. Both her mother and Rée reprimanded her and she asked herself why her most spontaneous action always led to disastrous consequences. If she had kissed Nietzsche she probably thought nothing of it. It was merely an expression of friendship. But clearly no one else in the party regarded her action in such an innocent light. She was shocked and a little frightened when she realized how Nietzsche interpreted her kiss. It was a spark that set his highly combustible brain aflame. Her efforts to withdraw after she noticed what she had done merely added fuel to the fire.

Rée was particularly outspoken in his criticism. He warned Lou that her behavior had been indiscreet and that she was to blame if Nietzsche had misunderstood her. When he heard that they were to meet again in Lucerne, he knew why. If Nietzsche proposed, Lou would have to handle the situation herself. Rée asked her to be firm and unambiguous in her refusal. No wonder Lou came to the Lucerne meeting with misgivings.

Nietzsche had requested that she meet him in front of the lion's statue in the Lucerne park. It was a beautiful May day. Spring had come to the Swiss mountains and the air was perfumed with the scent of flowers and blossoming trees. Love was in the air. As Nietzsche waited for Lou he saw the diverse pieces of his life fall into a pattern. All around him, life was renewing itself; perhaps his life, too, would be renewed. With Lou at his side a new movement would start. Perhaps they would have a son. He wanted a son, he had told Mrs. Overbeck. Everything made sense now—his suffering, his solitude, his long wait for a disciple. Fortune, with one stroke, was to grant him all his wishes.

Who knows the turmoil that went on in Nietzsche's heart as he saw Lou's slender figure approach? He scanned her face eagerly for any sign of her Monte Sacro tenderness. But there was none. Lou was friendly but detached. Nietzsche felt there was no time to lose. Solemnly he proposed marriage. Lou listened to him, and then with equal solemnity told him that she did not want to get married. She wanted to remain free but he also wanted them to remain friends. Now it was Nietzsche's turn to listen, and he noticed, as she described her plans for the future, that Rée was always included. He suspected that Lou's real reason for rejecting him was Rée. But whatever jealousy he felt, however keenly he was disappointed, he accepted Lou's refusal with apparent good humor. It seemed to Lou he was almost relieved when she turned him down. She had expected a scene but much to her surprise Nietzsche behaved with great calm. He may have been considering other means to get her away from Rée; on the surface, however, he agreed with every thing she said. They would go ahead with their study plan. Certainly sharing Lou was preferable to losing her altogether. When the meeting was over, Lou felt she had handled the situation perfectly. Together they walked back to her hotel, where an anxious Rée was waiting for them. There was no need to tell Rée what had happened. He sensed it and he also sensed that this was no time for asking questions.

It was Nietzsche who then suggested that, to celebrate their trinity, they have their picture taken together. He knew just the right person for it—Jules Bonnet, one of the best-known photographers in Switzerland. Rée at first balked at the idea He did not like to have his picture taken anyway, and to pose with Lou and Nietzsche seemed rather grotesque in view of their strained relationship. But neither Nietzsche nor Lou would take his no for an answer. They felt in the mood for a celebration and Rée had to come along.

Monsieur Bonnet was a man of impeccable bourgeois taste. His photographs, portraits of solemn-faced men and women in Victorian attire, or stiffly arranged family scenes with children dressed like ladies and gentlemen and staring at the camera with a curiously unchildlike, *fin-de-siècle* lassitude—even an occasional Pekingese, facing the camera with an expression of bored indifference—were in wide demand because they mirrored the spirit of the times, solemnity and boredom. Among the props in Bonnet's studio was a small farm cart which came in handy for rural scenes. It could be photographed drawn by dogs or donkeys, or simply left standing as background. When Nietzsche saw it his eyes lit up. He demanded that it be placed in the center of the stage and told Lou to kneel in it. A rather awkward gesture, Bonnet thought, and not at all suitable for a young lady. But his protests went unheeded. Then Nietzsche asked him for a piece of rope which, he insisted, should be tied to his and Rée's arms and held by Lou like a rein. Thus the two men were harnessed to the cart in which Lou knelt. Over Rée's protests, Nietzsche claimed that no other pose could more fittingly represent their relationship. Lou, who felt rather cramped in her half-kneeling posture, told them to hurry, but Nietzsche was not satisfied yet. As their driver, Lou must have a means to enforce her authority. A small stick was found, a piece of rope tied to it and thus a whip fashioned. Nietzsche gave it to Lou; as a finishing touch, he tied a sprig of lilacs to it. A second later the camera clicked and the picture was taken.

It turned out well. Some people laughed when they saw it and treated it as a joke; others, like Malwida, were shocked by it and thought it showed Lou's depraved sense of humor. Lou and Rée were ashamed of it and tried to forget it. But it exists. It can neither be explained away nor dismissed from memory. Monsieur Bonnet's camera caught the rapt ecstasy on Nietzsche's face. It remains a grotesque and terrifying reflection of the way his mind worked, a mind that a few months later, when his dream of marrying Lou had been shattered and Nietzsche was alone once more, would coin the savage phrase: "You go to women? Don't forget the whip."

After the events in the Löwengarten and in Monsieur Bonnet's studio, the pilgrimage to Wagner's former home at Lake Lucerne came as somewhat of an anticlimax. Rée excused himself. He had had enough for one day and refused to go. Once again Nietzsche and Lou were alone. But much had happened since Monte Sacro and both were in a somber mood. Lou was uneasy in Nietzsche's presence and Nietzsche was burdened by his mixed feelings, love and hate, for Wagner: "I have suffered so much because of this man and his art. It was a long, long passion, I find no other word for it. The required renunciation, the necessary return to myself belong to the hardest and most melancholic experiences of my life."

In a soft and subdued voice he told Lou the story of his friendship with Wagner, recalled the happy hours he had spent in this house, this garden and by this lake. Richard and Cosima Wagner had been his friends. They had understood him and he had loved them. Even now, he said, he dreamt of those happy days, but they were gone forever. And here he was again in the company of someone he loved and was fated to lose. As they sat by the lakeside, Nietzsche's voice dropped to a whisper. With his walking stick he drew figures in the moist sand and when he looked up Lou noticed that he had tears in his eyes.

Was it pity she felt for him then? Was it pity that made her accede to his urgent plea to spend a few weeks with him in

Tautenburg? She had grave doubts about the wisdom of giving Nietzsche any further encouragement. And yet she did. Did the spectacle of this lonely man weeping disarm her suspicions? Was she flattered by the admiration of one who had suffered so much? Or did she feel she owed him something for having shattered his Monte Sacro dream?

7

The Tautenburg Idyll

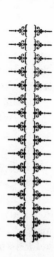

IN LUCERNE THE PARTY SEPARATED. NIETZSCHE WENT BACK TO BASEL and from there to his family in Naumburg. Rée accompanied the women to Zurich where he left them to return to his home in Stibbe, West Prussia. Lou and her mother stayed a few weeks with friends in Zurich and then traveled to Hamburg for a reunion of Madame von Salomé's branch of the family. The question of Lou's future was still not settled. Madame von Salomé's call for help had brought her son Eugene to Germany. But even he could do no more than fight a rear-guard action. Lou had made up her mind not to return to Russia and gradually she wore down her mother's resistance. It was finally agreed that her brother should accompany her to Stibbe, where the Rées owned a large estate, and entrust her to Mrs. Rée's care. Lou would spend the summer months with them.

The Overbecks noticed a change in Nietzsche when he returned from his brief excursion to Lucerne. His exuberance was gone. He was moody and looked tired. But he made no mention of any change in his plans and spoke of Lou as enthusiastically as before. He told Mrs. Overbeck that Lou had expressed the wish to meet her and he asked her to talk to the girl about him "with complete frankness." No third person should be present on that occasion, not even her husband. Mrs. Overbeck was somewhat puzzled by this request, and to allay her fears, Nietzsche wrote her a few days later from Naumburg: "I was too excited during our last meeting and left you and friend Overbeck worried and disturbed. There was no reason for that—quite the reverse. Fate always turns out to be my good fortune, at least my good fortune in wisdom—why then should I be afraid of my fate, particularly if it comes to me in the completely unexpected person of Lou?"

In the same letter he told Mrs. Overbeck that he had not said anything about Lou to his family. This, of course, was not true. He had told his sister. Only his mother had been kept in the dark. Even this simple woman must have wondered what Elizabeth and Fritz meant by their frequent and rather mystifying allusions to a popular comedy entitled *Somebody Must Marry*. But she was used to being excluded from the private world of her children, which she did not understand in any case.

Soon after he arrived home, Nietzsche received a postcard from Rée, who told him that everything had finally been settled; Lou was going to spend the summer in Stibbe. The next day Nietzsche left Naumburg. He told his mother and sister that he wanted to explore the environs of Berlin. A Swiss forester, he said, whom he had met on a hot afternoon in Messina, had spoken in glowing terms of the beautiful woods that surround the Prussian capital. He suddenly felt the urge to visit the Grunewald. If he liked it there he would stay awhile, if not he would return to Naumburg.

That again was not the real reason for Nietzsche's sudden journey to Berlin. He hoped he would see Lou there before she went to the Rées' in Stibbe. But in that hope he was disappointed. Lou had just made the acquaintance of yet another young philosopher, Heinrich von Stein, and was quite happy to see Berlin in his company. Nietzsche did not see her, and when he sought refuge in the famed Grunewald, he experienced another bitter disappointment. He discovered that it was not really a forest at all. It was a popular excursion ground overrun with picnickers, children and dogs. Disgusted, he fled back to Naumburg.

There was nothing for him to do now but wait. "It has been a strange year," he wrote his friend, Peter Gast. "All kinds of important things have happened or are about to happen. I am watching this singular game of dice with amazement and I am waiting, waiting. Everything must turn out for the best for me. I am living with fatalistic resignation in God." He asked his friend to help him proofread *Gay Science*. He said it was to be his last book because in the autumn he would start his studies at the University of Vienna.

During this period of waiting, both Lou and Nietzsche corresponded with Malwida about their winter plans. Malwida was pleased to hear that Lou liked Nietzsche, and she was "genuinely happy that this poor man enjoyed your company. . . . It would be my wish, if you are not going back to Russia, that you go to the Nietzsches and come with Miss Nietzsche to Bayreuth." This is exactly what Nietzsche had in mind. He wanted Lou to meet his sister and hoped that Elizabeth would prevail upon her to join him in the Thuringian resort of Tautenburg where he proposed to spend the summer months. Nietzsche was grateful for Malwida's support and he wrote her that a firm friendship now united him with Lou "as firmly as anything of this sort can be arranged on earth. I have not made a better acquisition in a long time. I am truly grateful to you and Rée for having helped me to it. This year, which in many important respects means a new crisis in my life ('epoch' is the right word, an interval between two crises; one behind and one in front of me) has been made very beautiful, thanks to the charm and the graciousness of this young, truly heroic soul. I hope to have in her a pupil and, if my life should not last much longer, an heir and disciple."

"Incidentally," he added, "Rée ought to have married her to remove many difficulties in her position, and I for my part have not spared giving him encouragement. But it now seems to me hopeless. He is, in an ultimate sense, an unshakable pessimist and I admit I respect him for having kept faith with himself, in spite of all the objections of his heart and of my reason. The thought of propagating mankind is unbearable to him, he cannot bring himself to increase the number of unfortunates. In this respect he has too much pity and too little hope for my taste. In confidence."

Considering what Malwida knew about Rée's feelings for Lou, this letter must have puzzled her. She would have been even more puzzled had she known Nietzsche's own feelings for the young Russian. But her puzzlement changed to alarm when Lou wrote her that they were going ahead with their three-way study plan. Lou said that she hoped to share an apartment in Vienna with both Rée and Nietzsche.

"You cannot possibly live with the two young men," Malwida wrote in reply. "Not only because it would be a slap in the face of the whole world (that would not be the worst) but because of the very serious inconvenience of such a situation, its really offensive aspects, which you would only discover afterward. I have no idea how you imagine this 'living and working together.' A serious consideration seems to me the fact that it would again be a completely mistaken enterprise for Nietzsche. He cannot attend lectures any more than he can give them. And the very bad climate of Vienna when he has definite proof that he can live only in the south.

"It is all perfectly naïve nonsense which in a moment of enthusiasm seems possible, but which would soon turn out to be entirely impracticable. Poor Nietzsche! I wish it were possible for him but I think it is presumptuous even to consider it. . . . And finally this 'Trinity.' No matter how much I believe in your neutrality, the experience of a long life and my knowledge of human nature tells me that it is not possible without at best cruelly hurting one heart and, at worst, destroying a friendship."

Malwida was not the only one who uttered such warnings but neither Nietzsche nor Lou paid any attention to them. Lou had won the last round of her bitter struggle with her mother. Reluctantly Madame von Salomé had yielded to her daughter's wishes and to the persuasive arguments advanced in Lou's favor by both Rée and Nietzsche.

"It may be," she told Nietzsche, "and I won't deny it, that my point of view, which holds that a woman's life and sphere of activities lies in other directions than that of striving after intellectual improvement of the kind my daughter seeks, is old-fashioned and out of season. But then the opinions with which one has grown old cannot be changed like an old dress, particularly not before the value of the other point of view is clear and evident. . . . Only the future will show whether she [Lou] will find true happiness in her perfectly free life. I wish it for her from my whole heart and shall not count the many sacrifices it has cost me, nor the long and hard struggles; and I shall be content."

With the tacit approval of her mother, Lou was making plans to attend the Bayreuth Festival in July, while Nietzsche was trying to persuade his sister to invite Lou to spend the month of

August with them in Tautenburg, although he told the Overbecks that, "as regards my sister, I am determined to keep her out of it; she could only get things mixed up (and herself most of all)."

It was almost six weeks after he had said good-by to Lou at the Lucerne railroad station before he heard again directly from her. She wrote to him from the Rées' estate at Stibbe. He was delighted. He asked his sister to write immediately and invite Lou to join them. Much to her later regret, Elizabeth carried out her brother's wishes. After another two weeks of waiting, the longest two weeks Nietzsche had ever known, Lou's letter of acceptance arrived. He wrote her at once:

MY DEAR FRIEND:
Now the sky is bright over me! Yesterday noon it seemed as though I had a birthday! You sent word that you would be coming, the most beautiful present anybody could make me now; my sister sent cherries; Taubner sent the first three proof sheets of *Gay Science;* and, to crown it all, the last part of the manuscript had just been finished and with it the work of six years (1876–1882), my entire "free-thought." O what years! What torments! What solitude, what disgust with life! And against it all, against life and death as it were, I have brewed my medicine, these my thoughts with their small, small patches of cloudless sky:—O, dear friend, when I think of it all I am shaken and moved and do not know how I have succeeded. A feeling of self-pity and of victory fills me. For it is a victory, and a complete one—even my health has come back, I don't know from where, and everybody tells me that I look younger than ever. Heaven help me from follies! . . . But from now on, when you will advise me, I shall be well advised and need not be afraid.

As regards the winter I am thinking seriously and exclusively of Vienna: my sister's winter plans are quite independent of mine, and there are no afterthoughts. The south of Europe has receded from my mind. I do not want to be lonely any more, I want to learn to be human again. Alas! This is a lesson I have to learn from the beginning!—

Accept my thanks, dear friend. As you say: everything will turn out for the best. With the kindest regards to friend Rée.

Entirely yours, F.N.

There is something pathetically naïve about this letter. The first part with the description of Nietzsche's six years of torment and solitude is indeed filled with "self-pity," but the victory he claims sounds rather hollow, like somebody whistling in the dark to keep his courage up. The talk about his good health, for example, when Lou knew that he was not at all well. As to his curious boast that he looked much younger, it must have made her smile. Did he want to convey that he was young enough for her? At any rate young enough for all sorts of follies. And what was she to think of the pledge that he made—that he would put his entire trust in her? He, a mature man, a university professor, seeking the advice of a twenty-one-year-old girl! And what about the strange phrase: "there are no afterthoughts"? Did he want to reassure Lou that he was content with being her friend and had no other designs? If so, he promised more than he could keep.

After he had written to Lou he again waited impatiently for an answer. But Lou remained silent. She had agreed to meet Elizabeth in Bayreuth and, together with her, join Nietzsche in Tautenburg. There was no need to continue corresponding about that. Besides, she was having such a good time with the Rées and had become so fond of Paul, who did everything in his power to make her feel at home, that she hardly noticed how quickly the weeks went by. She was almost sorry now that she had promised to join Nietzsche in Tautenburg. Rée, too, was sorry. He could hardly bear the idea of her leaving him. When Nietzsche did not get an answer from Lou he wrote her again:

"Now, my dear friend, everything is fine and we shall meet again Saturday week. Perhaps my last letter did not reach you? I wrote it two weeks ago Sunday. I would feel sorry if you had not received it. I described a very happy moment: many good things had suddenly come to me and the 'goodest' of them all was your letter of acceptance. . . .

"I have thought a great deal of you and have shared with you in my mind so many serious, happy and moving moments that I have lived as if I were in the company of my friends. If you only knew how strange this seems to an old hermit! I have often had to laugh at myself!

"As regards Bayreuth, I am quite happy that I do not have to be there; and yet, if I could be near you like a spirit, murmuring this and that into your ears, I could bear even the music of *Parsifal* (otherwise I cannot bear it). Before you go I wish you could read my little book, *Richard Wagner in Bayreuth.* Friend Rée may have it. . . . Wagner's last written words to me are in a beautiful, dedicated copy of *Parsifal: To my dear friend*

Friedrich Nietzsche; Richard Wagner, Oberkirchenrat. Exactly at the same time Wagner received my book *Human, All Too Human* and with that everything was clear but also everything was finished.

"How often, in all sorts of circumstances, have I not experienced just that: 'Everything clear but also everything finished!'

"And how happy am I now, my beloved friend Lou, that I can think with regard to us two that 'everything is beginning and yet everything is clear.' Trust me! Let us trust each other!"

The tenor of these letters is hardly that of a rejected suitor resigned to his fate, and if Lou had been emotionally more mature she would have thought twice before agreeing to join Nietzsche in his Tautenburg retreat. He obviously expected more from her than she was willing to give.

There is no doubt that Lou was fascinated by Nietzsche's ideas and by the way he expressed them. Perhaps she wanted to see how far she could go without committing herself. If so, she played a dangerous game. Her later silence about the affair and her refusal to defend herself, even when she was publicly attacked by Nietzsche's sister, may have been caused by a sense of guilt. She may have realized later that her behavior was indiscreet and open to serious misunderstanding.

Nietzsche certainly was aware that his relationship to Lou could be misunderstood and he vigorously protested that it was not a love affair. But he protested too much. What, for example, was Peter Gast to think of a letter he received from Nietzsche in the middle of July in which his friend exhorted him to dismiss from his mind any notion that he, Nietzsche, was having a love affair with the young Russian? Gast had not even heard of Lou before that letter and the idea of Nietzsche in love with a twenty-one-year-old girl must have struck him as absurd. Why did Nietzsche mention it? There were other reasons for Gast to be mystified by the sudden entrance of Lou into Nietzsche's life. At the beginning of July he had received a poem in his friend's handwriting, entitled "Hymn to Pain." Since there was no accompanying letter he assumed, of course, that Nietzsche was the author of the poem and complimented him on it. But two weeks later Nietzsche informed him:

"That poem, 'Hymn to Pain,' was not by me. It belongs to those things that have complete power over me; I have never been able to read it without tears: it sounds like a voice for which I have been waiting and waiting since my childhood. This poem is by my friend Lou, of whom you have not heard yet. Lou is the daughter of a Russian General and twenty years old. She is as keen as an eagle and as brave as a lion, and yet she is also a very maidenly child who will perhaps not live long. I owe her to Miss von Meysenbug and Rée. At present she is visiting the Rées and after Bayreuth she is coming to Tautenburg. In the autumn we are going to Vienna together.

"I am sure, dear friend, you have sufficient respect for both of us to dismiss any notion of a love affair. We are friends and I shall honor this girl and her trust in me.—Besides, she is incredibly self-assured and knows very well what she wants, without asking the world for permission, nor caring what the world thinks of her. All this is for your ears only and for nobody else."

Could anything be more revealing? He protests that there is no love affair between them, but it is evident that Lou, the girl with the mind of an eagle and the heart of a lion, has complete power over him. It is amusing and a little pathetic to hear from Nietzsche himself that so far Lou's resistance had proved stronger than his desire. But she would be with him soon and Rée would not be present. Was he not entitled to interpret her willingness to come as yet another omen that at last the star of his own fortune was rising?

While Nietzsche was hopefully waiting in the solitude of the Tautenburg forest for the great turning point in his life, his rival, Richard Wagner, was making preparations for the grand finale of his amazing career, the première of *Parsifal*. For years his friends had begged Wagner to finish this work, begun six years previously, and to present it at Bayreuth. And for years Wagner had hesitated. Not because he felt unequal to the task, but because it seemed to him almost a profanation to stage *Parsifal* in the contemporary theatre.

"And, indeed, can a drama in which the sublimest mysteries of the Christian faith are shown upon the stage he produced in theatres such as ours, before such audiences as ours, as part of an operatic repertory such as ours?"

But eventually Wagner had succumbed to the wishes of his

king and the entreaties of his friends and had agreed to conduct the first performance of *Parsifal* in Bayreuth in the summer of 1882.

It was a spectacular occasion. Wagnerians from all over the world attended and during the last week of July the little Bavarian town was the center of the world of music. Even Wagner's enemies had to admit that the old magician had once again scored a complete triumph. 1882 became known as the *Parsifal* year.

In this setting of fervent Wagner-worship, Elizabeth Nietzsche met Lou Salomé. Two more different women it would be hard to imagine. Like Kriemhild and Brunhild, they came from different worlds and represented diametrically opposite ideals. Bold and unconventional one—self-righteous and petty the other. They were fated to clash, even if they had met under more favorable circumstances. But meeting as they did, in the shadow of the giant with whom Nietzsche was carrying on a personal vendetta, their relationship was strained from the beginning and reached a breaking point a few days later.

Elizabeth Nietzsche was thirty-six years old at that time. She had spent most of her life with her mother in the prim little town of Naumburg on the Saale, where her father had been a Protestant pastor. Her upbringing had followed the conventional pattern. As a result she was deeply imbued with the ideal of that genteel, middle-class respectability to which most young girls of her time and class gave unquestioned obedience. She went to church regularly, helped her mother and later her brother with household chores, was socially active, liked going to parties and was a popular member of Naumburg society. She was an attractive girl with a pretty face, a nice figure and a quick mind. And yet, in all her thirty-six years, she had never been really in love, was still unmarried and, apart from her affection for her brother and her devotion to her mother, she had not formed any close attachments. Her large circle of acquaintances and friends were chiefly important to her, one suspects, as a source of gossip. For, like many aging girls who are not yet resigned to spinsterhood, Lisbeth Nietzsche was always thinking of marriage and experienced a vicarious pleasure by talking about other people's affairs. It gave her great satisfaction to find flaws in the moral character of others, to catch them off guard and to discover what her brother called their "Human, All Too Human" failings.

If Elizabeth Nietzsche had made a deliberate effort to meet someone who was bound to offend her frustrated emotions, she could not have done better than with Lou. Lou represented everything she abhorred. Her unconventional habits, her shockingly free behavior with men, her indifference even to ordinary cleanliness caused Elizabeth to feel an almost physical revulsion. How could her brother want to associate with such a creature? And Lou, sensing Elizabeth's instinctive disapproval of her, reacted, as she always did under such circumstances, by exaggerating her eccentricities. There were plenty of opportunities for that in the cosmopolitan society of Bayreuth.

Malwida von Meysenbug was a guest of honor at the Bayreuth Festival. It was well known that she was one of the composer's closest friends. As Malwida's protégée, Lou was introduced to Wagner's intimate circle and became very quickly a popular member of the master's entourage, especially among the men. The women were more reserved toward her. She was often seen in the company of the gifted young Russian painter and stage designer, Joukowsky, one of Wagner's long-time friends, who had been entrusted with the job of designing the sets for *Parsifal*. It must have rankled Elizabeth to see these two Russians frolicking so close to the master's throne while she, because of her brother's feud with Wagner, had to keep a certain distance. Was not Lou ridiculing her brother by so blatantly associating with his enemies? And the stories one heard about the girl! It was rumored that she had taken off her dress in public and had permitted Joukowsky, who was also a noted dress designer, to design a dress right on her body. She was also said to have attended nightly séances as the only lady present. God knows what went on then! It was not hard to imagine what kind of a girl Lou was. The more Elizabeth heard and saw of Lou the more alarmed she became and the more determined to open her poor blind brother's eyes to the true character of his new disciple.

But what really incensed Elizabeth was a scene at the Bayreuth railroad station. She had accompanied Dr. Bernard Förster, a young man of her acquaintance, to the station and was happily chatting with him on the platform, prior to his departure from

Bayreuth. Förster, a notorious anti-Semite, who had played a leading role in the campaign of 1881, during which over a quarter of a million signatures were collected to petition Bismarck to stop Jewish immigration into Germany, had attended the Bayreuth Festival chiefly because he revered Wagner as an exponent of genuine Germanism and a supporter of the anti-Semitic movement. Another reason for Förster's coming to Bayreuth was Elizabeth Nietzsche. He had known her for some time and had grown very fond of her. He may have proposed to her during the festival week. At any event, the unexpected had happened. In her thirty-sixth year Elizabeth suddenly found herself loved and in love. Perhaps she was secretly engaged to Förster, whom she married two years later, when she accompanied him to the Bayreuth station. Imagine her chagrin when she discovered that Lou and her friend were traveling together on the same train!

Lou had decided, almost on the spur of the moment, to leave Bayreuth somewhat earlier than Elizabeth because, as she freely admitted, Wagner's music fell on deaf ears with her. They had agreed to meet at a friend's house in Jena and to travel to Tautenburg together from there. Elizabeth had not been sorry to see Lou leave Bayreuth. She wanted to talk to Wagner privately, to try to patch up her brother's quarrel with him, but she did not want her brother to know of it. She feared, and with good reason, that he would have resented it. As long as Lou was in Bayreuth and closely associated with Wagner's friends, it was obviously difficult to keep such an interview secret. Lou was bound to hear of it and would, Elizabeth thought, report it to her brother. She was therefore quite pleased when she heard that Lou intended to leave. But her pleasure was short-lived. To her horror, she noticed as the train was pulling out of the station, that Lou had entered Förster's compartment and at once engaged him in animated conversation. It was outrageous. Here she was, left standing on the platform and forced to watch this "terrible Russian" carry on with her friend. There and then Elizabeth decided that Lou was a menace—a menace not only to her brother. The sooner she got rid of the girl the better for all concerned.

Their reunion in Jena gave Elizabeth an opportunity of telling Lou what she thought of her. It started innocently enough.

Elizabeth took Lou aside and told her "younger sister" that a girl's most precious possession was her reputation. Alas, it was easily damaged and hard to repair. Then she sighed and said that Lou was perhaps too young to understand how careful a girl had to be—an incautious gesture, a glance, a rash word and everything was lost. At this point Lou burst into laughter. There was no need for her "older sister" to go on, for if Elizabeth was right, then, indeed, everything was lost. But Lou said she had no regrets. She had enjoyed every minute of it.

Elizabeth reprimanded her sternly. It was not proper for a young lady to talk like this. In fact, she considered it her duty to tell Lou that she was quite shocked by Lou's behavior in Bayreuth. The way Lou had flirted with Joukowsky had been a public scandal. Everybody had said so. Malwida had told her in confidence that she was sorry now to have introduced Lou to her Bayreuth friends. And she, Elizabeth, had felt terribly embarrassed when people had asked her if it was true that Lou was joining her and her brother in Tautenburg. Did Lou not realize who her brother was? Did she not know that he was one of the greatest thinkers alive, a man of the highest principles, almost a saint? Did she not feel cheap for having publicly associated with his enemies?

Lou was startled. She knew that people had talked about her and Joukowsky, but she had paid no attention to it. She considered it beneath contempt to take notice of gossip. What she did with her life was nobody's business but her own. As for taking sides in Nietzsche's quarrel with Wagner, it had never occurred to her. Rather pointedly she replied that nobody could have cared less about Nietzsche than Count Joukowsky. He never even mentioned his name.

Elizabeth was stung by Lou's remarks. Joukowsky was Wagner's favorite. He occupied the position that Nietzsche had held ten years previously. It was a bitter blow for Elizabeth to be told that not even her brother's name was mentioned in Wagner's circle any more. As far as Wagner was concerned, Nietzsche was dead. Vehemently she replied that Joukowsky was a charlatan who did not deserve to be mentioned in the same breath with her brother. Obviously, Lou did not know the difference between a genius and an impostor. And since they were talking so frankly, she might tell Lou that her proposition to share an apartment with her brother and Rée was downright indecent. Among Russians such an arrangement, masquerading as friendship, might be possible, but not among civilized people. To suggest it to her brother was an insult.

This was too much for Lou.

"Don't get the idea that I am interested in your brother, or in love with him. I could spend a whole night with him in one room without getting excited. It was your brother who first soiled our study plan with the lowest intentions. He only started to talk about friendship when he realized that he could not have me for anything else. It was your brother who first proposed 'free love.'"

When she heard that, Elizabeth became hysterical. Uncontrolled sobs shook her body, she covered her face with her hands, and before she could get to the bathroom, she vomited.

Lou was dismayed and angry. What a beginning for a joint vacation! She wished she could go back to Stibbe where Rée was waiting for her. She should have known better. She should not have accepted Nietzsche's invitation. Rée was right: whenever you do something from kindness it turns out badly. But it was too late for such thoughts now. She had to calm down that hysterical goose.

The next day the two women patched up their quarrel after a fashion. Elizabeth said she was sorry she had lost her temper. She suggested that the incident be mentioned to no one. Unpleasant experiences are best forgotten. But she hoped that Lou would never again talk to her about her brother in that way. She could not bear it. Obviously Lou had a completely wrong impression of him. Perhaps Rée had misinformed her. On the surface Elizabeth pretended friendship, but her resentment of Lou was still great. It suddenly crossed her mind that Rée was Jewish. Perhaps that was it, perhaps Lou, too, was Jewish? That would account for many things: her disrespect for tradition, her blatant behavior, her sly undermining of authority. Bernard Förster called the Jews "elements of decay" and said they were corrupting the German people. Was not that what Lou was doing to her brother? She would watch the girl and warn Fritz. He must know how dangerous she was and what people had said about her. She could ruin him if he were not careful. With such thoughts Elizabeth brought Lou to Tautenburg.

Nietzsche met them at the Dorndorf station. He was in a very cheerful mood. Lou's arrival ended his long wait. At last his Monte Sacro dream had come back. She was here with him and he had almost a month to win her. Gallantly he helped her from the train, kissed her hand, and bade her welcome to his Thuringian forest retreat. His eyes sparkled, he smiled and chatted happily, telling them the latest local gossip. Elizabeth noticed with dismay that his emotions were dangerously involved. She had never seen him like that. "Fritz is madly in love with Lou," she wrote her friend in Jena. There was no time to lose. She must disillusion him before any damage was done.

While Lou was getting settled in the little room in the vicarage that Nietzsche had rented for her, Elizabeth told her brother briefly what had happened. She did not go into details. There were some things that were too painful to relate. Her main charge was that Lou had betrayed him by making common cause with his Bayreuth enemies. It was a clever approach. She knew that if anything could break the enchantment her brother felt for Lou it was the charge that she had ridiculed him in Bayreuth. And she was right. Nietzsche listened to her story with visible pain. He felt hurt and humiliated. That Lou, Lou of all people, should have betrayed him in Bayreuth was more than he could bear.

When Lou came down she knew at once that something was wrong. Nietzsche's cheerfulness was gone. He looked at her reproachfully and wanted to know why she had been so indiscreet. Had she forgotten what he had told her about Wagner and himself? It hurt him to think that she had made fun of him in front of his Bayreuth enemies, especially in view of the fact that she had accepted his invitation. There was a scene. Lou resented being asked to give an account of herself. Nietzsche had no right to tell her with whom she could associate. His quarrel with Wagner did not concern her. And as for accepting his invitation, she was ready to leave at once. But Nietzsche would not hear of that. He apologized for his touchiness on the subject of Wagner and asked her to come for a walk. He wanted to show her where the village elders planned to put up a bench in his honor, a bench with the inscription: *Gay Science*. He might be dead in Bayreuth; in Tautenburg he was a famous writer.

Again Lou was amazed by the sudden change in Nietzsche's mood. A minute ago he had been bitter and reproachful, now he was cheerful and light-hearted. Had he been serious before? Was his humor genuine now? She could not tell, but she agreed to go with him. Elizabeth excused herself. She said she had to unpack. Once again they were alone and their misunderstanding was gone. They talked freely and easily, as if they had known each other for years. When they came to the spot in the forest where the memorial bench was to be placed, Nietzsche told Lou that the joke was still on him. For according to a local legend, a dead man had once been found there and the place was still popularly known as "Toter Mann." He seemed to think that this was a great joke and he laughed heartily. But Lou shuddered— Dead Man—it was really rather morbid. How could he joke about it? But Nietzsche did not give her time to reflect. He continued talking with the abandon of a child just home from school. His good humor was so contagious that Lou was carried away by it. Again she noticed that it was difficult to resist him when he was in the full flow of his spirit.

In order to have a record of her thoughts and sentiments during her Tautenburg vacation, Lou kept a diary in the form of letters addressed to Rée, who had not liked the idea of her spending a month with Nietzsche and wanted to be kept informed of what went on. Her first entry, dated August 14, 1882, reads:

"Nietzsche, on the whole of an iron will, is a man of powerful moods. I knew that once we would get to know each other— which we failed to do in the beginning because of the turmoil of our feelings—we would soon discover, beyond all petty gossip, how deeply akin we are. I had already told him so in writing in reply to his first strange letter. And so it has happened. After a day of being together with him, during which I tried to be cheerful and natural, our old intimacy was re-established. He came up to my room again and again; and in the evening he took my hand, kissed it twice, and started to say something which he did not finish. During the following days I had to stay in bed; he sent letters to my room and spoke to me through the door. Now my fever is gone and I got up. Yesterday we spent the whole day together and today we spent a beautiful day in the dark quiet pine woods, alone with sun rays and squirrels. Elizabeth was at Dornburg with friends. At the Inn where we ate under a large, broad-branched linden tree, people think we belong together, just as you and I, if I am wearing my cap and Nietzsche arrives without Elizabeth.

"Talking with Nietzsche is very exciting, as you know. But there is a special fascination if you encounter like thoughts, like sentiments and ideas—we understand each other perfectly. Once he said to me in amazement: 'I think the only difference between us is that of age. We have lived alike and thought alike.'

"It is only because we are so much alike that he reacts so violently to the differences between us, or what seem to him differences. That is why he is so upset. If two people are so unalike, as you and I, they are pleased when they discover points of agreement. But if they are as alike as Nietzsche and I, they suffer from their differences.

"I had intended to take notes of our conversations but that is almost impossible because they range from the nearest to the most distant realms of thought and do not lend themselves to precise formulations. And, actually, the content of our conversations is not as important as this halfway meeting of our minds. Nietzsche enjoys talking with me so much that he confessed to me yesterday that even during our first quarrel upon my arrival, and while he felt very miserable, he could not resist experiencing a kind of joy because of my way of arguing.

"He has read my essay on women and thought the style of the first part was horrible. It would take too long to write what else he said. . . . He advised me to continue my little work and wrote down some books that would be helpful. I was glad when he said that he hated all creative work unless it was excellent. He would not advise me to go on with it if he could not do so with a good conscience. He said I could learn to write in a day because I was ready for it.

"I have a very great confidence in his teaching ability. We understand one another so well. But I am wondering if it is good for him to talk with me all day long from morning to night, instead of doing his own work. I told him so today. He nodded and said: 'I have had so rarely an opportunity for it that I enjoy it like a child.' But the same evening he said: 'I must not live too long near you.'

"Memories of our time in Italy often come to us and yesterday, as we were walking up a small path, he said softly: 'Monte Sacro . . . I owe to you the most beautiful dream of my life.'

"We are very cheerful. We laugh a lot. To Elizabeth's horror (who, incidentally, is hardly ever with us) my room is immediately visited by 'ghostly knocks' when Nietzsche enters. We must have even this cursed gift in common. I am glad the mournful expression that hurt me has disappeared from his face and that his eyes are again clear and sparkling.

"We are also spending happy hours at the edge of the forest on a bench near his farmhouse. How good it feels to laugh and to dream and to chat in the evening sunshine when the last rays fall on us through the branches of the trees. . . ."

It was an idlyllic existence and yet there were moments when Lou felt uneasy. Nietzsche had a way of talking about Rée that displeased her. He called him a coward, a candidate for suicide who enjoyed suffering pain and was always carrying a phial of poison in case life should become unbearable. Although said half-jokingly, Lou sensed that these words were meant to influence her against Rée and she resented them. And there were many times when she felt Nietzsche was still harboring hopes which she thought had been buried. He was too attentive to her, too eager to please her. She noted in her diary that in their talks they often reached forbidden territory.

"If somebody had listened to us they would have thought that two devils were talking." And she asked: "Are we really close? No, we are not. Those hopes that Nietzsche cherished but a few weeks age lie like a shadow over my feelings and separate us. And somewhere in a hidden depth of our beings we are worlds apart. Like an old fortress, Nietzsche has within him many dark dungeons and hidden passages which one does not see at first sight and which yet, perhaps, contain his true character.

"Strange, the other day the thought suddenly struck me that one day we might even be enemies."

This thought must have struck Nietzsche too, for it was obvious that his sister hated Lou bitterly. It was also obvious that she tried to turn him against Lou. What should he do now? He had hoped to have an ally in his sister; instead, he had to reckon with Elizabeth's active hostility. In trying to win Lou he risked losing his sister. It was a formidable dilemma. After all, Elizabeth was his own flesh and blood. She was closer to him than anyone else. They had grown up together and had lived together almost like husband and wife. Elizabeth was much more to him than a sister. She was his helpmate, his confidante, his "Faithful Llama." It was terrible to be forced to choose between her and Lou, and yet he made that choice. That is what Elizabeth never forgave Lou.

There are hints in Nietzsche's letters to Gast of his struggle between his love for his sister and his love for Lou. They leave no doubt that Elizabeth lost. For example, on August 4 he told Gast:

"One day a bird flew past me; and I, superstitious like all lonely people who stand at a crossroad, thought I had seen an eagle. Now everybody tells me that I am mistaken and there is a pretty European gossip about it. Well, who is happier? I, the 'deceived one,' as they say, who has been living in a higher world of hope all summer because of this bird omen—or those who 'cannot be deceived'?"

And ten days after: "I have had to pass a hard test and I have passed it.—Lou is going to stay two more weeks. In the autumn we shall meet again (in Munich?). I have an eye for people. What I see exists, even if others do not see it."

And again, a week later, on August 20: "Lou is staying another week. She is the most intelligent of women. Every five days we have a little tragic scene. Everything I have written you about her is nonsense—including, probably, what I have just written."

Elizabeth watched Lou and her brother with undisguised indignation. It was infuriating to see Fritz fall under the spell of the "terrible Russian." She would have left Tautenburg if it had been possible without causing a scandal. As it was, Lou and her brother behaved as if she did not exist. The way they treated her was downright insulting. She sensed they were making fun of her behind her back. And she was outraged by the behavior of Lou, who let her brother stay in her room half the night. "Discretion" was a word that did not seem to exist in Lou's vocabulary. She prided herself on her frankness. Frankness indeed! To Elizabeth, Lou's frankness was simply immodesty. She blushed when she caught snatches of their conversation. They seemed to have no shame left. They talked about everything—God, religion, morals, sex—with complete disregard for the most ordinary decencies. And what was more, as far as she could tell, they turned everything upside down: religion was a childish dream, meekness was weakness, God a man-made ideal, love nature's trick to reproduce itself. She was horrified by such talk. If that was her brother's new philosophy, and Lou the kind of disciple to whom it appealed, she would have nothing more to do with him. Let him perish in his own hell!

Heaven and hell were the main topics of conversation between Lou and Nietzsche. "The basically religious trait in our character is what we have in common," Lou noted in her diary. "It is perhaps so strong in us because we are free-thinkers in the most extreme sense of the word. In the free-thinker, the religious emotion cannot relate itself to some divinity or heaven outside, where those forces that give rise to religion—like weakness, fear and greed—can be accommodated. In the free-thinker, the religious need . . . thrown back upon itself, as it were, can become a heroic force, an urge to sacrifice himself to some noble purpose. In Nietzsche's character lies such a heroic trait. It is the most essential part of him and gives unity and structure to all his other properties and drives. We shall yet witness his becoming the prophet of a new religion and it will be one that seeks heroes for disciples."

This uncommonly shrewd insight into Nietzsche's future role, voiced at a time when that role was still quite obscure, caused derision among Lou's friends. Malwida thought it was almost comic to see in Nietzsche the founder of a new religion and she advised Lou not to waste her time on futile speculations. But to Lou such speculations were not futile at all. She realized—again anticipating events it took half a century to unfold—that the growing secularization of life would not solve the problem of religion, just as in her own and in Nietzsche's case loss of faith did not mean they had found the answer to the problem of how to live in a godless universe. Man will have gods and when the old gods die he will have new ones. In her first book, *A Struggle for God*, published three years after her meeting with Nietzsche, Lou touched on many problems she had discussed with him. And Nietzsche acknowledged, although still smarting under the pain of having lost her, that Lou had made good use of her Tautenburg summer.

The book's main interest lies in the fact that it demonstrates the proximity between religious and erotic exaltations. Imperceptibly the climate changes from the purest spiritual love to the grossest forms of physical indulgence. In a highly intellectualized setting, wanton acts occur. Under the strain of great spiritual tensions the women in the book commit all manner of crimes: adultery, suicide and, practically, incest. And the men are driven by a sense of guilt because of their loss of faith. The book's main theme is how to find peace of mind after you have lost faith in God. Rudolf, a character in the book who seems to be modeled after Rée, finds it by embracing Buddhism. He feels that there is no real happiness and that all we can hope for is the negative bliss of Nirvana. But his older brother, Kuno, who has some of Nietzsche's features, says he will go on fighting for dying gods. For the grave is not the end. The only attitude worthy of man is a defiant acceptance of his fate—*amor fati:* Here I stand, I can do no other! In that spirit he finds fulfillment and peace.

Lou's book, reflecting as it does the Tautenburg atmosphere—tense and questing and charged with emotion—offers a commentary on Nietzsche's feelings during that fateful summer. It explains the state of excitement in which he found himself. All year he had lived at the brink of great expectations. His spirit had soared into dizzy heights. Lou's coming had been the climax of all his hopes. She was very close to him, closer than anybody had ever been, closer even than Elizabeth. It was an exciting sensation, as if their spirits had been married. Carried away by his exultation, Nietzsche wrote to Lou's mother that he considered himself secretly engaged to her daughter. At least this is what Lou says. She also says she did not know that Nietzsche had written such a letter and would have been shocked if she had known. But she must have known what feelings she aroused in Nietzsche, for in her book she writes: "While no road leads from sensuous love to spiritual love, many roads lead from the latter to the former." And again: "All love is tragic. Requited love dies of satiation, unrequited of starvation. But death by starvation is slower and more painful." Did she not know that she condemned Nietzsche's love to that slow and painful death?

The uninvited guest at the Tautenburg idyll was the dark river-god of the blood, enticed to the surface by the spiritual kinship Nietzsche and Lou felt for each other, by their intimate talks, their walks through the woods, their long nightly vigils. Lou must have known the cause of Nietzsche's tension. She had only recently experienced something very similar with Gillot. She must have known that the longer she stayed with Nietzsche the greater his tension would become until it would either find its natural release—and that possibility does not seem to have occurred to her—or end in an explosion.

The explosion came. It led to a complete break between Nietzsche and his sister. By then, however, Lou had left Tautenburg, giving him as a parting present a copy of her poem, "A Prayer to Life," with the prophetic ending:

> If you have no more happiness to give:
> Give me your pain.

8

Reunion and Farewell

FROM TAUTENBURG LOU WENT TO BERLIN, WHERE RÉE WAS ANXIOUSLY waiting for her. He had been uneasy about her spending a month with Nietzsche and had warned her before she left to be on guard in case there was a change in Nietzsche's "physical behavior" toward her. He remembered clandestine nightly visits from the Neapolitan girl that Nietzsche had received during their stay in Sorrento and was suspicious of the philosopher's platonic intentions. He was glad when Lou returned from Tautenburg apparently none the worse for her experiences, but he had serious misgivings about their joint study plan in which Lou still firmly believed. Rée was deeply in love with Lou, addressed her with the familiar *Du* and called her his "dearest little snail." He freely admitted that he was jealous of Nietzsche.

There was actually no reason for Rée to be jealous. Lou made no secret of the fact that she preferred him to Nietzsche and that she would gladly live with him, provided he did not insist on marriage. She wanted him to treat her like a sister. Rée could not quite see himself in that role and feared the rest of the world would look upon it even more skeptically. He was afraid there would be a scandal involving not only himself and Lou but their families. Nietzsche's presence was still the lesser evil. For this reason he kept his doubts to himself and when Nietzsche wrote and called Lou his "sister"—"after I have lost my natural sister I need a supernatural one"—he replied in the same vein: "Nothing can now or in the future separate us since we are united by a third to whom we subordinate ourselves, not unlike medieval knights."

Nietzsche, too, claimed his feelings for Lou were merely chivalrous, but he deceived no one, least of all Elizabeth. When Lou left Tautenburg Elizabeth vented all her pent-up emotions on her brother. She was so angry about the whole affair that she refused to return to Naumburg with him. Worried about what she might tell their mother, Nietzsche pleaded with her to forget her quarrel with Lou. He reminded her that Lou had not started it and that she had as much reason as Elizabeth to feel upset.

"For the rest," he continued, "if I think of the future I would be sad if I had to assume that you do not share my feelings for Lou. We are so much alike in our thoughts and plans that sometimes our names will be linked together and all slanderous attacks on her are attacks on me too."

But it was useless. Elizabeth had made up her mind about Lou and would not be appeased. She wrote her mother that she refused to come home as long as her brother was there. Fritz had fallen into the clutches of an evil woman and she, Elizabeth, would have nothing more to do with him. This news came as a complete surprise to the good pastor's widow. With a great show of Lutheran righteousness, she told her son when he arrived that he was a disgrace to the family and that his behavior would make his pious father turn in his grave for shame. Offended and angry, Nietzsche left Naumburg, vowing he would never return. He went to Leipzig and waited for Lou and Rée to join him there. He had never felt more miserable. After his break with his family he was now really alone. The only other friends he had were the Overbecks and Peter Gast. To them he poured out his heart:

"The weeks in Tautenburg have done me a great deal of good, particularly those toward the end; and, on the whole, I have a right to talk of recovery, although I am still often enough reminded of the precarious equilibrium of my health. But I need clear skies above me, otherwise I lose too much time and strength. . . . This long and rich summer was a testing time for me. I have taken leave of it proudly and courageously for during this time the otherwise so ugly gap between intention and achievement seemed bridged. There were hard demands on my humanity and

I measured up to the hardest. I call this whole interval between the usual and the unusual, *in media vita*. And the demon of music which, after many years, once again visited me forced me to talk of it even in sound.

"But the most useful experiences I have had this summer were my conversations with Lou. Our minds and tastes are very similar; on the other hand, there are so many contrasts that we are the most instructive subjects and objects of mutual observation. I have never known anyone who could gain so much objective knowledge from experience, no one who obtained so much insight from what she learned. Rée wrote me yesterday: 'Lou has undoubtedly grown several inches in Tautenburg'—well, I perhaps, too. I wonder if there has ever existed such a philosophic candor as exists between us. . . . I am afraid her health will not last more than six or seven years. Tautenburg has given Lou a goal. She left me a moving poem . . .

"Unfortunately, my sister has become Lou's deadly enemy. She was full of moral indignation from beginning to end and says that she knows now what my philosophy means. She wrote to my mother that she had seen my philosophy come to life in Tautenburg. I love evil but she loves the good. If she were a good Catholic she would now go into a convent and atone for the evil that would result from it. In short, I have the Naumburg 'virtue' against me. There is a real break between us—even my mother once forgot herself so much that I packed my suitcase and went to Leipzig early in the morning. My sister, who refused to come to Naumburg as long as I was there, commented ironically: 'Thus began Zarathustra's downfall.' She is wrong, it is the start of the beginning."

It was a trying time for Nietzsche, this waiting in a small furnished room in Leipzig. He knew that Lou was with Rée and he wanted her back but there was nothing he could do. Fortunately, he had the poem she had given him in Tautenburg and the music he had written for it. He would surprise her by getting it published. He sent it to Gast and asked him to transpose his music. Then he took it to Professor Riedel, President of the German Musical Society, and suggested that it be performed by the Riedel choir. There is no evidence that Riedel seriously considered Nietzsche's suggestion but that did not deter him from joyously telling Lou in a letter from Leipzig that her poem quite possibly would be sung by Riedel's choir, "one of the best in Germany. That," he added significantly, "would be only one small way for us to reach posterity *together*—other ways being reserved." In the same letter he told her:

"Your idea of reducing all philosophical systems to the personal lives of philosophers is truly an idea from a 'sister brain.' That is the way I myself used to teach the history of ancient philosophy in Basel. I often told my students: 'This system is refuted and dead—but the man behind the system is irrefutable, the man cannot be silenced—for example, Plato.

"As regards your 'characterization of myself' which is correct, there came to my mind my little verses from *Gay Science* entitled '*Request.*' Can you guess, my dear Lou, what I request?"

He requested somebody "closer than his closest friend," somebody midway between his closest friend and himself. Did he mean a wife? In any case, mysterious allusions of this kind must have made Rée and Lou wonder, for Lou showed Rée all the letters she received from Nietzsche. Did they not imply that Nietzsche still hoped to establish a closer relationship with Lou than she desired? Was he out of his mind—as Rée suspected—or merely trying to be amusing as Lou thought? They could not make him out. The letter's final paragraph left room for both interpretations. In it Nietzsche told Lou of a happy afternoon he had spent the previous day:

"The sky was blue, the air mild and pure. I was in Rosenthal, lured by the music of Carmen. I sat three hours, drank the second glass of brandy this year in memory of the first (O, how awful it tasted!) and reflected in all innocence and malice whether I did not have some predisposition for madness. I finally said 'no' to myself. Then the music of Carmen began and for half an hour I walked about with tears in my eyes and a wildly beating heart.— When you read this you will probably say 'yes' and add another note to my characterization.

"Please come to Leipzig very very soon. Why only the second of October? Good-by, my dear Lou."

The longer Nietzsche waited the gloomier he became. "I have never had such melancholic moments as during this autumn in Leipzig," he confided to Overbeck. And to Gast he wrote: "Ah, my friend, if I could tell you of the fivefold darkness that wants to envelop me and how hard I have to fight against it. Avoid people. Men like us are like glass and break easily—that is the end." But in a postscript he added: "News item: Lou is coming here the second of October. A few weeks later we leave for Paris. —My proposal."

Again and again Nietzsche tried to get a commitment from Lou about where they would study together, and the date of their meeting. But Lou evaded the issue, either because she did not know herself or because she, too, was having doubts about the wisdom of having Nietzsche join them. No wonder that he became sad and irritable. However, when she finally arrived in Leipzig, his spirits rose quickly and once again he overflowed with ideas and plans. Paris was beckoning, he wanted Lou to come to Paris with him. He seemed to have forgotten that Rée also was in the picture and that even Rée's mother planned to join them. He tried to establish the same intimate relationship with Lou that had existed—or he felt had existed—in Tautenburg.

Rée, whose claims to Lou's favors were by now much more substantial—there were rumors that they lived together in Leipzig, as they certainly did a few months later in Berlin—was thoroughly annoyed by Nietzsche's persistent refusal to face facts. He tried to tell his friend as gently as possible that his behavior embarrassed Lou because she did not share his feelings and never had. Nietzsche would not hear of it. Had Lou not told him in Tautenburg that Rée was hopelessly caught in the net of his shallow "réealism"? Had she not told him that she had much more in common with him, Nietzsche, than with Rée? Had she not called him her "brother in spirit"? What right had Rée to insinuate that Lou preferred him? Nietzsche could not help noticing, of course, that Lou and Rée were on very intimate terms but that knowledge merely increased his ardor. Sensing Rée's irritation he thought he could sweep Lou off her feet by leading her deeper into the mysteries of his new philosophy. Whenever he had a chance to talk with her alone—because of Rée's watchful presence that was not often the case—he hinted darkly about the impact his ideas would have on the world. Eternal recurrence: the very words made one shudder. To think that there was no relief from life, that we were chained to it like galley slaves, returning again and again to the same miseries. Was that not enough to make the bravest cringe? Once the world had understood the meaning of eternal recurrence it would crucify him, even his friends would crucify him. Or did Lou think Rée could bear such thoughts? He who always carried a phial of poison and thought he could sneak away from it all like a thief in the night. No, Rée was not the man for his new philosophy. He lacked courage and imagination. What good was intellect without imagination? With an air of mystery, Nietzsche invited Lou to explore with him the far reaches of the soul that lie beyond the bounds of intellect; "for intellect," he told her, "what do I care about intellect! What do I care about knowledge! I respect nothing but drives and I would swear it is *that* which we have in common. Try to see through this phase in which I have been living the last few years, see behind it. Do not let yourself be deceived about me. I hope you do not seriously believe that the 'free-thinker' is my ideal! I am . . . pardon, dearest Lou!"

Such confessions troubled Lou. She understood too well why Nietzsche scorned Rée's rationalism. She had doubts about it, too; and she could not help being fascinated by Nietzsche's appeal to the irrational forces in life. Would a world devoid of awe, faith and mystery be worth living in?

"A span of time that has no meaning except that we creep through it on all fours in the morning, on two legs at midday and on three in the evening—merely to die."

What scale was there when reason had conquered faith? The mystic at least could hope to find peace in God and that hope gave meaning and color to life. But without that hope . . . ? Of course, nothing could be more hopeless than Nietzsche's eternal recurrence, and yet he somehow managed to give it the fascination of a glacier: silent, white and menacing.

But there always came a point when Lou was annoyed with herself for being carried away by Nietzsche. While her emotions were stirred by his ideas, her mind rebelled against them. There was absolutely no proof for anything he said. Rée was right, Nietzsche was not really a philosopher at all. He was a mystic and a rather cloudy one. It was amusing to listen to his oracular pronouncements and almost comic to hear him comment on the world-shaking impact of his ideas. More and more often, particularly when Rée was present—who listened to Nietzsche's prophecies with undisguised scorn—Lou found it hard to keep a straight face. What had sounded convincing in the twilight of the Tautenburg forest made less and less sense in a gaslit room in Leipzig.

Rée watched Lou's growing disenchantment with satisfaction. He had long suspected that something was wrong with Nietzsche and he told Lou that their friend's vanity had now become pathological. The less people took him seriously the more he tried to shock them. His entire philosophy was aimed at shock effects. It was really a mixture of madness and nonsense. In order to impress them Nietzsche alternately issued imperious commands in the name of a future philosophy or made hushed allusions to the wheel of eternal recurrence. It was pathetic. He behaved, Rée thought, like a jilted schoolboy, at once boastful and awkward, theatrical and shy.

At last Lou began to feel sorry for Nietzsche and remonstrated with Rée when she thought he went too far in ridiculing their friend. Nietzsche was a tragic figure. It was unkind to make fun of him.

Rée decided that the best way to handle this delicate situation was to pretend that everything was fine. As long as they were in Leipzig he would leave both Lou and Nietzsche under the impression that their plan to study in Paris might materialize, although he had definitely decided against it now. He knew it would require a great deal of tact and diplomacy to disengage himself and Lou from Nietzsche. Nietzsche was firmly committed to the plan; he had broken with his family because of it. There might be serious consequences if he were told that they would not join him. And there was no telling what Lou would do in the event of a crisis. She might be moved by Nietzsche's pleas and insist on going ahead with their plan. Rée decided that she too must be kept in the dark. He would let her think that they would join Nietzsche in Paris, but first he would propose that they return to Stibbe once more, ostensibly to get ready for the winter semester. They would not commit themselves to any definite date for the Paris meeting. Nietzsche would realize when they did not return that their plan had been abandoned. This rather Machiavellian scheme, Rée thought, offered the best solution and the least painful for all concerned. It was, of course, very cruel, and Nietzsche had reason to feel betrayed.

By the end of October Nietzsche seems to have sensed that he was losing Lou. He could not recapture the mood of Monte Sacro, nor their Tautenburg intimacies. He blamed Rée for that, and, becoming more and more desperate, he began making remarks about Rée that really angered Lou. Rée was a coward and quite incapable of any profound thought or feeling, a petty bourgeois with a sniggering little soul. What could Lou possibly see in him? Let her think of the heights their thoughts had reached in Tautenburg, those intoxicating moments of truly creative joy. How could she hesitate? Here he was offering her a chance to mature, a chance to participate in the deepest mysteries of the age. Mistaking Lou's surprise for emotion, his language became more and more lyrical. He began to allude to his love in sensuous images. And again Lou was perturbed. She noted in her diary:

"Just as Christian mysticism (indeed all mysticism) at the point of its highest ecstasy returns to crude religious sensuousness, so too, the most ideal love can become sensuous again, precisely because of its emotional intensification of the ideal. It is an unpleasant fact, this revenge of the body. I do not like circular feelings that return from whence they came, for that is the point of false pathos, of lost honesty and truth of feeling. Is it this, perhaps, which alienates me from Nietzsche?"

It was a sad Sunday, the first Sunday in November, when Nietzsche said good-by to his friends at the Leipzig railroad station. Many unspoken things lay between them, although outwardly everything seemed the same. They would soon meet again and live together as they had planned in the perfect harmony of their "holy trinity." But Nietzsche was not sure. Grave doubts filled his mind as he watched his friends depart; Lou cheerful and relaxed as always, Rée reticent and serious. But hope dies hard and just before the train left Nietzsche gave Lou a copy of his *Gay Science* inscribed with the poem "The New Columbus." But in Lou's version the last two lines read:

> Courage! For you hold the rudder,
> Loveliest Victoria!

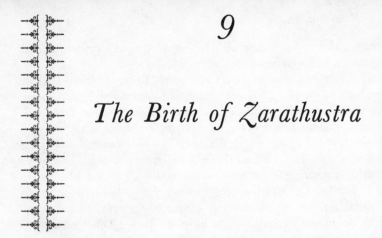

9

The Birth of Zarathustra

AFTER THE DEPARTURE OF LOU AND RÉE, NIETZSCHE STAYED ALMOST two weeks longer in Leipzig. He felt sick at heart and did not know where to turn next. Peter Gast was with him and tried to cheer him up by playing him passages from his recently composed opera, *Matrimonio Secreto*. It was ironic. Here Nietzsche was asked to listen to a work, the very title of which reminded him of his loss. Gast soon realized that it was hopeless to try to cheer up his friend. Nietzsche could not get Lou out of his mind. He hoped against hope that he would see her again. He told the Overbecks that Lou and Rée had gone to Berlin to meet Rée's mother and from there they would travel to Paris where he would join them. He still pretended to believe that, although he added significantly:

"Lou's health is woefully bad. I give her a much shorter time now than last spring."

But it was not Lou's health that prevented her from returning to him. Gradually Nietzsche was forced to realize that she would never come back. This realization came as a terrible shock although—or perhaps because—it was not altogether unexpected. It was a shock that all but unhinged him. Like a wounded animal, his instinctive reaction was to hide from the world. He could not bear the sight of people. When he left Leipzig in the middle of November his only thought was to get away from it all, from Germany especially, where he had been so terribly humiliated.

On his way south he stopped in Basel and paid a brief visit to the Overbecks, who were appalled when they saw him and begged him not to let his despondency get the better of him. He must not eat out his heart in solitude. They invited him to stay with them but Nietzsche would not hear of it. He must be alone now, he insisted; he would go to the furthermost point of loneliness.

He returned to Genoa where he had started his fateful journey. But it, too, had changed. The spring sun was gone. He encountered a cold and dreary winter and, although badly in need of creature comforts, he could not find them. The rooms in Genoa were unheated. He could not get warm, and what was worse, he could not find sleep.

"If only I could sleep! But the strongest doses of my opiates do not help me now, nor do six or eight hours of walking. . . . I am lost unless I succeed in discovering the alchemist's trick of turning this dirt into gold."

Almost to the end of the year he harbored lingering hopes that everything might still turn out well. Even when he heard that Lou and Rée were living in Berlin together and had no intention of asking him to join them there, he wrote and begged them to give him a clear answer. What did they intend to do? Why all their distrust? Would not Rée please tell him "what now concerns us most—what stands between us."

In letters and especially in drafts of letters jotted down on the spur of the moment, the depth of his anguish is starkly revealed. He pleaded for clear skies above them. He could not live in this atmosphere of deceit and distrust. Calling Lou his "dear heart," he begged her to lift the cloud of suspicion from his mind:

"A solitary suffers terribly from suspecting the few people he loves; particularly if he suspects that they harbor a suspicion of his whole being. Why was there never any cheerfulness in our relationship? Because I had to use too much restraint. . . . I am talking obscurely. Once I have your confidence you will see that I shall find the right words. So far I have always been forced to be silent."

To Malwida he confided that his sister considered Lou "poisonous vermin that has to be destroyed at all costs and she acts accordingly. This is a most exaggerated point of view and thoroughly repugnant to me. On the contrary, I would like to help her [Lou] as much as possible from my whole heart and bring out the best in her. Whether I can do it, whether I have been able to do it so far, is a question I don't want to answer. I have honestly tried. But she has shown very little interest in me: to her I am, so it seems, more superfluous than interesting." He called Lou's intelligence "extraordinary" and added that "Rée thinks Lou and I are the most intelligent people alive." He still persisted in the pathetic effort to have Lou linked to him, and by Rée of all people! Again and again he asked who was at fault: "How did it all happen?" And his bitterness rose when he received only evasive answers.

"Please don't write me such letters," he admonished Lou. "Remember: I want you to rise in my esteem so that I do not have to despise you."

Or again: "I do not reproach you today with anything except that you have not been honest with me at the right time. . . . What would you answer if I asked you: 'Are you loyal?' 'Are you incapable of treason?' "

The more he brooded over the affair in his cold and dreary room, the angrier he became.

"Watch out," he warned Lou, "if I now reject you that is a terrible indictment of your character. . . . Who can keep company with you if you give way to all the pitiful traits of your nature? . . . You have done harm, you have caused injury not only to me but to all people who love me. This sword hangs over you. . . . I have not created the world or Lou. If I had created you I would have given you better health and, above all, something that is much more important than health—perhaps also a little more love for me (although that is what you are least interested in). . . . Remember: this cattish selfishness of yours that is incapable of love, this feeling for nothing, are to me the most repugnant traits in man, worse than evil. . . . Farewell, my dear Lou, I shall not see you again. Preserve your soul from similar deeds and make good with others, especially with friend Rée, what you cannot make good with me. . . . Farewell, I have not finished your letter, but I have read too much already."

However, try as he might, he could not forget Lou. If she were a man, he wrote Rée, he would challenge her to a duel. She had shamefully deceived him. Frustrated in his efforts to hurt Lou, who did not see most of these letters because Rée kept them from her, Nietzsche's disappointed love turned against himself. He talked of suicide. He called himself a madman and boasted of taking overdoses of opium.

"My dears, Lou and Rée, do not worry too much about these outbreaks of my paranoia or my hurt vanity. Even if, perchance, in some fit of despondency, I should take my own life, there would not be much cause for mourning. What do you care about my fantasies—you did not even care for my truth. I want you both to consider that I am, after all, nothing but a semi-lunatic, tortured by headaches, who has been completely unhinged by his long solitude. I have arrived at this, as I think, reasonable insight into my situation after taking an enormous dose of opium from desperation. But instead of thereby losing my mind, it finally seems to have come. Besides, I have really been sick for weeks and if I say that I have had Orta weather for twenty days I don't need to say any more. . . . Please, friend Rée, ask Lou to forgive me everything. She will perhaps give me an opportunity to forgive her. For, so far, I have not forgiven her. It is much harder to forgive one's friends than one's enemies."

Late in December he told Overbeck that his friendship with Lou was "dying a painful death. At least, so I believe today. Later, if there is a later, I shall say a word about this. Pity, dear friend, is a kind of hell."

What should he do now? Could he go on living? Would it not be better to put an end to it all? Suicide—the longer he brooded the more convinced he became that there was no other way out. He felt like a gambler who had staked everything on one card and had lost. His friends were horrified by the suicidal tone of his letters.

"I had the impression of a light that flickers," Overbeck wrote Gast, "and was prepared for the worst."

Nietzsche's family, too, were prepared for the worst but for different reasons. They felt offended because Nietzsche did not tell them where he was after he left Leipzig. They were afraid he had gone to Paris with Lou and was living in sin with the Russian adventuress. To them that was a fate worse than death. If that were the case, the pastor's widow told Elizabeth, her son had a choice of three alternatives: "Either he marries the girl, shoots himself or goes mad."

One gets the impression that the first of these choices was the least acceptable to the Naumburg ladies. They did not know what had really happened; that it was not Lou who was running after Nietzsche but quite the reverse. This basic misunderstanding distorted all the accounts of the "Lou Affaire" given by Nietzsche's sister and by those who took their cue from her. Strictly speaking there never was a "Lou Affaire." It was a "Nietzsche Affaire" from beginning to end.

How little Lou was affected by it can be seen from an entry she made in her diary at the end of 1882. Summing up the events of that fateful year, she writes only of Rée.

"It was during the first days of January when I came, sick and tired, to the sunshine of Italy, in order to take away from there sunshine and life for a whole year. How brightly this sun shone on our Roman walks and talks, on the idyll of Orta with its boat rides, its Monte Sacro and its nightingales, on the journey to Switzerland through the Gotthard and on the days in Lucerne. And then, when I left Mama, and wanted to live my newly won life, we started that unusual friendship upon which up to this day our lives depend. A friendship of such intimacy and restraint as perhaps does not exist anywhere else in the world. Rarely or never have two people entered into a relationship so imprudently and, at the same time, with such prudence. To be sure, we did not know what would come of it when I arrived in Stibbe that evening alone and unknown, a stranger among strangers. Stibbe, which became a home for me through you. But then came the day when we left Stibbe together, hand in hand, like two good comrades entering the great world confident that we could not be misunderstood."

As it turned out this assumption was wrong. When Lou and Rée, a young man and woman who were not married, began to live openly together, criticism was heard from all sides. Elizabeth Nietzsche became so indignant that she felt it should be brought to the attention of the Prussian police. Nietzsche, too, was outraged.

"Every other man would have turned away from such a girl with disgust," he wrote Overbeck, "and to tell the truth, I too felt it but I overcame it again and again. I have shed countless tears in Tautenburg, not for my sake but for Lou's. I deplored seeing the decadence of a nobly endowed character. This trick pity played on me. I lost the little I still possessed, my good name, and the confidence of the few people I love. I am perhaps even going to lose my friend Rée. I lost a whole year through horrible torments which I am still suffering to this day. I found nobody in Germany who would help me and I am now exiled from Germany. And what hurts most, my entire philosophy has been compromised. I myself really do not need to feel ashamed of the whole affair. I have felt the strongest and most genuine emotions for Lou and there was nothing erotic in my love. At most I could have made a god jealous. Strange: I thought an angel had been sent to me when I returned once more to people and life, an angel who would mitigate what had become too hard through pain and solitude, and above all, an angel of courage and hope for all that still lies in front of me. But she was no angel. For the rest I do not want to have anything further to do with her. It was a completely useless waste of love and heart. Well, to tell the truth, I am rich enough for it."

Completely unaware of how deeply she had hurt Nietzsche Lou started the year 1883 with the happy assurance that her struggle for independence was over. The pattern of the life she wanted to live emerged. In the company of her "brother" Rée, she moved freely in a small circle of young scholars and scientists, took part in their discussions, shared in their work and was accepted as one of them. She enjoyed this unique position enormously, and if she had any regrets that Nietzsche was not among them, she kept them to herself.

At this time the crisis in Nietzsche's life reached its climax. Exactly a year after that glorious *Sanctus Januarius* which he had celebrated in *Gay Science* and which had given rise to such great expectations, he found himself literally at the end of his rope. He knew that only a supreme effort of his creative will could save him. Lou's betrayal had thrown him into a "veritable abyss of emotions." If he could not rise above them he was lost.

The first part of *Thus Spoke Zarathustra*, written at the beginning of February, 1883, in a few days of intense concentration, marks Nietzsche's ascent "vertically from that depth into his height." He wrote the book as a challenge hurled against a world that had so cruelly disappointed him.

His spokesman is Zarathustra, that legendary Persian prophet, also called Zoroaster, who is supposed to have lived some eight hundred or a thousand years before Christ. He was the first moralist, Nietzsche said; the first to see that "the wheel in the working of things" is the struggle between good and evil. Since Nietzsche believed that there is nothing either good or bad but thinking makes it so, he felt that Zarathustra's doctrine of a universal moral law was a false doctrine and had been refuted by the course of history in the past three thousand years. "Zarathustra created morality, this most fateful error," Nietzsche wrote, "hence he must also be the first to recognize it." That is why he resurrected him. Nietzsche's Zarathustra is the Persian turned around.

In rhapsodic language that abounds in Biblical allusions Zarathustra preaches the ideal of Superman: "Man is something that is to be surpassed." He is a rope stretched between the animal and superman—a rope over an abyss. The future belongs to the strong, the ruthless, the powerful in mind and body. Overflowing with health, they are the creators of new values. They love the earth and laugh at any thought of a hereafter, for they know that all gods are dead. Fearlessly they follow the dictates of their will to power. They pursue greatness, not happiness. They live dangerously and accept without flinching the terrible truth that there is no peace ever from the wheel of eternal recurrence. They are the lords of the earth and despise the herd, the many-too-many, the meek, the sick and the poor in spirit.

As one ponders Nietzsche's grandiose vision of a new Adam and a new Eve and remembers the wretched life of the man who had it—poor and suffering and half-mad with solitude and disillusionment—one suddenly realizes that Superman is everything that Nietzsche was not. He is the violent projection of a brilliant brain, tortured beyond endurance, a defiant protest against his fate. He is Nietzsche turned around. Bearing this in mind makes it easier to understand Lou's part in the creation of this amazing book.

Eagle and serpent are Zarathustra's animals. "Keen as an eagle and brave as a lion," Nietzsche had called Lou. But Lou had betrayed him. Eve and the serpent had betrayed Adam. Zarathustra, the spokesman of the new Adam, would enlist the aid of the serpent, the cleverest animal under the sun. Lou's betrayal had brought on insomnia. Zarathustra heard of a sage who knew much about sleep. "Fortunate who lives near this sage; such sleep is contagious."

Rée, too, had betrayed him. Nietzsche was bitterly jealous of Rée. Says Zarathustra: "He who is consumed by the flame of jealousy turns at last, like the scorpion, the poisoned sting against himself."

Elizabeth Nietzsche claims her brother was a saint and incapable of carnal desires. But Zarathustra refutes her claim. The book abounds in erotic allusions and thinly veiled images of Nietzsche's repressed sexuality. "Do I counsel you to chastity?" asks Zarathustra. "Chastity is a virtue with some, but with many almost a vice."

Having failed to rouse Lou, Nietzsche noted angrily that she suffered from "sexual atrophy." Zarathustra turns it around and says: "Is it not better to fall into the hands of a murderer than into the dreams of a woman in heat?"

Forsaken by his friends, Nietzsche had fled into solitude. "Flee into solitude," counsels Zarathustra. "You live too closely to the petty and spiteful. Flee from their invisible revenge."

"It is easier to forgive one's enemies than one's friends," said Nietzsche. And Zarathustra: "One should honor in one's friend even the enemy."

Zarathustra says: "Woman is not yet capable of friendship. Women still are cats and birds or at best cows." And Nietzsche noted that Lou had "the character of a cat, a beast of prey that pretends to be a domestic animal."

In her essay on women, which she had discussed with Nietzsche in Tautenburg, Lou wrote: "Pregnancy is the cardinal condition which has gradually, in the course of time, determined the character of women." Zarathustra says: "Everything about women is a riddle. And everything about women has one solution—its name is pregnancy."

In Lucerne Nietzsche gave Lou a whip to hold over him and Rée. Says the old woman to Zarathustra: "You go to women? Don't forget the whip."

It has been noted that no one among Nietzsche's friends was blond and blue-eyed, except the girl he loved. "Be on your guard against the assaults of your love!" warned Zarathustra. But he warned in vain. The bitch sensuality, whom Nietzsche castigated in Zarathustra, took her revenge on him. Tormented by his desire for a blond young girl, his alter ego transformed her into the fierce image of a "blond beast."

How much Nietzsche's fascination for Lou contributed to the creation of *Zarathustra* is, of course, a complex question. It will be remembered that after the completion of *Gay Science* Nietzsche said he had no intention of writing another book in the near future. He needed time to work out a systematic presentation of his philosophy of eternal recurrence. There was no indication that he would rush into print as the prophet of Superman. The whole tenor of the book, its erotic overtone, its quasi-Biblical style, its religious-prophetic utterances, sets it apart from Nietzsche's other writings. In this respect it reflects Lou's presence. Elizabeth Nietzsche is quite right when she says that Zarathustra is her brother's "most personal work." What she does not say, indeed what she most vehemently denies, is that it was Nietzsche's encounter with Lou that provided the personal background to Zarathustra. Less biased witnesses than Elizabeth have stressed this fact. Mrs. Overbeck writes that, "in spite of various contributory impulses that led to Zarathustra, Lou had a direct share in it by inspiring Nietzsche to make this philosophic-religious and moralistic-prophetic statement as a substitute for religion and morality." And Peter Gast noted: "For some time Nietzsche was really enchanted by Lou. He saw in her somebody quite extraordinary. Lou's intelligence, as well as her femininity, carried him to the heights of ecstasy. Out of his illusion about Lou grew his mood for Zarathustra. The mood is indeed entirely Nietzsche's own but, nevertheless, that it was Lou through whom he was propelled into such Himalayan heights of feeling makes her an object of reverence."

Finally, Nietzsche himself acknowledged his indebtedness to Lou when he wrote to his mother in 1884: "You may say what you like against the girl—and certainly other things than my sister does—it still remains true that I have never found a more gifted and thoughtful person. And although we have never agreed, any more than I have agreed with Rée, we were both happy after each half hour we spent together that we had learned so much. It is no accident that I have accomplished my greatest work in the last twelve months."

In writing the first part of *Zarathustra* Nietzsche found release from the tensions that had built up in him during 1882 and had reached a climax in his encounter with Lou. But writing is not the only way to release creative tensions. It is anybody's guess what would have happened had Lou been willing to become Nietzsche's wife and disciple. Her rejection released, or helped release, *Zarathustra*. We do not know what kind of book, if any, Nietzsche would have written had she accepted him. But there is no doubt that Lou's acceptance would have altered Nietzsche's life fundamentally. Instead of being alone he would have had company. Instead of being dejected he would have been elated. Is it likely that such a mood would have given rise to *Zarathustra?*

Nietzsche himself maintained that all philosophical systems reflect the personal lives of philosophers. Hence, had his life been different, his philosophy would have been different. In view of the fateful consequences of Nietzsche's philosophy, especially his propagation of the "superman ideal," which attained such a powerful dominance on German thought, and became the bible of fascism, it is sobering to reflect that in 1882 the course of Nietzsche's life depended on the yes or no of a twenty-one-year-old girl.

The writing of *Zarathustra* enabled Nietzsche to master his despair and think of Lou with greater detachment. He had not committed suicide, instead he had created his son, Zarathustra. As far as he was concerned this creative act closed the Lou chapter of his life.

But this was not the way Elizabeth wanted the affair to end. She rejoiced when she heard that her brother had broken with that "terrible Russian," and now that she and her brother were reconciled through the good offices of Malwida, she wanted revenge. Lou had mortally offended her. She had alienated her brother's affection and must be punished. Besides, was she not a living disgrace to her sex? She should not be permitted to flaunt her immoral way of life in public. Cohabitation was a criminal offense. Elizabeth felt that the Prussian police should be informed of the goings-on in Berlin. There were means of getting rid of undesirable aliens. She would see to it that Lou learned a lesson that she would not forget.

With a will and determination worthy of a better cause, Elizabeth Nietzsche now started an action that had repercussions in many parts of Europe. Supported by Malwida, who was equally outraged by Lou's way of life, Elizabeth wrote a number of extremely damaging letters to Lou's family and to Rée's mother. She pointed out the immoral nature of Lou and Rée's relationship, threatened to inform the police and demanded that Lou be sent back to Russia. Her letters caused a sensation. They brought many unsubstantiated rumors into sharp focus and transformed private gossip into quasi-public accusations. Although they failed to achieve their purpose, they did succeed in arousing a great deal of animosity against Lou. There were urgent consultations in St. Petersburg among Madame von Salomé and her sons. In Stibbe, Rée's family also became alarmed. Mrs. Rée considered forcing Paul to come home by cutting off his allowance. She found it hard to share her son with anyone, let alone with such an unconventional creature as Lou. And in faraway Rome Malwida von Meysenbug joined in the epistolary attack against Lou and Rée.

One of her letters to Elizabeth fell accidentally into Nietzsche's hands. It tore the old wound wide open. To his horror Nietzsche now learned that it was not Lou who had betrayed him but his friend Rée. Rée had turned Lou against him. Rée had spread the ugly rumor that he, Nietzsche, had ulterior designs on the girl. Rée had ridiculed his philosophy and had called it the ravings of a madman. This was more than he could stand. His honor had been offended. He must challenge Rée to a duel. But Elizabeth quieted her brother. She insisted that it was "her war" and that she would fight it with her weapons. Bitterly Nietzsche told the Overbecks that his sister was bent on revenge on Lou but that, so far, he had been her only victim. "I have endured more, five times more, than would make a normal person commit suicide; and the end is not yet."

The Overbecks commiserated with him and advised him not to let himself be carried away by his sister's hatred. To their surprise he turned against them and replied, "My sister is quite right in this affair. She is just as much offended, perhaps even more than I, and if she wants to have Lou sent back to Russia she is probably doing more good (if she succeeds) than I with my charity who want to denounce all revenge. Last year my sister was far too considerate of me. Is it not maddening that I have not known the gravest facts of this bad affair until the last three weeks? . . . Rée now suddenly stands exposed. It is terrible to be forced to revise one's opinion so completely about someone with whom one has felt linked for years in love and confidence. . . . Perhaps there will be a little dueling in the autumn."

Once more Nietzsche fell to brooding over the affair. In his mind, Rée now played the part of Mephistopheles whose cold and calculating cynicism had destroyed his friendship with Lou. Something had to be done. He could not stand on the sidelines and watch his sister fight for his honor. He had to join the battle. He told Elizabeth that he had written some ten letters to Rée but had not sent any for fear that Rée would commit suicide upon receiving them. Finally, he decided to send a letter to Rée's brother George.

Like most letters Nietzsche wrote during this time, it tells a great deal more about his state of mind than about the facts in the case. He had discovered, he said, quite by accident that Lou had merely been the mouthpiece of Paul Rée's slanderous attacks on him and his sister:

"It is he who calls me a low character and mean egotist, who tries to exploit everything for his own purposes. It is he who reproaches me for having pursued, under the mask of ideal aims, the dirtiest designs on Miss Salomé. He preached to me about her, as if she were too good for this world, a martyr of knowledge from her earliest childhood, completely unselfish, as if she had sacrificed to truth all her happiness and joy of life. Well, Mr. Rée, once in a long, long while a human being like that is born into this world and I would travel around the globe to get to know it. I have met this girl and I have tried obstinately to retain the last vestige of that picture of her. Impossible! Her own mother warned me of her. I was simply deceived. But no matter how often I expressed to your brother my serious doubts concerning the character of this girl, do you think he ever had a word of excuse for her? He merely said again and again: 'You are completely right about Lou. But it does not alter my relation to her.' In a letter he once called her 'his fate.' *Quel goût!* This thin, dirty, evil-smelling little monkey with her false breasts— a fate!"

And so Nietzsche once again became embroiled in this tragic farce. "Since this affair has started again I am living in a state of madness and do not find peace day or night." Driven by the furies of Elizabeth's hatred and by his own sense of loss and injury, he hovered for weeks at the brink of a complete collapse.

The Overbecks watched with helpless indignation. They had never been very kindly disposed toward Lou, but even so they felt that Elizabeth's campaign of hatred was unpardonable. For the sake of her revenge she was destroying her brother's peace of mind and seriously damaging his reputation. But they knew that any intervention on their part would be resented. Even their counsel of moderation had been rebuffed. Elizabeth Nietzsche would not be deflected from her war of extermination. Lou must be punished even at the risk of her brother's life.

However, when the dust finally settled, Elizabeth found little cause for rejoicing. She had met her master in Lou. Standing calmly in the center of the storm that was raging around her, the young Russian warded off all blows aimed at her freedom. She did not go back to St. Petersburg. She did not give up her unconventional way of life. Neither Elizabeth's threats, nor her family's urgent appeals, nor the social ostracism to which she was subjected made her give up her intimate friendship with Rée. She had resolved to live her life according to her own insights and without regard to manmade rules. It was *her* life; the rest was unimportant. To become more and more herself, to grow according to the law and rhythm of her own nature—*that*, she believed, was her supreme task. It determined her actions and explains her obsession with freedom. For you have to be free to become yourself. That is what freedom meant to Lou: self-realization.

"It is released in us in the greatest hours of our lives, not when our ego says: 'I desire'—but: 'Here I stand, I can do no other.'"

Lou's commitment to the laws of her own nature ruled out

the possibility of her ever becoming any man's follower. Driven, like Nietzsche, by her daemon, she could not adapt herself to an alien pattern. Herein lay the tragedy of the Lou-Nietzsche encounter: like two stars they moved in the same orbit. They were fated to clash if they met.

The impact of this clash on Lou's life was profound, although she made light of it and tried to forget it. For one thing, Nietzsche's example showed her how precariously balanced the creative individual is, and how tenuous the line that separates genius from madness. It was an experience that focused her attention on the problems of psychopathology which were later to occupy such an important part of her life. Nietzsche had told her that it was not the intellect that matters but hidden and subconscious drives. In her work with Freud she learned that this was indeed the case. Man is not a rational animal. The mainsprings of his actions are his needs, desires and drives. Lou's meeting with Nietzsche, therefore, paved the way to her work with Freud a quarter of a century later.

She profited in another way from her stormy association with Nietzsche. It provided her with material for her own work as a writer. Nietzsche encouraged her first attempts to put down her thoughts on paper, and she decided she could gain her independence by making writing a career. She pursued this goal with her customary determination, but her quick success as a writer was due in no small measure to the rapid rise of Nietzsche's fame. While the philosopher lay dying in Weimar, during that long and agonizing period from his collapse in 1889 to his death in 1900, the world first began to take notice of him. Suddenly there was a great demand for interpretations of his work; and feeling that she was as well qualified as anyone, Lou wrote a number of newspaper articles and finally even a book on Nietzsche. Nietzsche's relatives and friends were shocked, and rightly so, by what they called Lou's "journalistic exploitation" of her personal acquaintance with the philosopher. Inasmuch as Lou made public a number of private letters Nietzsche had written her, giving her readers the impression that she had been on intimate terms with him, there is a good deal of truth in this indictment. It was poor taste, to say the least, for her to publish excerpts from Nietzsche's letters while the philosopher was still alive.

Being a young and unknown writer, Lou undoubtedly benefited from these disclosures, not only by gaining a certain amount of notoriety, but even financially. She was well paid for the series of articles she wrote for the Sunday edition of the *Vossische Zeitung* and for the *Neue Rundschau* in 1891. And if she did not make much money on her book, published in 1894, it certainly added to her reputation. It is an interesting book, rich in insights, and although it received only mixed notices when it appeared, it deserves a place in the huge library of Nietzsche criticism.

In one of his prophetic utterances Nietzsche had said that with Lou's "Prayer to Life" and the music he had written for it, they would reach posterity together. He was right. They did reach posterity together—but not through Lou's poem. His own tragic fate spilled over on the girl who had spurned him. For the rest of her life Lou bore the burden of having been Nietzsche's friend. It was a heavy burden and, although she bore it cheerfully enough, it had taught her to be more circumspect in the future.

PART III

Years of the Wild Duck
1883-1897

IO

"Brother" Rée

IN 1883 LOU AND RÉE LIVED TOGETHER IN BERLIN, WHILE NIETZSCHE ate out his heart in solitude in Italy. The "holy trinity" they had talked of so cheerfully a few months previously became a somewhat unusual twosome. For, although they shared the same apartment and kept very close company, they were not lovers. By the force of her will Lou kept the ardor of her "brother" under control. It did not worry her that he suffered from this enforced celibacy nor that her own reputation was hopelessly compromised by this strange living arrangement. They had agreed to live together like brother and sister for the rest of their lives. And for five years they did. Those five years were among the happiest of Lou's life. She was young and she was free. The monthly check she received from home assured her financial independence. She had a loyal friend and protector and she lived in a city that provided plenty of nourishment for her inquisitive mind. Everything had turned out exactly as she had planned. Life was magnificent. She was going to live it to the full.

Rée was a kind and considerate companion whose major fault was the low opinion he had of himself. It caused him to suspect the motives of others, especially with respect to himself. He did not believe in disinterested actions and was tormented by self-doubts and a deep-seated sense of inferiority. The fact that Lou, whom he adored, had chosen him as her life's partner was a source of constant wonder to him. He did not know what he had

done to deserve it and suspected that Lou needed him for ulterior purposes, as indeed she did.

To assuage his doubts Lou had to give him constant proof that
she was genuinely fond of him. This she did to the best of her
ability. And if it had not been for the memory of the Gillot affair
which, she insisted, ruled out any possibility of love, their friendship might have blossomed into love. There must have been many
moments during the intimate hours they spent together when she
may have wondered whether she should not become Rée's wife
and by this simple act bestow upon him a gift of love which
would have put all his doubts at rest. Her moral scruples certainly did not prevent her from yielding to his desire. But apart
from Gillot's invisible presence, there also seems to have been
something in Rée's physical make-up that was repugnant to Lou.
In any case, the intimacy of their relationship did not cause her
any sleepless nights, quite in contrast to Rée who often spent the
night restlessly walking through the deserted streets of Berlin. He
knew that any attempt to violate her trust would be fatal. All he
could do was wait and hope that his love would finally strike a
responsive chord in her. The only alternative was to leave her.
That is what he had wanted to do in Rome when he confided to
Malwida that he loved Lou. And that is what he tried to do once
or twice afterward.

"I am afraid we must part," he wrote her at the beginning of
their partnership, "for, although I am your protector and support,
you are too honest to want me in this role if there has been the
slightest change in the deep and intimate sympathy between us.
And there has been. For on the one hand, I am a weak character.
Weakness is the key to my whole being, at least that is what I
have become in the last four, five, or six years. . . . I was really
dead already. You have wakened me to a pseudo life. But a
pseudo life is repugnant to the dead. On the other hand, I cannot
rid myself of a feeling of mistrust because of a trait I have that
you do not like. The mistrust, I mean, of being unsympathetic to
you, of doing something that is repugnant to you. Hence let us
go our separate ways to our graves."

"No!" replied Lou. "Certainly not. We shall live together and
strive together until you have recanted the above."

Lou's self-assurance had a calming effect on Rée. He gradually

Lebensrückblick

Louise (Lolja) von Salomé
when she met Hendrik Gillot
in 1878.

Hendrik Gillot.

Lebensrückblick

Lou Salomé in 1882, at the time of her meeting with Friedrich Nietzsche and Paul Rée.

Lebensrückblick

"Friedrich Nietzsche, formerly a professor now a roaming fugitive." Nietzsche inscribed this picture for Lou Salomé in 1882. She published it in her book on Nietzsche in 1894.

Podach, *Friedrich Nietzsche und Lou Salomé*, Zurich: Niehans, 1937

The Holy Trinity: Lou Salomé, Paul Rée and
Friedrich Nietzsche, Lucerne, May 13, 1882.

Below: Elizabeth Nietzsche in 1882, the "Faithful Lama."

Above and right: Two views of Lou Salomé in 1897.

Friedrich Carl Andreas.

Lebensrückblick

Friedrich Pineles.

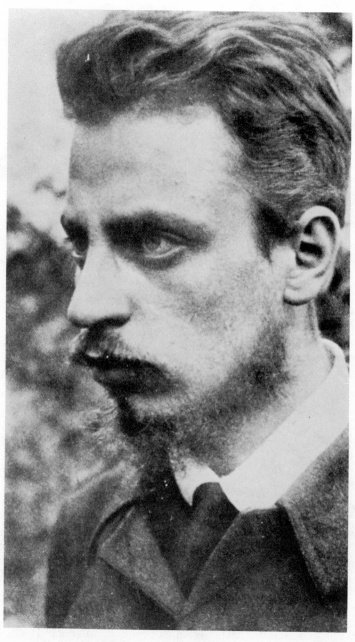

Rainer Maria Rilke in 1897, the year he met Lou Salomé.

Rilke and Lou Salomé travelling in Russia were the guests of the poet Spiradon Droshin and his family.

Lou Salomé (in furs) at the Weimar Congress, September 1911. Sigmund Freud stands behind her to the right.

accepted the role she had chosen for him and even seemed to enjoy it. Their friends called him Lou's "maid-of-honor." She mentions this epithet cheerfully without realizing that it is a devastating criticism of Rée's manhood. Perhaps he, too, treated it as a joke, the price he paid for being allowed to be near her. If so, he must have felt that once again the joke was on him.

In the same circle of their Berlin friends—a group of young scholars, philosophers and scientists—Lou was called "Her Excellency." This appellation, too, is revealing. It shows how she affected those closest to her. They admired her strength of character, her sovereign contempt of all petty virtues, her indifference to middle-class morality, fully as much as the unusual quality of her mind and her distinguished origin. Although she was the youngest member of the group and often the only woman present, she was the vital center, sparkling with ideas, daring in her speculations and entirely free of cant, pretense or prejudice. Considering the social taboos of the time, such qualities, unusual in men, were unheard of in women. Small wonder that this brilliant and exotic Russian fascinated them all and that, one by one, they fell in love with her.

Rée, who was the unofficial scorekeeper of Lou's conquests, had a hard time keeping track of them all. On more than one occasion he asked her with great concern if it was true that she had accepted a proposal of marriage. Once she borrowed an alarm clock from a young man of their acquaintance on condition that if she did not return it on a certain date he could assume that she would marry him. She promptly forgot both the clock and the condition, and was horrified when a dejected Rée bade her good-by, since she was now going to be someone else's wife.

Among Lou's passionate suitors at that time were Ferdinand Tönnies and Hermann Ebbinghaus. Lou considered the former, who became one of Germany's leading sociologists, the most brilliant man next to Nietzsche that she had met. His rival for her favors, Hermann Ebbinghaus, taught experimental psychology, a subject in which Lou was especially interested. Both men were very close to her, closer than Rée whose utilitarian mentality often struck her as pedestrian. And yet it was Rée with whom she lived and to whom she always returned. She followed this same pattern all her life. She let herself be wooed by ardent suitors, lived and traveled with them for a time, and then returned home again, home to herself, as she put it, to the shelter and protection, first of her friend Rée, and later of her husband, Andreas. The distinguishing feature of Lou's friendships and love affairs was that they always started on a high intellectual plane. For, although she was a very attractive woman, it was always her mind and the radiance of her being, her vitality and fervor, that attracted men. Nietzsche's friend, the philosopher Paul Deussen, who belonged to the Berlin circle of young intellectuals and who was one of the first to whom Lou gave a copy of her book *A Struggle for God* when it appeared in December, 1884, wrote: "I must confess that my love for Lou burst into bright flames during the reading of her book. My friend Ebbinghaus called it a 'nun's fantasies,' but I found much spirit in the book and I fell in love with that spirit."

It cannot have been easy for Rée, to whom she dedicated her book, and who was very sensitive about his appearance, to harbor the suspicion, warranted or not, that the real reason for Lou's refusal to belong to him was that she found him physically unattractive. He tried hard not to show any jealousy of the favors she bestowed on others, although there is no reason to suspect that, while she lived with Rée, Lou gave to others what she denied to him. But there were moments when Rée's self-control broke down and he gave vent to pointed remarks. Ludwig Hüter, a young man who was present at some of their meetings, although not a member of their group, reports that in a conversation Lou once mentioned Nietzsche's "beautiful mouth." Rée appeared piqued and asked her with his customary irony, "How do you know that? Nietzsche's mouth is hidden by a huge mustache." Lou replied, smiling, "Yes, but when he opens his mouth—and I have often spoken with him—you can see his lips very clearly."

Hüter concluded that Rée was jealous, "which is understandable for Lou Salomé is beautiful and enchanting. If she flirts she does it unconsciously, but she is nevertheless playing with serious, older men and it is not quite harmless that she always says what she thinks. For with such remarks, which may have been meant aesthetically but border on a naïve sensuality, she can play two rivals against each other."

Outwardly the Rée-Lou ménage was happy enough. They had

rented a three-room apartment in Berlin—not without experiencing some difficulty. Since they were not married their landladies
suspected that they were living in sin, a state of affairs that was
not encouraged in the Prussian capital. In Vienna, where Lou
and Rée also lived for a time, the situation was just the reverse.
Their Viennese landladies assumed that they were lovers and
went out of their way to be helpful and accommodating. Lou
found both attitudes amusing, and she often entertained her
friends with vivid accounts of house-hunting expeditions. She
loved shocking the bourgeoisie, loved watching the startled expressions on the faces of stolid German housewives when, after
telling them that she wanted to rent an apartment for herself
and her friend, she turned up with Rée. It was hilarious. Either
you were married or you were lovers, that was all they could
think of. Well, she was not going to let petty bourgeois minds
control her life. She was going to live it as she pleased.

In the company of a small congenial group of friends she did
indeed live as she pleased in the capital of Bismarck's Germany.
It was a stimulating existence. They went to concerts and lectures,
they discussed the latest plays and books, they organized a philosophic seminar at the home of the metaphysician Ludwig Heller,
they made excursions, went for boat rides on the lakes surrounding Berlin, and carried on an unending series of Socratic dialogues.
The intellectual air of Berlin was supercharged. The great post-
Kantian systems of philosophy were being replaced by positivistic
and Darwinistic movements; the scientific spirit claimed jurisdic-
tion over larger and larger areas of the human mind. The temper
of the times was critical and analytical. Lou called it a "heroic
period." Religious, philosophic, social and economic values were
undergoing profound change. Everything was in flux. Every tradition was subjected to rigorous scientific examination. Once again
the intellect attained dominance over the heart. It was a harsh
and unfeminine climate, but Lou thrived in it. Her enemies tried
in vain to find some weak spot in her intellectual or moral armor.
Asking for a confidential report on what was going on in Berlin,
Malwida received the following answer from Hüter:

"In your last letter you asked me what impression I had of
Miss Salomé. You know her very well and can easily see if I
judge her correctly. I shall simply tell you everything as I see it.

She made a very strong impression on me which I had to sort out first, for she is too unusual a girl to be easily understood. I encountered in her a completely different kind of woman from any I had ever met before. But let me say right here that I have understood and come to respect her. I believe that your anxiety is perhaps exaggerated. If there is a dual way of comprehending the world, a male and a female one, I would say that Miss Salomé comprehends it like a man. That is the striking and yet interesting aspect of her. The intellect thinks it can do everything, but without sentiment it is nothing. Both together govern mankind. Man creates the forms, builds the house, and woman gives warmth and content to it. Now I meet a charming, engaging, genuinely feminine creature who renounces all the means a woman has at her disposal and uses, instead, with a certain severe exclusiveness the weapons a man wields in the struggle of life. There is with her no trace of any quick judgment, or quick prejudgment, as with most women. On the contrary, a clear precision characterizes every word she utters. But the more precise her character is in one respect, the more one-sided it seems in another. There is indeed talk about music, art and poetry, but they are judged by strange criteria. Not by the pure joy of beauty, the delight of form, the understanding of content, the poetic pleasure of what is given with heart and soul—no, nothing like that. Instead, there is a cold, and unfortunately often, negatively destructive philosophizing about it. And behind her stands Dr. Rée, like Merk behind our great poet, a somewhat Mephistophelean character, dissecting everything, rationalizing everything.

"And yet I cannot believe that Miss Salomé will lose herself in this sort of criticism. She is not what one calls argumentative. With the marvelous clarity of her mind, she tries to approach the ideals of all men. Love of truth, not joy of argumentation impels her. You are afraid that her critical mind could gain dominance over her ideals. It is true her critical mind and its expressions are almost disquieting. But remember, she is too charming, warmhearted and friendly for her cold intellect to suppress her humanity. I think she is on the right track but I also think that, sooner or later, a reaction must occur against the one-sidedness with which she pursues it. If it brings to the surface her awakening feminine characteristics, something quite excellent will become of this richly endowed young girl."

Malwida does not seem to have been impressed with this glowing report. She felt that Lou had betrayed not only poor, suffering Nietzsche but her as well. Lou's way of life offended her
sense of propriety and she lent a willing ear to Elizabeth Nietzsche's sinister accusations. It was obvious that men were poor
judges of feminine character—how else was one to explain the
paeans of praise they all sang? The sooner the girl was sent back
to Russia the better for all concerned. Her behavior compromised
the whole feminist movement. If she did not leave Germany
voluntarily, pressure would have to be brought on her family.

As it turned out, it was Rée who bore the brunt of the attack
against Lou by the indefatigable Elizabeth and her allies, Malwida and Mrs. Rée. It was a bitter blow to him when his mother
joined the anti-Lou forces. He warded it off by appealing to his
brother George for understanding and support. George seems
to have been much more kindly disposed toward Lou than the
rest of his family. He noticed that Lou exerted a steadying influence on his financially irresponsible younger brother. Paul's
passion for gambling was kept within bounds. He no longer sent
those urgent requests for money that had so often been a drain on
the family finances. In this respect Lou's influence was all to the
good. It would be folly to break up a partnership that, whatever
else one might say about it, was financially sound. George told his
mother to stop meddling in Paul's affairs; he was old enough to
know what he was doing.

During the critical months in the spring and summer of 1883,
when Elizabeth's campaign against Lou was at its height, George
Rée's support proved invaluable. But there was always the
danger that Madame von Salomé, alarmed by the vituperative
attacks made on her daughter's character, would order her back
to St. Petersburg. She could stop Lou's allowance or ask one of
her sons to bring her home, by force if necessary. Something had
to be done to convince Lou's family that she was not merely having a good time in Berlin—she could do that in St. Petersburg
and with far greater propriety—but that she was engaged in
serious studies which could not be carried on in Russia. A book,
it was decided, was the answer. If Lou wrote a book her family
would have proof that Elizabeth's charges were unfounded.

As to her ability to write a book, there was no doubt. The only
question was could she write it in Berlin amid the distractions of
a large city. Since her health was still poor, Rée suggested that
they spend a few months in the south. They were both fond of
traveling and, being financially independent—they each received
250 marks a month from their families, a sizable sum in those
days—they could afford to live where they pleased. There may
have been an additional reason for Rée to suggest leaving Berlin.
He felt that too many of his friends paid too much attention to
Lou. It was true, she had rejected all proposals, but Rée would
have been less than human if the prospect of enjoying Lou's undivided company had not pleased him. They went to the idylli-
cally situated Austrian health resort, Gries-Meran, in the Tyrol.
There, surrounded by mountains, forests and rivers, they settled
down to write their books, Lou her psychological novel, *A Struggle for God,* and Rée his philosophic treatise, *The Origin of
Conscience.*

In retrospect Lou found it amusing that her first book, a command performance to impress her family, received better notices
than any of her later ones. Even such seasoned Berlin critics as
the brothers Hart were taken in by it. They failed to see that it
was a hodgepodge of two diverse ingredients: her St. Petersburg
notes on religious and metaphysical problems and a rather turgid
love story, originally written in verse. Today's reader will agree
with Lou that the literary value of *A Struggle for God* is slight,
but as a document of Lou's thoughts it is a book of considerable
interest. Like all her books, it contains a strongly autobiographical component: it poses the problem of what happens when man
loses faith in God. She presents it, naïvely enough Nietzsche
thought, in the form of an old man's diary.

After a brief account of Kuno's (the narrator's) childhood in a
vicarage dominated by the powerful figure of his father, a stern
old priest, Lou quickly comes to the point: Kuno's loss of faith.
At no time in his life have faith and reason been reconciled. In
his earliest childhood his piety had been so fervent that it inter-
fered with the normal development of his reasoning powers.
When they finally asserted themselves they had taken revenge,
as it were, by rising up in opposition to his faith. "The repressed
had become the repressors." The child's excessive piety had turned

into the brooding atheism of the adolescent. "I lost God," Kuno says, "as soon as I lost faith in the God of my childhood, the God whom I had created myself." As a result he felt forsaken and guilty, for "could there be a greater crime and a more deadly sin than this murder of God in my own heart?" Anxiously he asked himself whether he had indeed committed it or whether it had been committed against him by some daemonic power. And he became obsessed with the fear that he was predestined for evil.

The book's central theme, treated in various episodes and philosophic discourses, is Kuno's troubled feeling that his loss of faith is not so much an intellectual as a moral aberration. How can man live in a godless universe? Where are the moral co-ordinates upon which he can build his life? Kuno is not at all sure that the shifting sands of the human intellect can provide a safe substitute for the "Rock of Ages." But what else is there for a man of his intellectual honesty who is equally skeptical of the ancient faith in God and the modern faith in reason? Nothing, replies his younger brother Rudolf. He has to face the truth that life is meaningless, that there is no salvation, religious or secular, and that our best hope is to overcome it by embracing the Buddhistic ideal of Nirvana. But Kuno is passionately opposed to the doctrine of resignation. Beset by doubts and moral anxieties he still affirms the magnificence and grandeur of life and resolves to make it "the highest means of a highest goal."

When his brother protests that all religions consider life merely a necessary evil, Kuno replies that we can learn from religion, despite its denials, a genuine love of life, and the inspiring hope to endure for the sake of the realization of its ideals. As an example he mentions Jesus' agony in the Garden of Gethsemane. It was not, he insists, fear of death that made Jesus cry out, "Let this cup pass from me!" but love of life. He wanted to live because in his heart a world of glowing, passionate power demanded life and expression. But Rudolf remains unconvinced. The time will surely come, he says, when all the great revelations of all religions will seem to us like some forgotten dreams of our childhood. If this is true, replies Kuno passionately, then let us postpone this time, let us "fight for dying gods." He proclaims as the ideal of the modern atheist a "heroic attitude towards life, not resignation or despair."

In contrasting Kuno, the passionate skeptic, and Rudolf, the resigned agnostic, Lou portrays the contrasting attitudes of Nietzsche and Rée, with her sympathies clearly favoring Nietzsche. Kuno's life and actions are of particular interest, although admittedly, it would be absurd to equate the life and thoughts of her hero with Lou's own. The relationship between author and hero in a work of fiction is always complex. In a semi-autobiographical novel the author often transfers his problems to his hero, as Goethe did in *Werther*, and by so doing resolves them. While the problems are the same, the solutions are quite different.

The moral dilemma which Kuno faces is brought out in three major crises that occur at three different periods of his life as the result of his encounter with three women: his childhood friend, Jane; Margherita, whom he meets as a student; and his daughter, Mary. Each of these women is endowed with certain characteristics which are familiar to us from Lou's own life. Here again, fictional and biographical elements are intimately blended.

Jane, a pale but passionate girl, is an extreme idealist. She feels a strong need to admire, to worship, to kneel before an ideal, to deify it. This she calls a woman's religion. Margherita's need is for personal freedom. She becomes a student because she wants to live a fuller and freer life than she could otherwise. Finally, Kuno's daughter, Mary, who lives in a world of her own amidst the wonderful creatures of her vivid imagination, is a shy and sensitive child. Different though they are, all three women have a common fate: when they meet Kuno, tragedy enters their lives.

Until he meets Margherita, Kuno has lived an austere and ascetic life, devoted to his studies and pursuing his quest for knowledge with a Faustian zeal. He befriends Margherita because he is intrigued by her unusual way of life. He wants to know why she has chosen it. She tells him that only as a student can she hope to become emancipated from the chains that bind her sex to the narrow circle of home and marriage. Kuno questions the wisdom of her choice. In long and intimate talks they discuss the problems a woman faces when she tries to compete with men in the realm of ideas. Kuno thinks that the only way for a woman to attain greatness is through love. Margherita does not deny it but she rejects the exclusiveness of his statement.

Women, as well as men, have the right to live their lives to the fullest extent of their capabilities: intellectually as well as emotionally. She scorns the double standard of morality which keeps women in a state of inferiority and demands genuine equality for her sex.

Even when he disagrees with her, Kuno is charmed by her vivacity, her intelligence and her candor. But he is determined not to become emotionally involved with her and tries to keep their friendship on a high platonic plane. He wants to remain her friend and comrade. However, very soon a point is reached when a powerful sensuous element enters into their relationship, propelling them to closer and closer intimacy. To his horror Kuno feels passionate desires arising in him that seem to be "breaking out of him like wild beasts." Overnight the ascetic becomes a libertine. In such a mood he seduces Margherita, an act which at once fills him with disgust and remorse. He remembers his father's warning that "passions that are not guarded and guided by the Lord will lead to sin." With a great effort of will he tears himself away from Margherita, who is quite willing to remain his mistress, by telling her brutally, "You must know that a woman possesses two kinds of charm. She is either innocent and childlike in her purity, or she is a seductive mondaine versed in all the arts of coquetry. But you are merely a timid and unskilled beginner who has lost her innocence." The episode ends rather melodramatically by Margherita's poisoning herself after having turned down Kuno's belated and somewhat halfhearted proposal of marriage.

On a higher plane of tragedy is Kuno's reunion with his former childhood friend, Jane. When they meet again Jane is unhappily married to a dull and coarse husband who scorns his wife's idealism and uses her merely as a means of enjoyment. The fact that their marriage has remained childless has made it even harder for Jane to endure. Kuno is deeply moved when he senses how starved for affection she is. She in turn is filled with love and pity when she notices his intense moral anxiety resulting from his loss of faith. Her spontaneous response is to comfort him. With an almost Mephistophelean glee, Jane's husband watches their increasingly intimate friendship. He waits for the moment when their noble ideals will come crashing down on their heads. To prevent this from happening and to protect the spirituality of his love, Kuno decides to leave Jane. But it is too late. As he bids her good-by, at the moment of parting when love is strongest, Jane offers herself to him and he is too weak to resist. Once again the flesh proves weaker than the spirit. In trying to justify his weakness, Kuno declares: "Not I seduced Jane, she seduced me." But he knows that this is a poor excuse and again he is filled with shame and remorse.

When Jane realizes what she has done she becomes disconsolate and enters "into the loneliest of all lonelinesses that can grip a human heart, the abandonment of one who had betrayed the highest ideal of her life: self-abandonment." She confesses her adultery to her husband who merely laughs at her. Now, he feels, they are truly equal. But Jane cannot forgive herself. Tormented by a deep sense of guilt, she realizes that the wages of sin is death. "The Christian legend is right which says that hell started with a fallen angel." At the end of the summer she gives birth to a child and soon thereafter she dies.

The culminating tragedy in Kuno's life occurs when he decides to take Jane's child, Mary, who does not know that Kuno is her father, into his house. After the death of her mother, Mary has been brought up by an old peasant woman in a remote mountain village. Teased by her schoolmates because of her illegitimate birth she has become a withdrawn and shy child. Kuno takes her out of the village school and gives her private lessons much to the horror of the old woman who has tried to bring her up in the strict faith of the Catholic Church. She fears that Kuno's godlessness will bring misfortune to Mary. There are long discussions between Kuno and his brother Rudolf, who also lives with them, about the best way of bringing up the girl. Kuno wants to spare her the conflict between faith and reason with which he has struggled all his life. He thinks that by not compelling her to accept any ready-made God, but by encouraging her ability to admire and by instilling in her a reverence for life, he will permit her to remain capable of religious sentiments unencumbered by dogma or creed. He wants her to fight with "Promethean defiance" for her own ideals, compelling life to accept them. Then the word "God" will be more than an empty idea to her, it will be the name that comes to her lips in the greatest moments of her life.

He brings up his daughter in this spirit. She enjoys the lessons he gives her as much as he does, and he finds her intelligent and sensitive. Only in one respect is she her mother's child and a typical woman: "She does not want to reflect when she loves."

A shadow falls over the happy relationship between the two brothers and the girl when they notice that as she grows older Mary longs for an ever greater intimacy with Kuno. He plans to tell her on her seventeenth birthday that he is her father, but cannot bring himself to do it because he is afraid of making a humiliating confession to his child. In the meantime, the old peasant woman is shocked when she notices that Mary adores her father. She fears the girl will reap the bitter harvest of a god-less education. The story reaches its climax when Mary, sitting at the deathbed of the old woman who has suffered a stroke, tells her that she hopes to become Kuno's wife. Horrified, the old woman rises from her bed, utters a terrible shriek—"Lord Jesus, Thy judgment"—and falls back dead. Later that night Kuno asks Mary to call him Father. She suddenly understands, screams "Father!" and faints. That same night she drowns herself.

The tragedy of Mary's suicide forces the two brothers to reflect once again on the meaning of life and death. Rudolf, who now confides to his brother that he was deeply in love with Mary, cannot get over her death. Life, which has always seemed to him but a necessary evil, has now become empty and meaningless. He falls sick and wants to die.

"Death would mean liberation to me. Its peace and quiet which others dread, correspond to my innermost desire—to desire nothing."

But Kuno replies passionately: "The grave is not the end. From the graves of those we love most and where, with those we love most, are buried all our selfish drives and desires, we must draw the strength to dedicate ourselves wholly and unreservedly to the great purpose of our life: Behold: this is my religion."

In the final pages of the book, Kuno, now an old man, sums up his thoughts about life: "I have found no peace in old age, only the powerful and painful discontent of the creative spirit. . . . The longer, the more fiercely, a man fights in the struggle of life, the more it will become, beyond its deepest woes, a progress from God to God."

The book clearly reflects the one recurrent theme in Lou's life: her preoccupation with the problem of faith as well as her awareness of the dangers that lurk in the path of the atheist. Her hero Kuno, a Nietzschean figure with his passionate skepticism and his equally passionate affirmation of life, a projection of her own deepest convictions, is an elemental force that brings destruction to all who love him. He is directly responsible for Jane's death and for the suicides of Mary and Margherita. He knows it, he feels remorse for his actions but, driven by a Faustian discontent, he continues on his path, unable to change the course of his life. With supreme disregard for the suffering he causes, he pursues his quest—even as Lou did—wrestling with God like Jacob with the angel, while the people who love him perish by the wayside. It makes grim reading, this story of a man so dominated by his ideals that his "progress from God to God" is marked by the graves of his loved ones. Since it reflects Lou's own ideals, the book casts an ominous shadow over the course of her life.

Lou wrote *A Struggle for God* when she was twenty-three years old. Although hardly a literary masterpiece, the book served the purpose for which it was written: in the eyes of her family and the world she was now a writer and entitled to her freedom. That was all that mattered. Once her first book was out of the way, she was far too busy with her social life to waste any more time on writing. It took five years and another crisis in her life before she started her writing career in earnest.

During the months she spent working on *A Struggle for God* there was a remarkable improvement in Lou's health. She says she took a different body away from Meran, stronger and more resistant. Gone were the fainting spells and coughing fits that had troubled her during the greater part of her adolescence. From her personal standpoint the book was a great success, quite apart from the favorable reviews it received from Berlin critics, who praised its "psychological insights" and the boldness with which it treated the ancient conflict between faith and reason. They would have been even more amazed had they known that its author was a young woman. To protect her family, and because she felt a book written by a man had a better chance of success, Lou published *A Struggle for God* under the pseudonym of Henri Lou.

We do not know what Rée thought of Lou's book, nor whether he saw himself reflected in the figure of Kuno's younger brother Rudolf whose death-wish proved stronger than his will to live. Nietzsche remarked that, while all the formal elements in the "semi-novel" of Rée's "*soeur inséparable*" were almost comical, "the matter itself has gravity, even loftiness; and although it is certainly not the eternally feminine that pulls this girl upward then, perhaps, the eternally masculine."

Rée was probably too much occupied with his own book to pay much attention to Lou's. He, too, wrote it for a purpose. He hoped it would open the door to some academic appointment. Ever since he had obtained his doctorate in philosophy, it had been his ambition to become a university teacher. This meant he had to secure the *venia legendi*, the right to teach, by submitting a dissertation to the philosophic faculty of a university. If they accepted it, an academic career was open to him.

Rée had many friends among the young philosophers of his time and may have thought that if he could overcome his self-doubts and write the book, the thesis of which he had defended in countless discussions, he would gain admittance to the academic world. But he was mistaken. Wherever he submitted his book, after his return with Lou from Meran in the summer of 1884, it met with a polite but firm rejection. Nietzsche characterized it as "empty, boring and wrong"; and even Lou said it did not count.

In view of the immediate success of Lou's book his own failure must have preyed on Rée's mind. When it was finally turned down by the philosophic faculty of Strasbourg, he buried his hopes of becoming a university teacher and decided to study medicine. He did not intend to practice it for a living; since he was financially independent there was no need for that. He wished to offer his services to those who could not afford a doctor, the poor and forsaken. To this ideal he devoted the rest of his life with a single-minded selflessness that stands in marked contrast to his philosophic convictions. As a philosopher he maintained that there was no such thing as an unselfish act—"All men are equal, i.e. equally selfish, jealous and vain." But as a doctor his unselfish devotion to the poor became legendary. In the eyes of his patients this quiet and unassuming man who went out of his way to help them, although he himself seemed to suffer from an incurable sadness of the spirit, attained the stature of a saint. They noticed that he was always alone, shunned human companionship and spent his free time on solitary walks. What they did not know was that Rée mourned the loss of a sister who had sworn to be with him always and who had deserted him. He never understood why she had done it and he never forgave her. And Lou found it hard to forgive herself.

Perhaps their friendship really ended in Meran or as the result of the unequal fortunes of their books. The failure of Rée's hopes for an academic career and his decision to study medicine instead made certain changes in their living routine inevitable. They found that it was no longer practical for them to share the same apartment. Rée had to concentrate on his studies and had less time and inclination to participate in philosophical discussions. Lou, on the other hand, was more in demand than ever as the result of the favorable reviews of her book. She basked in the glory of being a young and successful author. They agreed that Rée would take a room near the university where he could work uninterruptedly and only spend weekends at Lou's. Since their friendship was meant for life, they felt that this slight separation did not matter.

And perhaps it would not have mattered if an event had not occurred which caused a decisive change in Lou's life, her encounter with Friedrich Carl Andreas. Rée was, of course, aware of the possibility that Lou might someday meet a man who would claim possession of her and whom she could not resist. And yet, when it happened, he was unprepared for it. She told him at first only that she had met Andreas and that if he, Rée, had no objections she would go on seeing him. Rée acquiesced. He hoped, no doubt, that she would return to him in the end, as she had always done. But when she told him one day that she had become engaged to Andreas and would marry him, although insisting that her condition on accepting Andreas' proposal was his agreement not to interfere with their friendship, Rée felt forsaken and betrayed. It was not in his nature to make a scene. Quietly he left her, but his departure made an indelible impression on Lou's mind:

"He left late at night, returned after a few minutes from the street because there was such a downpour, he said. After a while he left again and returned once more to get a book. It was already dawn when he finally left. I looked out of the window and was startled: above dry streets, pale stars looked down from a cloudless sky. Turning away from the window I saw in the lamplight a little photo of myself as a child which I had given Rée. On the piece of paper that was folded around it he had written: 'Be merciful. Do not search for me!' "

After that night Lou never saw Rée again, except in her dreams where he frequently appeared with an expression of infinite sadness. She tells of a particularly horrible one, a Kafkaesque nightmare:

"I found myself in the company of our friends who exclaimed joyfully that Paul Rée was present. I looked around and when I did not see him, I turned to the cloakroom where they had hung their coats. My glance fell on a strange fat man who sat quietly with folded hands behind the coats. His face was hardly recognizable under thick folds of fat which almost closed his eyes and lay over his face like a death mask.

" 'Don't you agree,' he said contentedly, 'here nobody will find me.' "

A workman found him on the 28th of October, 1901, in the river Inn where he had plunged from a steep cliff near the spot where he and Lou had spent their happiest hours together more than fifteen years previously.

II

Andreas

THE SUDDEN AND UNHERALDED ENTRANCE OF YET ANOTHER CON-
tender for Lou's favor came as a shock not only to Rée, who never
recovered from it, but to all of her Berlin friends and admirers.
Even Lou was taken aback by the vehemence of the stranger's
approach. For the first time in her life she felt the fatal fascination
of being in the presence of a man whose determination exceeded
her own. Her instinctive reaction was to turn to brother Rée for
help. But Rée was unequal to the task. If he had said no when
she asked him whether she should go on seeing Andreas, he might
have saved their friendship, he might even have won her love.
Failing to get help from Rée, Lou resigned herself to what seemed
to her an act of fate—not fate in the sense that in her twenty-sixth
year she had finally met the irresistible lover, the man who would
deliver her from her self-imposed maidenhood (she insists that
she was not carried away by a sudden physical desire), but fate
as the tragic involvement in the life of another, an elemental force
that cannot be denied. Even in the retrospect of a long life she
shuddered when she remembered the compulsion she was under
when she accepted Andreas' proposal of marriage. She felt it was
an irrevocable step that separated her not only from her friend
Rée but from herself.

The man who rang her doorbell unannounced one day and introduced himself as Friedrich Carl Andreas did not, at first sight,
strike Lou as a messenger of fate. He seemed gentle rather than

forceful, a man with the serious deportment of a scholar and the physical appearance of a monk. There was something exotic about his face, framed by a thick black beard and black hair and illuminated by a pair of bright, dark-brown eyes. But his figure was unimposing. He was a short and stocky man, a few inches shorter than she, and the black cape he was wearing made him look like a bird. Perhaps it was this first impression of a strange bird suddenly alighting on her doorstep that made her invite him in. She always responded to spontaneous actions with a guileless spontaneity of her own and was always surprised when, as a consequence, she found herself embroiled in serious difficulties. That she would be committed to this stranger for the rest of her life seemed to her in retrospect entirely incredible. She could only account for it by assuming that neither her own nor Andreas' actions had anything to do with the outcome. That was decreed by fate.

Andreas had come a long way to meet her, almost from the opposite end of the world. As he told her the story of his life, Lou must have felt that she was listening to a tale from *The Arabian Nights*. He came from the Dutch East Indies where his maternal grandfather, a talented North German physician, had settled at the beginning of the nineteenth century, taking as his wife a gentle and beautiful Malayan girl. Andreas' mother, born out of this unusually harmonious union between East and West, had married the scion of an ancient Persian family of royal blood, the Bagratuni. His branch of the family had been defeated in a family feud and had been forced to renounce their titles and names. They were called by their first name, Andreas. The boy, endowed with this rich and exotic heritage, was born in Batavia, on the island of Java, in 1846. He spent the first six years of his life there. Then the family returned to Germany and settled in Hamburg.

After receiving some private schooling, young Andreas was sent to a boarding school in Geneva noted for the excellent humanistic education it provided. It soon became apparent that he had an unusual gift for languages. He had learned German and English at home, probably also some Dutch; in Geneva he perfected his French and studied Latin and Greek. His interest in languages was not, however, merely philological. It encompassed the whole field of historic, geographic, ethnic and economic factors that make up a cultural pattern. Language was the key to unlock the life of a people. It was an important key, to be handled with the utmost care and precision, but it was not an end in itself. If it failed to open the door to a wider vision it was of little value.

In this spirit Andreas had devoted himself to his linguistic studies at the universities of Halle, Erlangen, Göttingen and Leipzig after graduating from the Geneva Gymnasium. He concentrated on Persian, the language of his ancestors, and in 1868 he obtained his doctorate from the University of Erlangen with a dissertation on the Middle Persian script-and-sound system. In addition he studied biology and had some training in medicine which stood him in good stead during his later travels in the Orient. After the completion of his formal studies he spent two years in Denmark, perusing unpublished Persian manuscripts in the Copenhagen Library and gaining deeper insights into the historic development of the Persian script. He also established close personal contacts with such leading Danish Orientalists as Westergaard, Fausbøll, Trenckner, and Thomsen, and made the acquaintance of Georg Brandes who introduced him to the Scandinavian languages and literatures.

The outbreak of the Franco-Prussian War forced him to return to Germany. He was called up and saw action in the battle of Le Mans. At the end of the war he went to the University of Kiel where he hoped to start his academic career by publishing his researches in the Pahlavi language. By now he was intimately familiar with the whole range of textual and linguistic problems that confront the scholar of ancient Oriental languages and his fund of knowledge in the field of his specialization was probably unequaled. And yet, at the end of two years of steady work, he still hesitated to commit his researches to print. He hesitated, not because he felt he did not know enough, but on the contrary, because his knowledge exceeded his ability to prove what he knew. He faced then and for the rest of his life the tragic dichotomy that not infrequently frustrates unusually brilliant scholars—the dichotomy between knowing and showing, between insights gained by the synthesizing force of the mind and the methodical step-by-step presentation of all the facts that have led to these insights.

At this stage the impasse was resolved by an event which promised to add actual experience to his theoretical insights. The Prussian Ministry of Culture announced it would send an expedition to Persia to make astronomical observations of the passage of the planet Venus. Andreas petitioned the Ministry to be included in the team of scientists that had been selected for this expedition. His memorandum explaining the importance of a first-hand investigation of the Middle Persian Sassanide inscriptions was "a work of such clarity and vision that even today, when these investigations are far advanced, it could form a useful introduction to their study." It had the desired effect. Appointed the archeological representative of the expedition, Andreas was given the chance to visit his ancestral homeland.

The journey proved far more hazardous than he had anticipated. He sailed for Persia by way of India in July, 1875, but a serious attack of cholera forced him to spend several months in Bombay. During that time he studied the religious customs of the Parsees, the descendants of those Persians who fled to India in the seventh and eighth centuries to escape Mohammedan persecutions. When he finally reached Persia in January, 1876, the work of the expedition was almost finished, the reports which he sent to the Prussian Ministry in Berlin were misunderstood, and he was ordered to come home. His answer was a defiant no! Although almost without funds, he decided to remain in Persia on his own. For six years he supported himself as best he could by giving language lessons, practicing medicine, and occasionally even taking official positions. Thus, he was for a time the Persian Postmaster General.

His extensive travels took him to all sections of the country and offered him an opportunity to make observations of the various Persian dialects, which he recorded carefully and which proved invaluable in his later work on the historic growth of the Persian language. Side by side with his linguistic studies he pursued a wide range of historical, archeological and scientific investigations. An active outdoor life brought him into close contact with the flora and fauna of the country. He became something of an expert on reptiles, many unusual specimens of which he collected and brought back to Germany.

There are many tales concerning his unorthodox medical practices. On one occasion he saved the eyesight of a child suffering
from one of the frequent eye diseases of the Middle East, by the
audacious remedy of burning away with silver nitrate the sticky
pus which had formed a thick layer on both eyes. On another
occasion he cured a prince in Baluchistan of a venereal disease by
administering a homemade medicine based on an Oriental variety
of peppers. As a result of such cures he was widely revered as a
sage and often consulted by members of the ruling families.
Sometimes they would invite him to spend an evening in their
rose gardens listening to a hafiz singer or watching the dancing
girls. Then the poetry and splendor of Persia's golden age came
to life, with effortless ease the problems of interpretation vanished, and the spirit of his royal ancestors awoke in Andreas'
heart. No longer did he have to grope for fragmentary knowledge;
he lived the past of his people.

His Western-oriented mind was powerfully impressed by the
mythic unity of man and beast. When he met a man who hunted
lions by stalking them in their mountain hideout, and armed
only with a dagger challenging them to mortal combat, Andreas
was reminded of similar scenes on Assyrian bas-reliefs. In the
presence of this lion-hunter, who proudly displayed the scars of
his deadly pursuit, he felt the force of the ancient equality that
once existed between man and the creature world. Adapting his
own mode of life to that of the Oriental, Andreas learned to live
simply and naturally and developed an uncanny power of imitat-
ing animal sounds. Later he often fascinated his friends by stalking through his garden at daybreak with the supple movements
of a creature, half man, half beast, and arousing with his calls a
host of birds from their sleep. Or, to test the scent of his watch-
dog, he would take off his clothes and try to approach it unseen,
"resembling one beast stalking another." When the dog, although
puzzled because he had never seen his master in the nude, made
no move to attack him but merely growled and drew back,
Andreas would laugh heartily and catch the surprised animal in
a loving embrace.

These and similar scenes endeared him to his friends but they
did not enhance his reputation as a scholar. When, after six years
in Persia, he finally returned to Germany in January, 1882, as the

traveling companion of Prince Ihtisam-ed-daule, he found himself at the prime of his life without employment and without
academic connections. The intense sunlight to which he had been
exposed in the Middle East had severely damaged his eyesight,
forcing him to undergo a protracted period of recuperation before he could continue his scholarly work.

Upon his return Andreas settled in Berlin, eking out a precarious living by giving private lessons in Turkish, Persian and
Arabic to Prussian officers and merchants. He was also employed
for a time by the Berlin Military Academy to instruct Turkish
officers in German and was commissioned to write a study on the
economic potential of the Middle East which was well received
by the experts. Bismarck's increasing concern with this strategic
region, and his insistence on sending well-trained diplomatic and
military representatives there led in 1887 to the founding of the
Institute for Oriental Languages in Berlin. Andreas was offered
a professorship in Persian, later also in Turkish. At long last his
future seemed assured. He was then forty-one years old.

And then he met Lou. If their meeting was fateful to her it
was equally fateful to Andreas. We do not know what made him
seek her out. Perhaps he had read her book, or perhaps someone
among her Berlin friends had told him of this unusually brilliant
girl whose unorthodox way of life proved an irresistible fascination to the men who met her. Like Nietzsche before him, and like
dozens of others afterward, Andreas was determined to win her
the moment he laid eyes on her. Nothing she said about her opposition to marriage or her relationship with Rée deterred him
from pursuing his goal. On the contrary, the more she resisted his
advances the more zealously he wooed her. He even accepted her
condition that if she should marry him she must still be free to
continue her friendship with Rée. A proud and passionate man, a
man moreover who was steeped in the Oriental tradition which
demands complete submission of the wife to the will of her
husband, Andreas must have exercised a great deal of self-denial
to accept such a condition. But he was in love with Lou and
firmly believed that he would ultimately win her.

It was a tragic belief, monstrous almost, Lou thought, and it
led to tragic consequences. For in a desperate move to force his
love on Lou, Andreas committed an irrevocable act by which he

both won and lost her forever: he made an attempt on his own life.

"Later it often occurred to me," Lou writes in her memoirs, "that on the eve of our engagement the suspicion of murder might easily have fallen on me. For his long nightly walks to his distant apartment, my husband used to carry a short and heavy pocket knife. . . . It had lain on the table opposite which we were sitting. With a calm movement he had suddenly seized it and plunged it into his chest. Half out of my mind, I rushed out into the street running from house to house in search of a doctor. . . . When I found one he asked me on the way up to my apartment what had happened. I answered that someone had fallen on his knife. While he examined the unconscious man lying on the floor, his glance and a few words made it clear to me whom he suspected of having wielded the knife."

Although he inflicted a deep triangular wound which did not heal easily, Andreas' life was saved because the blade had snapped shut when the knife fell from his hand.

We are not told why Andreas tried to kill himself. The only clue is that it happened on the eve of his engagement. Lou always insisted that he forced her to marry him. Had she just given him her final no when he stabbed himself? Whatever the reason, his suicide attempt made her consent to his proposal of marriage. But at the same time it hardened her resolution not to become his wife. The chain forged with one bloody stroke bound them together in an insoluble union which neither of them could break. In name Lou remained Andreas' wife for half a century; in fact, she resisted all his attempts to consummate their marriage.

Her refusal made the first years of their married life a veritable hell on earth. She mentions moments of utter despair when they both considered putting an end to it all. Andreas was a hot-tempered man. In the beginning he tried to assert his marital rights both by persuasion and by force. Lou says that on one occasion while she was fast asleep he tried to subdue her on a sudden impulse. Still half-asleep she pressed her hands tightly around his throat until his gasping woke her up. When she opened her eyes she saw to her horror that she was strangling him.

In trying to understand Lou's extraordinary refusal to have intercourse with her husband, one explanation has to be discarded at once: she was by no means a frigid woman, nor was she a prude. Sexual love seemed to her a very natural culmination of the total love play. The reason why she could not engage in it with her husband must be sought partly in the shock she suffered from his violent attempts to subdue her, and partly in the fact that she saw in him not so much a husband as a father. All her life she remained her father's child. Andreas, fifteen years older than Lou, could indeed have been her father, and he perhaps shared other similarities in character and temperament with General von Salomé. In her intimate diaries Lou often refers to her husband as "*Alterchen*," the "little old man," an expression that shows the ambivalence of her feelings. On the one hand, she was genuinely fond of him and did not want to hurt him, but on the other, his advances evoked in her something akin to the dread of incest. Her refusal to yield to him was not mere willfulness on her part. It was caused by a fear so deeply imbedded in her subconscious that it defied rational solution.

One might ask why Andreas did not admit defeat in the end and agree to a divorce. But that possibility never seems to have entered his mind.

"I could not stop knowing that you are my wife," he said when Lou suggested it to him. She insists that there was no trace of bitterness in his words, he merely voiced what, to him, was an irrevocable reality.

The climax of the first tense years of their marriage came when Lou met the writer-politician Georg Ledebour. A strong and self-assured man, he threw her into an emotional vortex when, in confessing his love to her, he told her point-blank that her marriage was a fake, and not only because she did not wear a wedding ring. He sensed that she was still a virgin. Lou was startled and dismayed. How could anyone know? The painful secret of her marriage had been locked deep in her own and her husband's hearts. Fascinated by Ledebour's personality, sympathy and understanding, she wavered for a time as to whether she should accept his love. But she soon realized that her husband's fierce temper ruled out any thought of an illicit affair. He would have killed them both if he had found out. As it was, he demanded that she stop seeing her friend.

She bowed to this demand, but in the months that followed, the bitter stalemate of their marriage entered a new phase. Pitting will against will, Lou fought for her freedom. Since Andreas refused to give her a divorce she consented to remain his wife only on the condition that he would no longer exercise any control over her emotional life. She wanted to be free to follow the dictates of her heart. The only way to make such a "marriage" work was for Andreas to find a "wife substitute" and for Lou to leave their common household the moment she sensed danger. After months of struggle some sort of agreement was reached. It left Lou outwardly bound but inwardly free. These were the years of her long travels through Europe.

For Andreas they were years of frustration and failure. Everything went wrong. His work at the Institute did not find favor with his superiors. He was accused of neglecting the practical aspects of language-teaching and of concentrating too exclusively on research. It was pointed out that the Institute's main function was to train diplomats and businessmen, not scholars. And he was told either to mend his ways or to find other employment. His proud contention that there was no other method, that language-teaching was and must be a total process with due weight given to historical, archeological, literary and economic factors, led to arguments and quarrels. He was told that there was no time for such utopian goals. Germany needed experts in Near Eastern trade and politics. But Andreas refused to be rushed. He had the Oriental's contempt for speed and paid no attention to schedules or deadlines. As a result his position at the Institute became untenable. He felt he was the victim of intrigues and became embroiled in a lawsuit about his severance pay with the Prussian Ministry of Education. Although settled in his favor, it jeopardized his chances of future employment with a university or any other state-controlled institution of higher learning. He was reduced to giving private lessons and to writing commissioned articles for business firms or trade journals. It was a precarious existence, providing barely enough income for one, let alone for a household. Fortunately Lou still received some financial support from home, and her work for literary journals, to which she now applied herself seriously, brought in some money. But it must have been humiliating for Andreas to feel that he was partly supported by his wife. Even on that score Lou was independent of him. She did not have to ask him for money when she wanted to travel.

Andreas would occasionally accompany her. But for the most part he stayed behind in their Berlin apartment with a house-keeper to take care of him. This woman, Marie, a simple and uncomplicated creature, was Andreas' "wife substitute." She became so much a part of the household that to all intents and purposes she took over Lou's duties. When in 1903 Andreas finally found the academic berth for which he was suited, the chair of West Asiatic Languages at the University of Göttingen, Marie went with them and took charge of their house on the Hainberg. She had two illegitimate children. One of them died young, leaving Andreas grief-stricken; the other, Mariechen, grew up and married but continued to live with Lou even after the death of Marie and Andreas. She took care of Lou in her old age and inherited Andreas' house when Lou died. In the eyes of the world she was an illegitimate child, but she always considered Andreas her father.

Andreas was married to Lou for forty-three years, from 1887 to his death in 1930, at the age of eighty-four. His life, like his marriage, was paradoxical. His personal tragedy as a scholar was that the Western tradition of scholarship ran counter to his power-fully intuitive mind. It resulted in a stalemate of his creative faculties. All his life he planned to publish the results of his re-flections and researches, but his major work remained unwritten. He failed to bridge the gap between intuition and analysis. What he did publish often lacked detailed documentation because to him it was evident, but not to his professional colleagues who scornfully referred to his Oriental studies as an "occult science." The small band of his students, on the other hand, with whom he often worked all through the night—that he held all his classes at home and at night was another reason for his Göttingen col-leagues to make disparaging remarks about him—his students were fascinated and inspired by him. One of them has written a vivid account of the first impression that Andreas made on him when he registered for a seminar in Persian:

"In his bright study with its large windows which offered a wide view over the valley of Göttingen and the hills opposite, the stocky black-haired and black-bearded man received me like an old acquaintance. Open in front of him lay the *Avesta*, of which I could not read one single letter. Stroking his hair, Andreas turned to me and said, 'I wonder when these fellows used a long and when a short i. That is something I cannot make out. Do you perhaps know the answer? Will you help me to find it?' I knew about as much of this problem as any reader of these lines. It was one that occupied Andreas at the moment. I was supposed to help him with it and had not the slightest idea what it was all about; incidentally, it is still unsolved today. Then there swirled around my head Aramaic papyri from Egypt, Sassanide coins, Chinese travelers, Jacob Grimm and the early writings of Franz Bopp, Byzantine historians, Pahlavi italics and Middle Persian inscriptions. Completely dazed I staggered away after a few hours, but happy and inspired."

By this unorthodox approach Andreas trained some of the leading European Orientalists and much of his work has been preserved in their writings. Still, there is no doubt that he suffered from his inability to publish. He gave vent to his frustrations by pouring bitter scorn on those of his colleagues who had nothing better to do than rush into print with their half-baked ideas, as he put it. On such occasions he could be vitriolic even in front of his students. He would then say "*der* so-and-so" has again presented us with a nice little piece of paper, or "*der*"—again mentioning the name of a colleague—has just committed another indiscretion in public. The use of the definite article "*der*" before a name became such an idiosyncrasy with him that a young French scholar, who worked with him, wondered whether the article in German generally had a derogatory meaning.

But such outbursts did not last long. Andreas was too vital a man to brood over his frustrations. Besides, he felt that his time to publish would come, there was no need to rush. On his eightieth birthday he surprised his well-wishers, colleagues and students, by presenting them with a long list of problems on which he was working and which he said would keep him busy at least another fifty years. This freshness of the spirit was the secret of his personality. It carried him over the many disappointments of his life. He refused to admit defeat. Resolutely turning his glance away from his personal problems, he submerged his whole being in the past of an ancient culture. There was his home, and there he found peace. And after the turbulent years of his marriage were over, he had the satisfaction that he had outwaited all his rivals. He may never have possessed Lou, as others did, but unlike others he never lost her either. She always returned to him in the end.

12

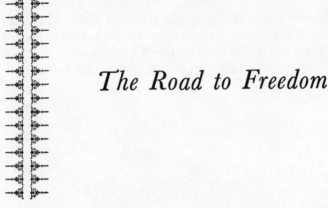

The Road to Freedom

Once upon a time there was an attic. Its low, slanting walls reached down to the wooden floor and the daylight had to force its way laboriously through cobwebbed dormer windows and cracks in the walls. But carefully spread-out fresh straw covered the floor and a barrel of water had been placed there. For in this attic all sorts of animals were kept prisoners and trained to get disaccustomed to a life of natural freedom.

This is the opening paragraph of a fairytale which Lou wrote, during the first difficult years of her married life, as an introduction to her book on the women characters in Ibsen's plays. She goes on to say that among the animals held in captivity—chickens, birds, pigeons, rabbits—was a wild duck, the noblest and the most pitiable of all the creatures robbed of their freedom. And then, in six brief passages, she describes what happens when the wild duck's innate instinct of freedom revolts against the forces that hold it captive. These six passages correspond to the six chapters in her book dealing with Nora (*A Doll's House*), Mrs. Alving (*Ghosts*), Hedwig (*The Wild Duck*), Rebecca (*Rosmersholm*), Ellida (*The Lady from the Sea*), and Hedda (*Hedda Gabler*). She finds that Ibsen gives six different answers to the quest for freedom in captivity.

The first deals with a wild duck that has joined the domesticated animals as a very young bird. It does not know its origin and grows up in the attic as if it were a cheerful playroom. Although it occasionally feels that the real world is outside, it is

quite happy with its life in the attic until the autumn storms remind it of its true nature. Then it longs to spread out its wings,
leave its cosy prison behind and soar into the wide-open sky. This
is Nora's case. Brought up in complete ignorance of herself and
treated by her husband like a spoiled and irresponsible child,
Nora is suddenly confronted with the fateful necessity of having
to act independently. She does so, but in a way that brings her
into conflict with the law. When her husband hears of her trans-
gression, which she has committed for his sake, he overwhelms
her with reproaches. Only when it appears that there will be no
serious consequences, no public scandal, does he offer to take
her back into her doll's house. But now Nora rejects him. She has
suddenly seen through the illusion that has been her life. She
feels that she must grow up, face reality and live according to
the laws of her own nature. We do not know what will happen
to her. All we know is that her longing for freedom and self-
realization is greater than even her love for her children.

Ibsen's second answer concerns a wild duck resigned to its fate
in the attic world. It knows that it leads a false and fraudulent
existence but it does not have the strength to rebel against it. No
autumn storms remind it of its lost freedom. It knows only in its
dreams that the real world is outside. Slowly dying in captivity,
it dreams of a life it might have led. This is the story of Mrs.
Alving. There is no future for her, no saving grace, nothing but a
glance back in sadness over a life of cruelly disappointed hopes.

A third answer treats the fate of the wild duck that has sought
refuge in the attic because it was wounded outside. It has made
friends with the other animals, especially with a young, blind
songbird. Growing fat and lazy in captivity the wild duck loses its
longing for freedom. Nothing reminds it of the free life it used to
lead, except the sweet sounds of the little bird. In the end it is
only the little bird who still believes in the wild duck's longing
for freedom. In an effort to arouse its friend it forgets that it is
blind, spreads out its wings and tries to fly away only to find itself
hopelessly caught in the cluttered attic. Crashing down with
broken wings, it dies. This is the story of Hedwig. Her love for
Hjalmar is like the love of the little bird for the wild duck. Her
suicide is a vain attempt to free what is great in him.

The fourth alternative is a wild duck that has invaded the attic world and, being stronger and more ruthless than the other animals, is lording it over them. But instead of resisting, the tame animals respond to its rule with love. And this is the danger: the taming of the wild through the forces of habit and love. Gradually the wild duck acquires the conscience of a domestic animal and develops such a sense of shame and remorse for the deeds of its primitive past that the only way to atone for it is by self-destruction. This is the case of Rebecca in *Rosmersholm*. Wild and lawless Rebecca, who is responsible for the suicide of Beate Rosmer, renounces her past and the call of the wild and follows her victim into the grave. She dies because she no longer has a life of her own.

The fifth possibility is the wild duck that strayed into the attic world by accident and cannot get used to captivity. In vain do the other animals try to cheer it up. Sunk in grief over its lost freedom, it hardly notices them. Finally, the tame animals decide to open the attic window and let the wild duck escape. But then the unexpected happens: the wild duck remains. Now that it knows it is free, the fear of captivity has lost its terror. This is the story of Ellida. She is married to a kind and considerate physician but she cannot forget a mysterious stranger from across the sea who has once loved her. With a daemonic power the sea lures and attracts her and she pines away in her sheltered home. Her marriage is a burden, because she thinks her husband does not understand her. For "understanding and love make the difference between a bond that unites two people and a chain that fetters them to each other." But she is mistaken. Her husband does understand her and, realizing that he cannot hold her against her will, he offers to let her go. She can choose her freedom at her own risk. This voluntary renunciation on his part breaks the spell under which she has lived and restores her peace of mind. To be free and to be responsible—that is what she needs. She longs to reconcile the conflicting demands made upon her by her own nature and by society.

This is the underlying problem in all the five plays. It leads to Nora's self-emancipation and to the voluntary subordination of Ellida. "In both cases it concerns the conflict between conjugal duty and personal freedom."

There is, finally, in Lou's fable a bird who is neither wild nor tame. It lacks the courage of a really free creature but, at the same time, is dissatisfied with its sheltered home. Its purposeless existence comes to a purposeless end. This is the case of Hedda Gabler. She is entirely surface, deceptive appearance, mask. Filled with envy and the malicious joy of harming others, she is the only character who remains unchanged. When her love affair becomes serious and she fears that she may be compromised and that there will be a scandal, she shoots herself. Only by destroying her mask can she prove that she, too, had a longing for freedom; a freedom, however, that lacked inner truthfulness, strength and purpose, and hence was empty.

It need hardly be stressed that Lou's interest in Ibsen and in the problems posed in his plays was personal as well as literary. After her marriage she herself felt like a wild duck that had been robbed of its freedom. In watching the struggle of Ibsen's heroines to free themselves, she thought of her own struggle and wondered how it would end. Would she succeed, as Ellida did, in reconciling her conjugal duties with her personal freedom? Or would her life end tragically like Rebecca's? There were moments when this seemed the only possible solution. More than once both she and her husband decided to put an end to it all, settled their affairs and all but closed the book of life. "Two people equally perplexed and desperate."

Lou's interest in Ibsen, whose plays her husband interpreted for her before German translations became available, brought her in contact with a group of *avant-garde* writers and editors in Berlin. Five years after the publication of *A Struggle for God* she began her literary career in earnest. The income she derived from articles and books helped cushion the bitter stalemate of her marriage by providing enough money for extensive travel. These periodic and often quite lengthy escapes from her home and her husband had a therapeutic effect. Like safety valves they prevented an explosion when the tension between them reached the bursting point. In a manner of speaking then, Ibsen led to Lou's emancipation. He enabled her to find a seventh solution to the problem of the wild duck.

Whenever life in captivity became unbearable, usually in spring, it would force the attic window open and fly away, sometimes for a few weeks, sometimes for so long that the other animals almost forgot it. But then one day it would suddenly return, tired of its freedom and quite content to join them again in their peaceful attic. The other animals would welcome it back and pretend that it had never been away. However, when it wanted to tell them of its experiences in the world outside, they would turn away. They preferred not to know.

"Once, in a moving hour," Lou writes, "I asked my husband: 'May I tell you what happened to me in the meantime?' Quickly, without hesitating a second, he answered 'NO'!" Thus a great unbroken silence grew up between them. They lived their lives together and yet separately. Since Andreas was in the habit of working at night and sleeping the better part of the day—he went to bed when Lou got up—their contacts were limited even when Lou was at home. Once this pattern had been set and tacitly accepted by both of them, a glow of mutual respect entered into their relationship. Gone were the days of despair, the bitter quarrels, the sleepless nights. Side by side they lived and worked, hardly noticing each other, and yet bound to each other by the invisible bond of sympathy and suffering.

During the first years of her marriage, Lou explored the limits of her personal and intellectual freedom. She was always on the go. From Berlin she moved to Paris, from Paris to Vienna, from Vienna to St. Petersburg, from St. Petersburg to Stockholm, and from there back to her husband in Berlin. The temper of the times reflected her own restlessness. Everything began to move faster. The automobile appeared, wireless telegraphy, and the first flying machines. The coming of electricity heralded a new age of speed and power. In the last decade of the nineteenth century the world lost its traditional moorings. While the bourgeoisie greeted every new discovery as a sign of progress, Europe's intellectual elite was deeply disturbed. They feared that so far from liberating man, as the apostles of progress believed, the machine would enslave him. It would rob him of his work and dehumanize his life. And events seemed to confirm their fears. The rapid rise of the factory system created huge wealth for some but misery and degradation for many. Dark satanic mills arose in England's pleasant land and in the peaceful valley of the Ruhr. Under conditions that defy the imagination young children were forced to work in coal mines, women in sweatshops. At the same time all workers were threatened by the spectre of enforced idleness. There were strikes and riots, armed clashes between the police and the proletariat. Political parties were founded, appealing to the solidarity of the working classes. All over Europe socialism became a political force to be reckoned with.

Lou's search for personal freedom coincided with the great ferment in the eighteen-nineties, the beginning of the social, political and intellectual transformation which culminated in the first World War. It started as a revolt against the smug self-satisfaction of the Wilhelmian bourgeoisie, its platitudinous Sunday-school morality and its brutal exploitation of the working classes—a revolt in the name of youth, honesty and social justice. One of the centers of this movement was in Berlin, where in 1890 a group of social-revolutionary writers under the leadership of Bruno Wille founded the *Freie Volksbühne,* a society dedicated to staging plays that were not allowed to be shown in public. They also published a journal, *Freie Bühne,* in which they advocated the liberation of the theatre from capitalist oppression, propagated socialism in politics and naturalism in the arts and, in the name of Ibsen, demanded a "revolutionizing of the human spirit." They were dedicated men, missionaries and idealists. A new dawn, they felt, was coming to Germany and Europe, another Renaissance.

"Resurrection! We live at a time of resurrection. The dead sod is breaking up and is bringing forth new life. Everywhere there are signs, everywhere the unconscious, imperturbable, prophetic spirit that precedes the new messiah. It is a joy to be alive!"

Always receptive to intellectual excitement, Lou was caught up in the spirit of the time and became an active member of the *Freie Volksbühne.* She formed personal friendships with its leading proponents: Otto Brahm, Maximilian Harden, Bruno Wille, Wilhelm Bölsche and the brothers Hart who had written such undeservedly favorable reviews of her novel, *A Struggle for God.* She often teased them about it. And she got to know some of the most promising and controversial writers, such as Carl and Gerhart Hauptmann, August Strindberg, Arno Holz, Max Halbe, Richard Dehmel and the "noble anarchist" from Scotland, John Henry Mackay, who had made his home in Berlin. Although Lou had shunned the "literary bohemians of Berlin" while she had lived with Rée, she now became one of them. Her intellectual brilliance, her outspoken contempt of middle-class values and, above all, her feminine charm made her entry into this *avant-garde* circle an instantaneous success. She frequented the "Black Pig," their place of rendezvous, took part in their heated political and literary discussions, and wrote articles, book and play reviews for their journal. In short, she threw herself wholeheartedly into a literary career, or rather was propelled into it by her need of self-expression and because it offered her a chance to escape from her domestic difficulties.

Her rapid rise to literary prominence proves that she had a natural talent for critical and creative expression and, her disclaimer to the contrary, a sound knowledge of modern literature. For one thing, she was familiar with Ibsen under whose banner the first great literary battles were fought. Indeed, she fired the opening gun of her literary career in defense of Ibsen by contributing two articles on *The Wild Duck* to the first volume of *Freie Bühne* in 1890. Then, too, she knew Nietzsche. On that account, the literary rebels of Berlin, who were imbued with Nietzschean ideas, considered her an almost legendary figure. Her friendship with the author of *Zarathustra,* and the rumor that there had been "an affair" between her and Nietzsche, added piquancy to her personality and authority to her writing. Finally, there was her Russian background, a considerable asset at a time when people began to take notice of the ferment in Russian society, and when Tolstoy's social-revolutionary ideals and the introspective art of Dostoevsky were hotly discussed. In these discussions Lou not only held her own, she was often the only one present who could speak on Russia with first-hand knowledge.

It was not, however, only the wide range of her knowledge that secured Lou a place among German writers at the end of the nineteenth century. Her articles and books, with their peculiar mixture of autobiographical elements and psychological insights, sounded a new and different note. Putting it paradoxically, one might say that as a writer Lou thought with her heart and felt with her head. This is a dangerous method for it lacks clarity and precision. It demands that the reader follow often rather clouded arguments based on personal experiences, insights and intuitions. A contemporary critic rightly remarked that Lou's "excessive emphasis on psychological factors removed her work from the sphere of the concrete. Her books lack the color of life."

At the same time, it was precisely her preoccupation with psychological problems that set her apart from and sometimes well ahead of her contemporaries. Does it not almost sound like an anticipation of psychoanalysis when, in an article about the creative impulse, she writes that artists are exposed to the same dangers that threaten neurotics: "those types of people with psychologically undigested remnants of life who can find relief only if fortunate circumstances or a successful hypnosis make them give vent to the cause of their disease, of which they are not consciously aware until it has, as it were, been thrust out of their souls." It was clearly unusual for a woman writer in the nineties to express such thoughts. No wonder that Lou was looked upon with respect and admiration by her Berlin artist friends, foremost among them Gerhart Hauptmann, whose early plays she reviewed in one of her first articles for the *Freie Bühne*.

Hauptmann's starkly naturalistic drama, *Before Sunrise* (*Vor Sonnenaufgang*), had caused a sensation when it was performed in 1889. The audience had wildly acclaimed the play or hissed furiously, and pitched battles had been fought in the theatre that reached a climax when a pair of forceps were thrown on the stage as one of the characters called for a midwife. Naturalism had arrived in Germany. The author of this tumult, Gerhart Hauptmann, was a young playwright who was then living with his wealthy wife and three sons in the Berlin suburb of Erkner. Like many budding artists he chafed under his role as *paterfamilias* and felt that his wife did not understand him. What a different woman Lou was! You could discuss all your artistic and human problems with her. She knew what you were talking about, she offered suggestions and helpful criticism.

"You must let me come and see you, dear and cherished woman," Hauptmann wrote Lou soon after he had met her, signing the note with his first name. There is an unmistakable tone of urgency in his request. But how close their friendship was can only be surmised. Lou was in the habit of asking her friends to destroy her more intimate letters, just as she destroyed theirs, which accounts for the loss of many important documents, among them her correspondence with Hauptmann. It is quite likely, therefore, that we shall never know with certainty the exact nature of their friendship.

But perhaps a clue can be found in Hauptmann's play *Lonely People* (*Einsame Menschen*), which he wrote in 1891 at a time when their friendship was at its height. It treats the theme of a young artist, Johannes Vockerrat, who is married to a woman intellectually beneath him. As a woman of means she can give him creature comforts and the opportunity to write unhampered by economic pressures. She is a good wife and mother, but she is no companion to him and does not understand his creative discontent. It is not difficult to see in her a reflection of Hauptmann's wife, the former Marie Thienemann. Vockerrat, moreover, bears certain features reminiscent of the young Hauptmann himself. His feeling of being misunderstood by everyone, especially by his family, his insistence on modern ideas concerning society and religion, his interest in social and philosophic problems as presented in the works of Darwin and Haeckel—these and a number of minor traits seem to be autobiographical.

Into this household comes Anna Mahr, a brilliant and charming girl student, disarmingly frank in her manner and endowed with a powerful intellect. She has just come from Zurich, where she has been studying philosophy, but her home is in the Baltic provinces of Russia. Her coming has a very stimulating effect on the young artist. At last he has found someone to talk to. The stultifying atmosphere of his bourgeois home is lifted from him. Anna's presence releases new and unexpected energies in him, making him feel that he is experiencing an artistic rebirth. But the point of the play is that during this process other than purely intellectual forces are also aroused. The emancipated spirit longs for the emancipation of the flesh. Sensing this danger, Anna decides to leave the Vockerrat household because she does not want to hurt the artist's wife. But it is too late. Vockerrat's passions are aroused to the point of madness. He cannot bear the thought of losing her, and rather than resume his frustrated previous existence, he takes his own life.

Anna's background corresponds closely with Lou's, and the effect her coming had on the young artist is certainly similar to Lou's catalytic impact on many of her friends. But with Vockerrat's suicide the similarity ends. Hauptmann did not commit suicide any more than Goethe did during the Werther period. His marriage, however, did not survive, and that there is a good deal of personal truth in *Lonely People* can be surmised from the dedication which reads: "I give this play into the hands of those who have lived it."

In her review of the play Lou quotes with approval the opinion of a Dutch critic who said that its strength lay in the fact that Hauptmann succeeded in presenting in Anna Mahr a new type of woman who, although stronger and a more independent character than Vockerrat, was no bluestocking. She added, however, that Hauptmann had failed to make a convincing case for Anna Mahr's intellectual superiority: "as a student from Zurich she comes alive only because she is presented as such." It is natural that Lou criticized Hauptmann's failure to understand those qualities of the mind and character of the modern woman which she valued most. Perhaps for this reason their friendship soon declined. Hauptmann is said to have remarked wryly that he was "too stupid for Lou."

But neither friendships nor more serious encounters, such as that with the writer-politician Georg Ledebour, could distract Lou from her major aim, the search for her freedom. To attain it she had to work. Her economic freedom depended, in part at least, on what she earned. And work she did. Article after article came from her busy pen, and book after book. In 1892 her book on Ibsen appeared, two years later her book on Nietzsche, the following year her novel *Ruth*, a year later *From a Troubled Soul* (*Aus fremder Seele*), followed in quick succession by *Fenitschka* (1898), *Children of Man* (*Menschenkinder*, 1899), *Ma* (1901), and *In the Twilight Zone* (*Im Zwischenland*, 1902). In addition she wrote more than fifty essays, articles and book reviews. Eight books and fifty articles in ten years is no mean achievement. While her husband was trying to make a living as a teacher of exotic languages, Lou made herself a name as a writer. And with her income derived from her writing she set out on her extensive travels, leaving Andreas for months in their Berlin apartment in the care of Marie. Paris, St. Petersburg, Vienna, Salzburg and Munich were the cities where she made temporary homes. Her literary fame and her reputation as a *femme fatale* brought her into contact with writers and artists wherever she went. Europe's intellectual *avant-garde,* determined to shock the bourgeoisie by presenting life in the raw and by advocating social justice and sexual freedom, welcomed her as a fellow fighter.

They were understandably surprised when they discovered that this bold and emancipated woman, who was quite ready to discuss the most intimate aspects of sex and love, was unwilling to practice what she preached. Whenever the question of physical intimacy arose—and because of her very free way of life this was often the case—she withdrew. She would not or could not surrender herself to any man. It was tantalizing. Here she was—young and attractive, an obviously passionate woman not bothered by moral scruples, and yet quite unattainable, neither wife nor mistress, a sort of sexless Messalina. Youthful and feminine in appearance but mature in her judgment and very sure of herself, she moved with ease among the literary bohemians of Berlin, Paris and Vienna.

She had started her literary career as a commentator on Ibsen, Nietzsche and Tolstoy because she saw in them the forerunners of a new movement in the history of the human spirit. She lived in that spirit intellectually, but emotionally she did not. And while her main concern was with her intellectual emancipation, she began to wonder what caused the strange dichotomy in her life. Why was she unable to complete the love act? Was the youthful intensity of her love for Gillot, and the shock she suffered when he made very human demands on her, responsible? At first she thought so. But the Gillot affair had been more than a dozen years ago. She was in her early thirties now, and among the many men who had crossed her path she had not yet found a lover. To be a married woman, a literary bohemian and a virgin all at once was a very improbable combination. It puzzled her friends and caused her enemies to spread all sorts of malicious rumors about her. They whispered that Lou was not a woman at all, that she was a hermaphrodite, frigid, a freak. Since she never paid any attention to what people said about her, she was completely untroubled by such rumors. She knew herself. She knew the time would come when she would meet the man who would liberate her. She did not coin the phrase "the emancipation of the flesh" which became one of the battle cries of the militant suffragettes, whom she despised, but it now began to preoccupy her.

Physical love in all its manifestations was one of the major themes in her writings and the only one of which she had no personal experience. "Not to have loved is not to have lived," she wrote. It was time to enter into the fullness of love.

13

The Emancipation
of the Flesh

"A WOMAN DOES NOT DIE OF LOVE, BUT IF SHE LACKS LOVE SHE wilts." This was one of the aphorisms Lou wrote during that memorable summer she spent with Nietzsche in Tautenburg. Even then, at the age of twenty-one, she knew that love was the regenerative force of life. She was more than ten years older now, a successful writer, much envied and much admired, the intimate of some of the most fascinating men in Berlin, Paris and Vienna—and still a virgin. At least so she says and so it would seem. Her appearance was still youthful although her face began to show signs that she was living too exclusively in the rarified air of the intellect. It lacked warmth; it lacked the glow, the soft luster that irradiates a woman's face who is loved and in love. Occasionally her bright blue eyes had a gleam of hardness. By way of softening her angular appearance she preferred to wear large, soft collars or wide-sleeved peasant blouses. For the rest she dressed simply, shunned stays and corsets and those other fashionable devices which imprisoned the bodies of most women of her generation. Her body, too, must be free.

It will, of course, be questioned whether a woman living as Lou did and arousing as violent passions could possibly have remained a virgin that long—and it has been questioned. Elizabeth Nietzsche, Malwida von Meysenbug and even Mrs. Rée suspected that there was much more to her innocent love affair with Gillot than Lou admitted. Others, like Rée and Andreas, were puzzled when they discovered that this very desirable and passionate woman resisted their advances so fiercely. Was there anything wrong with her? Nietzsche thought that Lou suffered from "sexual atrophy." And Lou herself wondered what caused the late flowering of her sex life. In Rée's case, she says, a slight physical aversion prevented her from becoming his wife. For Andreas she felt no such aversion and yet she resisted him. Was she a victim of those sexual inhibitions that afflict some women?

A clue to this problem can be found in her books. Since most of them reflect personal experiences, it is possible to use them, albeit cautiously, as biographical material. Her novel *Ruth*, for example, records the Gillot affair essentially as it happened. Similarly, her story *Fenitschka* is based on an actual incident that happened in Paris and involved the playwright Frank Wedekind.

Lou had gone to Paris in February, 1894. She spent half a year there, sharing an apartment for a time with her Danish friend Therese Krüger. France, like Germany, was then in the throes of political, social and literary turmoil. President Carnot's assassination by an Italian anarchist provoked widespread alarm and led to embittered debates in the Chamber of Deputies, followed a few months later by the outraged oratory over the Dreyfus affair. At the same time the literary life in the French capital was convulsed by fierce factional disputes. Naturalism was making its debut on the French stage. Storms of abuse or approval greeted each performance of a new play by Strindberg, Ibsen, Maeterlinck and Hauptmann in Antoines' Théâtre Libre and in Lugné-Poë's Maison de l'Oeuvre. Once again Paris was the battleground of revolutionary ideas.

Lou felt very much at home in this highly charged atmosphere. Accompanied by her black French poodle Toutou, she made the rounds of the literary cafés on the Left Bank, participated in innumerable discussions and made many friends in the cosmopolitan circle of the Parisian art world. She got to know the great Norwegian novelist Knut Hamsun, then in his thirties but famous already as the author of the starkly realistic novel *Hunger* and "handsome as a Greek god," the pale and sickly Danish journalist Herman Bangs, the German publisher Albert Langen, the young Russian émigré doctor Scawely, suspected of having participated in the assassination of Czar Alexander II, and the German playwright Wedekind whose powerful expressionistic drama of adolescent love, *The Awakening of Spring,* had caused such a scandal in Germany that Wedekind had retired to the more congenial atmosphere of Paris. Both as a man and as an artist Wedekind was obsessed with sex. He saw in it an elemental force that cannot and must not be denied. In powerful language, often bordering on the grotesque, he castigated the hypocritical morality of the bourgeoisie and became one of the most outspoken champions of sexual freedom.

It was Wedekind who provoked the incident that Lou relates in her story *Fenitschka.* She met him at a party given by the Hungarian Countess Nemethy. Like most men he was attracted to her at once and after talking with her half the night invited her up to his room. She accepted without hesitation and he assumed, of course, that her acceptance meant she was willing to spend the rest of the night with him. Much to his surprise he discovered that nothing was further from her mind. All his seductive arts, and they were considerable, failed to make the slightest impression on this bold and emancipated woman. In the end Wedekind, frustrated and feeling rather foolish, let her go. The following morning he appeared at her doorstep in formal attire, cutaway, black tie, gloves, and armed with a bunch of flowers, offering abject apologies for his ungentlemanly behavior. However, a few months later he took his subtle revenge by calling the main character of his play, *The Earthspirit,* "Lulu." A grotesque caricature, to be sure, for Lulu is a sex demon, insatiable and destructive.

In *Fenitschka* Lou relates this incident, enlarges on it and subjects it to some interesting psychological observations. Briefly, this is what happens. A young Russian girl, Fenitschka, who studies in Zurich and is determined to devote her life to the improvement of her mind, comes to Paris and spends an evening in the company of a group of friends in one of the smaller cafés of the Latin Quarter. Max Werner, a young German, joins them. Although he abhors the "intellectual woman," Fenitschka fascinates him. He marvels at the candor with which she discusses such delicate matters as the lives of Parisian grisettes, prostitution, free love and sex with a complete stranger in Paris in a café at night. Is her innocence merely a mask hiding a sensuous temperament, or is it genuine? He wants to find out, takes her to his room and tries to seduce her. But he meets with such a contemptuous refusal that he feels ashamed of himself and begs her pardon.

Thus far the story seems to be a fairly accurate account of the Wedekind episode. But it has a sequel. A few years later the young German meets Fenitschka again, this time in Russia. He finds that she has changed. She seems less intellectual and more womanly. Again they talk about love and marriage. He considers love the great excitement of life, while she compares it to "the good blessed bread with which we still our hunger." Gossip has it that Fenitschka now has a lover whom she meets secretly at night. She denies it indignantly: "How often had she not felt contempt during her student years abroad for those people whose cheap prudence had misunderstood her freedom?" But it is true nevertheless. The young German sees her one night in the company of a stranger. When he questions her she admits that she is in love with a man who has suddenly entered her life. He is not one of her university friends. In fact, intellectually, he is inferior to her. Although she hardly knows him she has become his mistress. The German is amused and wants to know what has become of her noble ideals? Has she lost faith in spiritual love? She becomes quite angry. It is a mistake to believe, she says emphatically, that the spirit is nobler than the flesh. Her intellectual friendships had never blossomed into love because there had always been something calculating about them. At last she had met the man who saw in her only a woman and treated her as such. With the abandon of a D. H. Lawrence heroine, Fenitschka had surrendered to him. There is reason to believe that Lou's own love life started with a similarly impulsive act of abandon.

In this connection the second story in *Fenitschka*, entitled "A Debauch," deserves attention. Although perhaps less autobiographical than the former, it does give an insight into the nature of the problem that occupied Lou. It treats the theme of masochistic love. The heroine is a young girl of artistic temperament who feels that a long debauch has made her incapable of love, because our "lives depend far less on what we experience or do consciously than on mysterious, uncontrollable, nervous impressions." She mentions that one of her earliest childhood experiences was seeing her nurse being beaten by her husband.

"I watched how she was beaten over the head by her husband, while her eyes hung on him with amorous humility." This picture had impressed itself deeply on her mind. It aroused memories of the slavish bliss of long-forgotten women. To subordinate herself completely to a dominating male had become her obsession. But her fiancé treated her with kindness and respect and did not understand what violent passions tormented her. Disillusioned, she left him. She felt his love would not satisfy her. What she longed for was the kind of brutal subjugation displayed in Klinger's engraving, *Time Annihilating Fame*, which shows a youth in armor with a face of iron resolution who pitilessly steps on a woman lying prostrate before him.

It is, of course, impossible to say whether masochistic tendencies troubled Lou's love life. That she dealt with them at all and not only in "A Debauch"—Renate, in a later novel, *The House*, is likewise consumed by the passion to subordinate herself completely to a masculine will—is significant. Equally significant, perhaps, is the fact that when Lou suddenly left Paris to escape the midsummer heat of the big city, she did so in the company of her Russian friend, Dr. Scawely, "a giant of a man who could tear the toughest nail from the wall with his strong white teeth." They went to Switzerland and spent a few weeks mountain-climbing in the Alps above Zurich. In her memoirs Lou says they stayed in an isolated Alpine hut, lived on milk, cheese, bread and berries and enjoyed most of all to walk barefoot across soft mountain meadows. It was an idyllic existence which was only once rather painfully interrupted when they accidentally walked into a maze of blackberry brambles. Crying with pain as she tried to extricate her bleeding feet, the thought suddenly struck Lou—"or was it an ancient memory? that man is always thrust from primeval bliss into the cruel realities of life." She goes on to say that she dismissed this thought and began to laugh when her friend admonished her cheerfully: "we should really offer our apologies to the blackberries for having stepped on them with our feet instead of kissing them with our lips." From the brief account Lou gives of this episode it is obvious that Scawely possessed to a high degree the qualities she cherished in men: strength and tenderness. Was he then her first lover? She does not say so. But since, with one exception, she makes no mention of any of her lovers, her silence does not mean much. And although her encounter with Scawely was brief, it was also passionate. She escaped with him from Paris, she lived with him in a lonely Alpine hut, and in his company she experienced "primeval bliss." He was a powerfully built man and, what is more, he was a Russian. That fact must be stressed. For Lou's sentimental attachment to Russia and her people grew in proportion to the length of time she lived abroad. However, if Scawely was Lou's first lover his place was soon taken by a mysterious stranger, never mentioned in her memoirs, whom she met in Vienna the year following her stay in Paris.

Lou had returned to her Berlin home and her husband in the late autumn of 1894 and started work almost at once on one of her most significant essays, "Jesus the Jew." She also compared notes with her Berlin artist friends on her Parisian impressions. In the spring of 1895 she became restless again and traveled to St. Petersburg to visit her family. She was accompanied by her new friend, Frieda von Bülow. In the past Lou's friendships had been mostly with men. Now they also included a number of unusual women, foremost among them Frieda von Bülow and Helene Klingenberg. Both were descended of old aristocratic families and both were writers, although neither attained Lou's literary prominence. Frieda, four years older than Lou, was the daughter of a Prussian Embassy Counselor; Helene's ancestors were Baltic Germans. Of the two Frieda was the more stimulating. A courageous and strong-willed woman, she had followed her brother to East Africa and participated in the struggle, led by Karl Peters, to establish a German protectorate there. She had founded hospitals in Zanzibar and Dar es Salaam. After five years of extensive work and travel in the newly acquired territory her health had broken down, forcing her to return to Germany. Lou met her in Berlin early in 1892 and they quickly became friends.

Lou was then at the beginning of her literary career and Frieda was already famous as an explorer and African colonizer. The attraction seems to have been mutual but both were strong-willed, and often had heated arguments. In an article, "Heresies about the Modern Woman," Lou took public issue with her friend who had insisted that a woman is just as much entitled to write books as to rear children.

"Certainly," Lou wrote, "only she should not take herself so terribly seriously. She should look upon her literary work as something additional, not essential to the full life of a woman."

But their disagreements did not diminish their friendship. They felt that they benefited from them and they frequently lived and traveled together. Lou introduced Frieda, who had been Karl Peters' mistress, to her family in Russia and for a while Frieda became romantically attached to Lou's brother Eugene.

The better she got to know Frieda the more Lou was fascinated by the strange mixture in her friend's character. Frieda seemed to oscillate between spurts of energy and periods of lassitude. The latter, a sign that she came from an old and weary race, can lead, Lou thought, to a longing for submission and self-surrender. Here again is the theme we have noted above: "the insane fascination with submission, the strongest impulse in all of us," as Renate confides to her friend Anneliese in Lou's novel *The House*.

At the end of April, 1895, Lou and Frieda left St. Petersburg and went to Vienna. There they made the acquaintance of Arthur Schnitzler, Richard Beer-Hofmann, Hugo von Hofmannsthal, Felix Salten, Peter Altenburg and other Austrian artists. Lou also met and became very fond of Marie von Ebner-Eschenbach, one of the most distinguished of Germany's women writers, an old lady of great charm and wisdom. Lou revered her as a wise and understanding woman who had not sacrificed the warmth of her femininity to her literary ambitions. By remaining true to her sex she had avoided the greatest danger that threatens the intellectual woman, that of "wasting her most intimate strength on reproducing herself on paper." Her example proved that it was possible to combine a literary career with the full and rich life of a woman. Lou needed that reassurance for nothing alarmed her so much as the sight of those militant bluestockings who, in trying to assert their equality with men, ceased being women. She was determined not to do that, not to subordinate her life to her work. Her writing was a sort of self-analysis, a probing of her own personality, an act of liberation. When it had served its purpose, when Freud had shown her a way to make therapeutic use of her psychological insights, she all but gave it up. Her success as a writer—and it was considerable: contemporary critics called her the "psychologically most profound among German women writers"—shows that her approach to literature was in accord with the spirit of the times.

Nowhere was that spirit better represented than in Vienna. While elsewhere in Europe political, social or economic problems occupied the most progressive minds, Viennese artists and scholars concentrated on the exploration of the human soul. Schnitzler's plays and stories—dealing with the vagaries of sexual love, promiscuity and infidelity in a slightly amused, slightly melancholy vein—or the overripe art of young Hofmannsthal, treated aesthetically what Freud and his fellow workers examined scientifically, the power of subconscious drives. To a born psychologist like Lou this was a fascinating climate. She noted that the literary life in Vienna differed from that in the other capitals where she had lived, by the easy interplay of intellect and eros. There were no sharp distinctions between the artist and the man of the world. The charm of the Viennese girls ennobled even the act of fleeting love and surrounded it with an aura of playfulness. As a result, the literary *bohème* of Vienna was easygoing and lighthearted. Absent was the sharpness of clashing ambitions, so marked in Berlin and Paris. Bathed in the warm glow of its setting sun, the capital of the Hapsburg Empire lived in a magic dreamworld of its own, shutting its eyes to the harsh realities outside.

The numerous friendships Lou formed in Vienna and her emotional involvements in the lives of unusual men and women deepened her insights into the human psyche and into her own soul. By subjecting these insights to a close intellectual scrutiny she reached conclusions that led her to the very threshold of psychoanalysis. But powerful though it was, her analytical intellect was not the most dominant trait of her character. That has been described as an "extreme readiness toward life, a humble and courageous holding-herself-open to its joys and woes, a fascinating mixture of masculine earnestness, childlike light-heartedness and feminine ardor."

According to her own testimony it took a long time before her feminine ardor was fully aroused, but once it was there was no holding back. She lost her slender, gaminlike figure and became a full-bosomed woman.

A good deal of mystery surrounds the man who wrought this change in her. She had withstood the passionate wooing of Gillot, Nietzsche, Rée, Andreas, Ledebour—to mention only a few. Now she was at an age when most women look back upon their first experience with physical love as an almost forgotten event of their adolescence. Lou, too, had come close to it several times but at the last minute she had always resisted it. So the question remains: who liberated her from her long protracted maidenhood? The answer is by no means easy. Lou herself draws a veil over this dramatic event. From her memoirs it would appear that the poet Rainer Maria Rilke was her liberator. And there is no doubt that Rilke was deeply in love with Lou and that she loved him. But was Rilke really the first man in Lou's life? It is much more likely—if she did not succumb to her Russian compatriot Scawely during those idyllic summer nights in the Alpine hut—that a quiet but powerful Viennese physician claimed her love. She met him two years before Rilke and he was her "unofficial" husband for years. His name sounds almost like a Joycean invention. It was Pineles, Dr. Friedrich Pineles.

Like Rée, Pineles came from an old and respected Jewish family which had emigrated to Austria from Galicia. Lou met him in Vienna in the late spring of 1895. She had been invited to a party in the home of Marie Lang, one of the leaders of the feminist movement in Austria. Among those present were Broncia Pineles, a gifted painter, and her brother Friedrich, called "Zemek" by his family and his closest friends, who was then an intern at the Allgemeine Krankenhaus in Vienna. His nickname Zemek, given him by his Polish nurse, means "Earthman." It suited him well. There was something earthy in his make-up, a quality of physical and moral fortitude. He was obviously not a man to be trifled with. In many respects he was a typical Viennese physician, cultured, widely read, interested in literary and philosophical questions and at the same time very learned, an authority in the field of his specialization. Even as a student he had carried on original research and was one of the first who tried to understand that peculiar disease of the central nervous system which causes a breakdown of the pupillary reflexes. He was one of seven students who registered for Freud's seminar on neuroses in the winter semester of 1895–96.

When he met Lou he was twenty-seven years old—seven years younger than she—dark-haired and with the swarthy complexion of the Eastern European Jew. His strong and clear-cut features, his distinguished bearing and his quiet intensity made him a conspicuous figure in any social gathering. Women adored him. They sensed a powerful masculine will behind his urbane exterior. And they felt something else, the profound sadness of a man of his race—a man whose brilliant dark eyes served notice that he had penetrated the surface of life and knew its illusions. He seems to have fascinated Lou at once. Like the heroine of her story *Fenitschka* she felt that here was the man who loved in her only the woman. Her intellectual qualities did not impress him.

They met about the same time that Zemek's beloved sister Broncia—the two were so close that they were sometimes mistaken for a married couple—met her future husband, the Styrian industrialist Koller. A whirlwind courtship ensued. Koller courted Broncia while Zemek wooed Lou. The two couples were inseparable. They went to parties and concerts together and together they roamed the Viennese woods. It was spring in Vienna and they were young and in love. Lou's friends knew, of course, that she was a married woman but they also knew or guessed that it was not a happy marriage. And being Viennese they felt that Lou had a right to happiness. She was obviously happy in Zemek's company and so was he in hers. They were therefore not particularly surprised when they heard that he had won Lou. Tradition has it that something like a double wedding took place with Broncia marrying Dr. Koller and Lou—unofficially—Zemek. Since she was married already, an official marriage was, of course, out of the question. But in the eyes of the Pineles family Lou became Zemek's wife and remained his wife for almost a dozen years. The only one who disapproved of this secret liaison was Zemek's mother. His sister understood and encouraged it. She invited the couple to her home in Hallein and later, when Lou was pregnant, to her country estate in Oberwaltersdorf.

Zemek's love provided Lou with "the good blessed bread" she needed. She stayed with him whenever she was in Vienna. And occasionally they met elsewhere and traveled together. Zemek, who longed for a more permanent union, chafed under this arrangement but Lou insisted that her husband would not give her a divorce. Besides, she was not at all sure that she could be faithful to Zemek if they were married. As it turned out she was right. Although it suited her to have an "official" husband in Berlin to whom she could always return, and an "unofficial" husband in Vienna whose love refreshed her, this arrangement did not, apparently, still her hunger completely. For after the earthman's embraces she once more yearned for a more heavenly love. She waited for a lover who could satisfy her treble needs of mistress, mother and madonna.

PART IV

Love and Poetry
1897-1901

14

"My Sister, My Spouse"

AT THE END OF APRIL, 1897, LOU WENT TO MUNICH WHERE SHE WAS joined by her friend Frieda von Bülow, who was to give a public lecture on her exploits in Africa. The Bavarian capital was one of the cities Lou liked to visit, although she did not particularly care for what she called the "Munich atmosphere," that peculiar blend of Bavarian patriotism, incense and beer. Most of her Munich friends were non-Bavarians like herself and congregated in Schwabing, the Munich Latin Quarter. Some of them, like Max Halbe and Frank Wedekind, she had met before in Berlin or Paris. In Munich she got to know Count Edward Keyserling, the architect August Endell, who remained a close friend the rest of her life, and the writers Michael Georg Conrad, Ernst von Wolzogen and Jakob Wassermann. The last, a promising writer whose novel *The Jews of Zirndorf* had attracted much attention, introduced Lou to the young and unknown Austrian poet Rainer Maria Rilke.

Rilke, then twenty-two years old, had recently moved to Munich from Prague, where he was born and brought up, ostensibly to carry on his studies at the University. Actually, he was far more interested in his literary career. He wrote poetry, plays, prose tales, book reviews, edited a literary journal and proposed the formation of a "League of truly modern writers." Although shy and retiring by nature he threw himself into a hectic literary activity because he wanted to prove to his skeptical family that he could make a living as a writer. He was a slender youth, gentle rather than robust, and with the chivalrous bearing characteristic of the young Austrian man-about-town. His small, pale face, dominated by deeply set eyes that looked at the world with anxious wonder, was framed by a thin straggling beard and a drooping mustache. In contrast to his full sensuous mouth was his slight, receding chin that sprouted a fuzzy goatee as soft and downy as the feathers on a young duck's head.

This was the young Austrian *littérateur* on the make, still known by his rather effeminate first name of René; and when Lou met him in Wassermann's apartment on May 12, 1897, he was a far cry from the great poet he was to become. A less likely contender for her feminine favors it would be hard to imagine. But Rilke's appearance was misleading. He was by no means the weak-willed youth he seemed. And what he lacked in physical prowess he made up for in an inner intensity that took Lou by surprise. Like most men Rilke was bent on her conquest the moment he met her. He applied himself to that objective with great skill and resourcefulness.

The day following their meeting he wrote her a letter in which he told her that it had not been the first time he had been privileged to spend a "twilight hour" in her company. Several months previously he had come across her essay "Jesus the Jew" in the April number of the *Neue Deutsche Rundschau*. It had been a revelation to him, for she had expressed with "the gigantic force of a sacred conviction" what he had been trying to say in a cycle of poems entitled "Visions of Christ." "I felt like one whose great dreams had come true," he told her, for she had said what he had merely dreamed. Her essay and his poetry were as mysteriously related as dreams are to reality. He had wanted to thank her for it but was incapable of doing so in the presence of others. Hence his letter. "For if one owes something very precious to another his gratitude should remain a secret between them." He added that it would give him great pleasure if he could read her some of these poems and closed with the hope that he would meet her the following night in the theatre.

Lou's reaction to the youthful fervor of Rilke's letter was mixed. On the one hand, she could not help feeling flattered by it. It reminded her of her own youthful impetuosity. And although she had long since learned to eschew romantic sentiments, she was still responsive to any spontaneous expression of feeling. The unbashful sentimentality of Rilke's letter made her smile. As she scrutinized his handwriting it dawned on her that he was the author of some mystifying anonymous letters she had received previously with poems enclosed. So Rilke was the young poet who had worshiped her from afar.

Lou would have been even more amused if she had known that Rilke had sent her poems because he was desperately eager to establish connections with prominent people. Having just embarked on a literary career he was anxious to be accepted by those who had made a success of it. He needed their encouragement both for reasons of self-assurance and because he wanted to impress his family with the illustrious names of his friends. Thus soon afterward he proudly informed his mother—herself an eager reader of the *Almanach de Gotha*—that he had made the acquaintance of the "famous Lou Andreas-Salomé" and her friend the African explorer Frieda von Bülow, "two magnificent women."

Whatever reservations Lou had when she met Rilke, she could not long resist his passionate pursuit. He sought her out with a single-minded zeal that surpassed anything she had encountered before. Wherever she went he tried to be there too. When he missed her in the theatre he looked for her all over Munich. "With a few roses in my hand I have been walking about the town and the entrance of the English Garden because I wanted to give you these roses. But instead of leaving them at your door with the golden key, I have been carrying them around, trembling with eagerness to meet you somewhere."

After every meeting he rushed home and poured out his heart in poetry. He knew instinctively that the spontaneity of his lyrical adoration was his strongest weapon. It disarmed her intellectual resistance by appealing to her own emotional spontaneity. The long and severe training to which she had subjected her mind had made her wary of uncontrolled emotions, but she could not long resist the intensity of Rilke's lyrical assault. When she succumbed to him a few weeks after they had met, he rushed into her arms like a child who has finally found his long-lost mother. But once she received him, she discovered to her surprise that the child was really a passionate young man, well versed in the arts of love. Suddenly their roles were reversed; it was now Rilke who played the dominant role. Mounted on Pegasus like another Bellerophon, he slew the Chimera that guarded the entrance to Lou's privacy and made her his wife. It happened so suddenly that even in retrospect Lou shuddered when she thought of it. In her memoirs she writes:

"I was your wife for years because you were the first reality, body and man undistinguishably one, the incontestable fact of life itself. I could have said literally the same you said when you confessed your love: 'You alone are real.' In this we became husband and wife even before we had become friends, not from choice but from this unfathomable marriage. It was not that two halves were seeking one another: shudderingly, our surprised unity recognized a preordained unity. We were brother and sister, but as in the remote past, before marriage between brother and sister had become sacrilegious."

On the face of it the whole affair was, of course, ridiculous. Here she was, a mature woman and almost old enough to be Rilke's mother—a woman, moreover, who was passionately desired by many men, some of them far more virile than Rilke. She had resisted most of them and now, in her thirty-sixth year, she succumbed to a boy. Why? Rilke's friends and admirers cast Lou in the role of a wily seductress who took advantage of an innocent youth and lured him into her nets. But it was more complex than that. Rilke was by no means an innocent youth when he met Lou. He had had his fair share of erotic adventures and knew that the surest way to win a woman's love was by appealing both to her motherly instincts and her feminine ardor. This he did with consummate skill. He penetrated Lou's intellectual armor and aroused her passion, but soon after their first embrace her critical faculties reasserted themselves and she began to look upon her young lover with increasing suspicion. His tremulous state worried her. She wondered whether his lyrical exultations, alternating with fierce moods of depression, were not the danger sign of mental sickness. There seemed to be two Rilkes, one confident and self-assured, the other morbidly introspective. In her letters and memoirs she writes that it was a frightening spectacle to see "the other" suddenly emerge, trembling with fear and giving vent to bitter self-reproaches and self-pity. She hoped at first that her love would cure him, but gradually her fears increased and she decided to end the affair. However, between its sudden beginning and its equally sudden end lay almost three years of love and poetry.

When Rilke met Lou he had already published a great deal of poetry. Under the signature of René Maria Rilke there had appeared in quick succession the slender volumes of *Life and Songs* (1894), *Wild Chicory: Songs Given to the People* (1896), *An Offering to the Lares* (1896), and *Crowned with Dreams* (1897). It was pure poetry of mood, vaguely yearning for something to come, vaguely nostalgic for something that has been; perfect of its kind; sentimental, sensitive and subtle. Its recurrent theme was the strangeness and mystery of life—life not lived or observed but felt, intuitively felt, as oneness:

> Dreams seem to me like orchids
> Rich and gay.
> They draw their strength from life's
> Gigantic tree.
> Proud of their borrowed blood
> They boast and flee
> A minute later: pale and dead.
> And as the worlds above
> Move silently
> Do you not feel a fragrance overhead?
> Dreams seem to me like orchids. . . .

Although Lou was struck emotionally by Rilke's verbal virtuosity, by the melodious rhythms, evocative alliterations and ornate assonances of his poems, they did not appeal to her intellect. She did not deny that many of them were beautiful, some even beguilingly so, but if you tried to grasp them they dissolved, like dreams just beyond recall. She complained that she could not understand them and Rilke made a conscious effort to write more simply and about simple things.

Helped and encouraged by Lou, the young poet entered upon a long period of severe self-discipline which came to fruition many years later in the plastic splendor of *New Poems*. One sign of Lou's influence can be seen in the striking change in his handwriting. Before he met Lou, Rilke wrote sloppily and often illegibly. Now his writing became as neat and precise as hers. When she scorned the somewhat effeminate French form of his name, René, he changed it to Rainer. Even after their break, when Lou told him that she could help him no longer, his letters bear moving testimony to the great debt he owed her.

"I felt it then and I know it today, that the infinite reality that surrounded you was the most important event of that extremely good, great and productive time. The transforming experience which then seized me at a hundred places at once emanated from the great reality of your being. I had never before in my groping hesitancy felt life so much, believed in the present and recognized the future so much. You were the opposite of all doubt and witness to the fact that everything you touch, reach and see, *exists*. The world lost its clouded aspect, the flowing together and dissolving, so typical of my first poor verses. Things arose. I learned to distinguish animals and flowers. Slowly and with difficulty I learned how simple everything is and I matured and learned to say simple things. All this happened because I was fortunate enough to meet you at a time when I was in danger of losing myself in formlessness."

Lou's failure to respond to his poetry as wholeheartedly as he wished made Rilke concentrate on that theme which he knew occupied her deeply, religion. Here they were on common ground. They were both extremely fond of the Bible, especially of the Old Testament. And when they were alone together in the privacy of Lou's rooms, Rilke sometimes read to her. He selected those passages that corresponded most closely to his feeling for the beloved woman. "Thou hast ravished my heart, my sister, my spouse; thou hast ravished my heart with one of thine eyes, with one chain of thy neck. How fair is thy love, my sister, my spouse! how much better is thy love than wine!" On and on, Rilke read and he could feel the current of sympathy that his words aroused in Lou's heart.

Sometimes their discussions touched on the significance of the Christ figure which Lou had pondered in her essay "Jesus the Jew," and Rilke in his poetry. It is possible, indeed likely, that Rilke received further stimulus for his poems "Visions of Christ" from Lou's essay. He read it about the time he started the cycle, and certainly there are striking similarities in the treatment of the theme. Both saw in Christ, not the son of God but of man, a religious genius infinitely moving in the solitary agony of his assion.

Starting from the premise that all gods are manmade, Lou's concern was with the retroaction, as she called it, of these manmade gods on those who believe in them. The intensification of man's emotional response to figures originally created to assuage his fear of death and the unknown seemed to her to be the heart of the religious phenomenon. It propelled men to become saints. The classic example of that process was Jesus. Here was a young Jew brought up in the stern tradition of Judaism and taught to believe in the messianic promises of Jehovah, the God of Wrath. But he had concentrated the rays of his fervent heart on this forbidding deity, transforming Him into a God of Love. His childlike, unwavering faith, his absolute trust in Him whom he called his heavenly Father, had resolved the contradiction that lies at the root of all religions: men kneeling in front of a manmade God. For it is the human heart in which the mystery of the religious experience takes place, causing a manmade God to give birth to a godlike man. This happened to Jesus and made him the Christ, the begetter of a new religion.

But Lou insisted that in order to understand the real tragedy of the historic Jesus it must be remembered that he grew up in the Judaic tradition of an essentially just, if stern, God. It was this God whom he loved and to whom he cried out in the hour of his greatest need. Who knows what terrible doubts assailed him on the road to martyrdom from Gethsemane to Golgotha, and what despair filled his heart when he finally realized that his heavenly Father had forsaken him.

"Even at the last moment, when he was already hanging on the cross, he must have forgiven his God, for a miracle was still possible and it *had* to happen: a just man could not be made to perish miserably, handed over to his enemies, least of all could he be forced to suffer that form of death most dreaded and most shameful to Jewish eyes—death on the cross, even if he was not the Messiah but merely another just Jew. God's firm and sacred promise preserved him from such a fate."

And yet it happened. Hence Christ's agonized outcry: "My God, my God, why has thou forsaken me?"

These anguished words, spoken by a martyr of his faith, sum up the suffering of all religious men. They pose the problem of

God's very existence. But while Jesus may have died with thi
doubt in his heart, his disciples succeeded in transforming hi
moment of deepest despair into his greatest triumph by th
grandiose paradox of asserting that God punishes those He love:
Christ's death on the cross became the prologue of his ascent t
heaven, his solitary agony the symbol of a new religion. Howevei
"amidst the triumphant shouts of a solid faith, useful to all, thei
echoes very gently and painfully the ultimate word of religion t
which only now and again a poor solitary genius can rise wh
has experienced it deeply: *Eli, Eli! lama sabachthani.*"

Christ's anguished cry on the cross is also the theme of Rilke
poem "Annual Fair," written six months after Lou's essay. In hi
first letter to her Rilke told Lou that he had read her essay at th
suggestion of a Dr. Conrad, one of the editors of the journal *Di*
Gesellschaft who, having seen a few poems of his "Visions c
Christ," thought that her essay would interest him. Rilke adde
that Conrad was going to publish five of these poems, a clain
which he had made earlier in a letter to Ludwig Ganghofer. Bi
he was mistaken. They never appeared in *Die Gesellschaft*, nc
anywhere else until they were published more than sixty yeai
later in the third volume of his collected works. What caused th
long delay? One thing is certain: Rilke had no doubts about the
poetic merits. At a time when he was very critical of his earl
verses he referred to them as "these great poems." The mystei
heightens if we ponder the significance of Rilke's reply to Wilhel
von Scholz who, in 1899, wanted to publish them. "I have man
reasons," Rilke told Scholz, "to conceal the Christ figures for
long, long time. They are the future which accompanies me a
my life."

Between these two dates—1897 when he seemed eager to pu
lish them, and 1899 when he rejected any thought of publicatic
—falls Rilke's encounter with Lou. How intimately these poen
are linked to Lou is further evidenced by the fact that it was Lc
to whom he turned when in 1912 his publisher, Kippenber
urged again that they be published:

"Unfortunately, I have once hinted that the *Visions of Chri*
exist and since Kippenberg now attaches great importance
offering unpublished work in this new edition, he urges me
include these great poems (which I myself have not seen fc

many years) in this new publication. Under no circumstances will I do this without knowing what you think of it. Do you think that there is something else from that time which might rather be published, or has the time really come for these things?"

Lou's answer to this request appears to be lost. But whatever she said, Rilke decided against publication. He mentioned them once more to Lou eighteen months later in the postscript of a letter written in the home of his publisher in Leipzig.

"Perhaps the Visions of Christ in a yellow folder have remained with you? In this case, please read them."

This time Lou replied at once telling him that he was right, his poems were in her bank safe. She had reread them and, for the first time, had been struck by amazing relationships, difficult to explain in writing.

"In tone they [Visions of Christ] are very different from the two recent ones [a reference to the first two Duino Elegies] and yet everything you have written moves with an inner unity between these old Visions of Christ and the coming visions of the angel."

Rilke felt comforted by these words. Once again he was torn by self-doubts and needed reassurance. If Lou still believed in him, could he not believe in himself? Perhaps he recalled those intimate hours in Munich, now long ago, when he had first read his poems to Lou. It had been an unforgettable experience. She had listened with a quiet intensity that forged an invisible bond between them. Imperceptibly she had become involved in his poetry and, through it, in him. He could feel that it was more than sympathy he aroused in her. It was an upsurge of wonder, admiration and love. Her whole being responded; her heart to his music, her head to his words. They sounded so familiar to her that she might have written them herself and perhaps she had, perhaps she was listening to an echo of her own voice? It was certainly the voice of her brother in spirit.

In his poem "Annual Fair" Rilke treated the Christ theme in the context of a visit to the Munich Oktoberfest. In colorful images he describes the gay and noisy life at the fair, the huge beer tents, merry-go-rounds, ferris wheels, and the multitudinous attractions from all over the world that assail the eyes and ears of the visiting throng. He strolls among them until he comes to a

booth at the end of the fair where a sign says that here one can
see the life and death of Christ. Without knowing why, he pays
ten pfennigs, gets a ticket and enters. He finds himself in the
presence of waxen figures representing various scenes from the
life of Christ: his birth at Bethlehem, his visit to the Temple,
his entrance into Jerusalem, his solitary vigil in the Garden of
Gethsemane and finally his crucifixion. As he watches the figure
of Christ on the Cross his heart suddenly stops, for:

> The waxen God opened and closed his eyes,
> his glance concealed by thin and bluish lids,
> his narrow, wounded chest heaved and sighed,
> his sponge-drenched lips in deadly pallor tried
> to grasp a word and force it through his teeth:
> My God, my God—hast thou forsaken me?
> And as I, horrified and at a loss
> to understand these martyred words, remain
> fixed to the spot and stare and stare
> at him, his hands let go the cross.
> He groans and says: "It is I."
> I listen speechless to his anguished cry,
> look at the walls covered with glaring cloth
> and feel the cheap deception of the fair,
> the smell of oil and wax. But there
> it starts again and says: "This is my curse;
> Since my disciples stole me from the grave,
> deluded by their vain and boastful faith,
> there is no pit that holds me—none.
> As long as rushing brooks reflect the stars
> and life bursts forth under a spring sun,
> I must go on and on across the earth,
> I must pay penance now from Cross to Cross . . .
>
> Do you know the legend of the Wandering Jew?
> I am myself that ancient Ahasver
> Who daily dies and daily lives anew."

This was language that Lou understood and with it Rilke
gained her love. Two weeks after their first meeting his letters
already sound ardent and intimate. He sent her poems, songs of
longing, that were different from his former songs because "I have
looked into the eyes of longing beside me." The only clouds on
the bright horizon of their love were Lou's husband in Berlin and,
more immediately, a call from Rilke's Austrian draft board order-

ing him to appear before them. He was disconsolate and grasped every second to be with Lou. At the end of May they spent two days together in search of solitude and mountain air in the little Upper Bavarian village of Wolfratshausen. When the dreaded day of departure came Rilke was heartbroken. Fortunately, his draft board decided, after examining him, that he was not needed after all. He communicated this good news to Lou in a joyous telegram from Prague and a few days later he rejoined her in Munich. From then on they were inseparable.

The growing ardor of Rilke's letters and poems shows how quickly his love found fulfillment. On June 6, Whitsunday, he sent her greetings, told her that this spring had a particular significance for him and submitted himself humbly to her "sweet slavery." Two days later he vowed that it would be many years before she understood how much he loved her. What a mountain spring means to a man dying of thirst, her love meant to him. He said he wanted to see the world through her for "then I do not see the world but only you, you, you." In a poem three days later he called her his "Empress." She had made him rich, and even though he tried to hide his riches, everybody could see his happiness shining in his eyes. He wanted to "lose his separate identity and dissolve completely" into her. "I want to be you. I don't want to have any dreams that do not know you, nor any wishes that you cannot grant. I do not want to do anything that does not praise you. . . . I want to be you. And my heart burns before your grace like the eternal lamp before the picture of Mary."

Lou's answers to these rapturous effusions are unfortunately lost, because of their joint decision to destroy all documents of their love. In her memoirs she says that "the prevailing and unalterable condition of their lives"—an allusion to her marriage —made this action necessary. And there is no doubt that Andreas' fierce pride made it imperative that they be discreet and avoid an open display of their affection. For this reason Lou was not altogether happy with the lyrical adoration in prose and verse with which the young poet pursued her and she hints at black-inked corrections that resulted in the mutilation and destruction of many of Rilke's love poems. She then quotes a fragment that had somehow survived, still in the original and by now faded envelope in which Rilke had sent it to her:

> With gentle blessing did your letter greet me;
> I knew that distance cannot stop our love.
> From all that's beautiful you come to meet me,
> My spring wind you, my summer rain above.
> You my June night on thousand pathways lead me,
> Upon which no initiated walked before:
> I am in you.

It is easy to imagine what Andreas' reaction to this poem would have been if he had seen it. For it describes, although veiled in poetic language, the course of his wife's love affair. It was obviously a reply to a letter she had written Rilke, and obviously, too, he had been waiting impatiently for it. When it came his pent-up emotions burst into song. In rhapsodic language he recalls the passionate hours they had spent together. They had met in May, hence the allusion to spring wind, had become lovers in June—"my June night"—and had spent the summer months in close proximity in a small peasant house in Wolfratshausen. All these events are faithfully recorded in the poem. But most revealing, and from Andreas' point of view, most painful, is the penultimate line with its oblique reference to Rilke being Lou's first lover—or so he thought. It is understandable that Lou felt embarrassed by his lyrical indiscretions and tried to suppress them. She was not altogether successful, for many of the poems she eliminated from a manuscript collection of love poems, *In Your Honor*, which Rilke gave her were preserved in Rilke's notebooks.

However, the occasional displeasure Rilke's lyrical exuberance caused Lou was far outweighed by the pleasure she derived from his company. They had left Munich in the middle of June and had retired to Wolfratshausen accompanied, one suspects mainly for the sake of appearances, by Frieda von Bülow and August Endell. Wolfratshausen, a typical small Upper Bavarian town with a charming old market square, baroque churches with onion-shaped steeples, and a fair number of the traditional Bavarian inns, is situated in the broad valley of the Inn at the foot of the Kalvarienberg. Pleasant walks lead up to the top of the hill and offer magnificent views of the Alpine range to the south. They had rented a small peasant house with a garden and a shady arbor in the back—an idyllic setting for a love tryst. Lou recalls that her room was on the ground floor facing the street, and that Rilke always closed the shutters when he visited her, to prevent passers-by from looking in. In the semi-darkness of these summer days they celebrated their honeymoon.

It was a passionate affair, with Lou always, at first, being overawed by Rilke's male aggressiveness before her greater maturity asserted itself. Then she would take her young lover into the garden behind the house and teach him to walk barefoot over the dewy grass. She would tell him the names of her favorite flowers, make him listen to the wind in the trees and the rushing water of the brook. Her husband had taught her to observe the animals at daybreak and now she passed this knowledge on to her young lover. For the first time in his life Rilke entered into a real relationship with nature, a simple, direct and non-literary relationship. Lou communicated to him her sense of wonder at the oneness of the world, her joy of living, and her vitality. The healthy vigor of her sensuous enjoyment made him feel ashamed of the mawkish sentimentality of his adolescent dreams. A new world opened before his eyes, less tortured than the one he had known. He felt as if reborn. His whole life, he now realized, had been influenced by the false piety and the artificial values of his mother. She was responsible for the unhealthy exaltations which alienated him from reality. He had met Lou just in time. She would help him find himself. Inspired by his love for her, and with her guidance, he tried to express his feelings more simply and directly. This was not easy and many poems he wrote during this extremely productive time reflect his "pre-Wolfratshausen mood," as he called it, that floating between day and dream which is so typical of his first verses. But with others one feels the effort toward greater concreteness:

> The land is bright and darkly glows the arbor.
> You speak in whispers while I watch with awe.
> And every word you say is like an altar
> Built by my faith upon my quiet shore.
> I love you. You're sitting in a chair, your cool
> white hands asleep as in a bed.
> My life is lying like a silver spool
> within your hands. Release my thread.

Boldly this poem comes to grips with the love theme, first by setting the scene—land and arbor: an allusion to the arbor in Wolfratshausen, where they spent so much of their time. Lou is talking. We get an idea of how intently Rilke listened from the image "altar" to which he likens her words, thereby elevating his love to the level of religious adoration. But this feeling is immediately brought down to earth again by the simple statement, particularly moving in this context: "I love you." With it the poem returns to a concrete image. Lou is sitting in a garden chair, her hands folded in her lap. As he watches her the poet realizes that he is completely in her power. She holds the thread of his life in her hands. The image is completed with the gentle request, stated with the utmost verbal economy, that she untangle his life and set him free: "Release my thread."

It is in poems such as these that one can see how much Rilke was under Lou's influence. He clung to her with an almost desperate helplessness, and could not bear the thought of being separated from her. Periods of separation were, however, unavoidable. Lou could not subordinate her life completely to his as he wanted her to. This would have been against her nature. She had to interrupt even their Wolfratshausen honeymoon to keep a prearranged appointment in Hallein with her friend Broncia Koller. But no sooner was she gone than Rilke's passionate letters with their pale-blue seals followed her. He wrote her daily, protesting his love and imploring her to return to him. Perhaps he sensed the danger of another man in the background, although Lou had not told him much about Zemek. To her dismay she noted that he indulged once again in the most extravagant language, and once again she felt uneasy and disturbed.

To make matters worse her official husband, Andreas, who had been in Berlin all this time, announced his arrival and said he would spend a month in Wolfratshausen with her. It was therefore particularly important that her young lover learn to control his emotions. Since there is no record of discord, Lou and Rilke seem to have succeeded in keeping Andreas in the dark. To be sure, cynics have said that so far from trying to conceal her affection for Rilke, Lou confessed it to her husband and that he acquiesced in it. But in view of Andreas' well-known temper this is hardly likely. The fact that he did not notice anything is a tribute to Lou's expert handling of the affair. She had always been surrounded by adoring males and Andreas may have thought that of all his wife's numerous admirers Rilke was the least dangerous. He seems to have grown quite fond of the young poet and raised no objections when Rilke proposed to return to Berlin with them. Thus ended the first chapter of Lou's affair with Rilke. Henceforth she would become more and more his friend, his teacher and his mother-confessor. Their honeymoon was over.

15

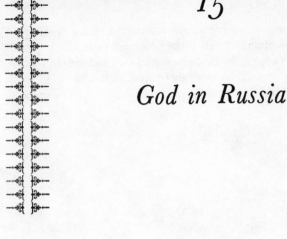

God in Russia

LOU AND RILKE SPENT THE WINTER OF 1897 IN BERLIN. LOU IN HER small apartment in Schmargendorf at the edge of the Grunewald —the same Grunewald from which Nietzsche had fled in bitter disappointment—Rilke in the neighboring village of Wilmersdorf. They were both cramped for space. The largest room in Lou's apartment was her husband's library, where he worked and gave his lessons. She had to receive her own visitors in the kitchen, not one would have thought, the most suitable milieu for her poet-lover. But Rilke seems to have loved it. While Andreas was secluded in his study, he assisted Lou with her household chores, cut wood, helped clean up, and watched her prepare his favorite Russian dishes, gruel and borsch. Or they went for long walks in the woods, frolicked in the company of tame deer, and watched silently, hand in hand, the setting of the pale winter sun on the western horizon. They were great nature lovers, especially Lou, who always returned home refreshed and at peace.

For Rilke these were moments of creative bliss. For the first time in his life he experienced something greater than his own emotions. Lou's presence gave him a feeling of completeness, a sense of reality he had not known before. In her arms his frustrations vanished, he felt confident and happy. She was his love and more than his love, she was life itself—present and future. Some day she would be the mother of his children:

When we have children sweet and fair
I'll give each boy a crown to wear
and a garland to each girl.

That possibility must have occurred to Lou, too, and she probably dreaded it. It would further complicate her already complicated life. But she was not in the habit of brooding over the consequences of her actions. Rilke's love gave her fulfillment. That was all that mattered now. Should there be consequences she would know how to take care of them.

Sometimes Lou and Rilke spent an evening in the city, went to the theatre or attended a concert, and afterward she introduced him to her literary friends. On such occasions Rilke could be an animated talker with a quick eye for the humorous and a contagious laugh. But there were other times when he remained silent and withdrawn. During these fits of depression Lou felt ill-at-ease in his company and wondered what she could do to help him. She thought of seeking medical advice and she did discuss Rilke's case with her friend Zemek, but for the time being she decided that the best cure was to keep him occupied. He had a good but undisciplined mind. He needed to learn that even a poet could not rely exclusively on a few inspired moments. She taught him the value of work, hard sustained work. She was a great worker herself, a new article for the *Neue Deutsche Rundschau* had to be finished and her publisher urged completion of her book *Fenitschka*. The summer of love was over. Lou was ready for a winter of work.

Her example inspired Rilke to do likewise. Realizing that his unmethodical education had left serious gaps in his knowledge, he decided to enroll as a student at the University of Berlin and attend lectures on art history and aesthetics. Under Lou's supervision he also began to study the art of the Italian Renaissance. He had been in Italy several times and was planning to spend the coming spring in Florence. Lou unfortunately could not come with him but he promised to keep her informed of his Italian impressions by writing a diary especially for her, both as a token of his love and as proof that he had learned his lessons well.

The product of this promise was Rilke's *Florentine Diary*. It opened with a poem in which he deplored his having been "banished" from their wintry landscape into this distant spring. He felt lost in it, bewildered by this new and shimmering land. "Whether I am already calm and mature enough to begin the diary which I have promised to bring home to you—I do not know." But then he remembered the previous spring, when he had met Lou, and thought it was a good omen to start writing this "proof of his longing" now. He would spread out before her dear bright eyes what he had captured of Florence, his personal impressions, thoughts and pictures.

There follow several pages of descriptive prose rich in color and atmosphere. Florence was not an easy town to get to know. Unlike Venice it did not invite the stranger in at once. He found its palaces dark and forbidding, monuments of a strong and martial time. "But once you have gained the confidence of these palaces, they tell you gladly the legend of their lives in the magnificently rhythmic language of their courtyards." These he loved and lovingly describes in a few inspired pages. Then, all of a sudden, the diary stopped. He left Florence, fled from it because he could no longer bear the overpowering impact of its art. He went to Viareggio to be closer to nature and, in spirit at least, closer to his love. In one of his first poems written there he told Lou:

> Believe me, beloved, we are still
> far from our origin;
> Your summer silk you're spinning yet,
> and when my longing cries for you
> I feel I'm much too much afraid.

It was a wise move; it inspired a whole cycle of poems in which Rilke conjured up in strangely haunting melodies the mysterious state of maidenhood. "Maidens are like gardens on an evening in April, spring on May pathways, but nowhere a goal." They are queenly sisters waiting in a state of tremulous excitement for the coming of their bridegrooms. Their songs and prayers relate their subconscious fear of what lies ahead of them, as well as their secret longing for it. "Let something happen to us—look how we long for life," Rilke's young girls implore the Virgin Mary.

In some entries the poet similarly implored Lou. He praised the state of motherhood and reminded her that it meant peace and fulfillment:

"Today a mother who was much afraid before the miracle happened to her, wrote me," he told Lou, and went on to describe the happiness Countess Reventlow felt for her recently born illegitimate son Rolf. "I have sat all afternoon in the garden with Rolf and in the air he blossomed out like a rose. He has become much prettier since you saw him." Rilke added that he had read this passage "like a hymn," and "I long for the moment when I shall read it of you. Then it will become melody."

Does this reference mean Rilke thought that Lou was pregnant? His British biographer, Miss E. M. Butler, thinks so and Eudo C. Mason, another British Rilke scholar, points out that sixty years ago the knowledge of contraceptives was not so advanced that a chance pregnancy must be ruled out. However, there is no record that Lou was pregnant at this time; and the rumor still current in London that Ellen Delp, whom Lou sometimes called her "chosen daughter" (*Wahltochter*), was her natural daughter by Rilke, is certainly unfounded.

But, whether true or not, Rilke may have thought, and indeed hoped, that Lou was carrying his child. There is no doubt that during his Italian journey he was preoccupied with the twin themes of maidenhood and motherhood: "The artist's effort is to find himself. The woman finds fulfillment in the child." Or again: "A woman's way always leads to the child, before she is a mother and afterwards."

But there is no doubt either that Lou dreaded the thought of motherhood. Not because she had any moral scruples—she would cheerfully have born an illegitimate child—but because a child did not fit into the pattern of her life. Rilke, on the other hand, may have felt that if Lou had a child by him there would be less danger of his losing her. That was what he dreaded most. Perhaps it was Lou's refusal to bear his child which caused the sudden outburst of anguish in his diary:

"After a day of prayer a day of atonement. That is what happens often. I found your letter after dinner and was dismayed and afraid. Even now I am sad. I have been looking forward to the summer with such joy. And now doubts and worries come, and all paths are confused. Whither? Everything is suddenly dark around me. I do not know where I am. I feel only that I must travel among strangers one day and another and a third before I reach you—perhaps to say good-by."

But this mood did not last. He went for long walks and recovered his peace of mind. "There is no anxiety in me any more, only the bright joy of having you again, darling." This joy gave him strength to write. He felt sure that in the great happiness of their reunion they would find a way to the future. He told her how much he had learned and how rich he would return to the "festival of their love." Proudly he told her that he had become the confidant of all that is beautiful, a friend and brother of all quiet things. "Even now, and I am only at the first threshold of understanding, evenings come to me in the forest that remove all precaution from the things around me, all the strange bashfulness of their austere chastity." He has learned to look and to listen. He no longer tries to force his love on nature. He waits for her to come to him.

When a young Russian girl, a casual acquaintance with whom he took a long walk by the Ligurian Sea—during which his mind returned to those unforgettable walks with Lou in Wolfratshausen—asked him if he had always had such an intimate relationship with nature, he replied: "No—and I was surprised how tenderly my words sounded—it is only a short time since I have been able to see and enjoy it."

Later the young lady said, "I am ashamed to confess it, but I feel dead. My joy has become weary and I don't want anything any more."

Rilke pretended not to have heard but suddenly, pointing with quick eagerness, he said: "A glowworm, do you see it?" She nodded. " 'There, too, and there, and there,' I continued, and carried her away. 'Four, five, six,' she counted excitedly, and then I laughed: 'You ungrateful one! This is life: six glowworms and many, many more. And you want to deny it?' "

One can almost hear Lou speaking here. It was her joy of life that Rilke echoes.

He had conquered his doubts. He would return to his love with confidence in himself and in his future as an artist. "I wish very much to come to you quickly, quickly, for I know something in me that you do not know yet, a new great brightness that invigorates my speech and gives me a wealth of images." Exultantly he exclaimed: "You magnificent one, how vast you have made me! That I am returning so serene, darling, is the best thing I bring you."

But when they finally met at the Baltic seaside resort of Zoppot his anxiety returned. He had wanted to surprise Lou with his newly found confidence. This time he wanted to be the lord and master. He wanted to assert the independence of his manhood and dreamed of Lou rushing into his arms with the tremulous excitement of the girls in his songs. Poor Rilke! He should have known Lou better than that. She was not the woman to rush into the arms of any man. Although ardent when aroused, her will put a brake on any such romantic notion of passion. She received him kindly enough but she made him feel that he was still a child, a child she loved but did not take too seriously. He felt crushed and outraged, and in a sudden uprush of anger he said that he hated her. He had not come to relive the past. "I did not want to find the memory of those winter days in Berlin, you were to be more than ever my future." But in her presence he felt small and insignificant, worthless, like a beggar: "I felt so miserable and wretched that I lost or threw away my last remaining riches, and in my despair I had the uneasy feeling that I must leave the sphere of your kindness that humiliates me."

But his anger did not last long. He could not tear himself away from her. While he was still in the grip of such turbulent emotions Lou calmly asked him what he planned to do. This question shocked him into facing up to reality. He spent a sleepless night over it and when they met again the next morning he told her simply that he loved her and would always love her. She was his future, his hope and his life. "Be always ahead of me, dear one, only one, holy one. Let us ascend together to a great star. . . . you are not one goal for me, you are a thousand goals, you are everything." And so another crisis passed. Once again Rilke accepted Lou on her own terms. In the ensuing discussions Lou suggested that he devote some time to the study of Russian. Here she could really help him. Besides, she herself would benefit from a return to the scenes of her childhood.

It was a sensible suggestion. Interest in Russian life and letters was rapidly growing in Germany and there was much demand for translations of Russian books. Perhaps Lou thought that if

Rilke knew Russian he could make a living as a translator. She was concerned about his future; obviously he could not live on poetry. She knew, of course, that her husband did not earn much money as a teacher of languages but he did not have to starve. Rilke, she feared, was heading toward economic disaster. She surmised, and probably correctly, that her young lover's sudden moods of depression which made her fear for his sanity were caused by his subconscious fear of the future. He had to find a goal other than that of writing poetry or of clinging to her in desperate love. That responsibility she refused to accept. Since he was a gifted linguist, it would not take him long to learn Russian, and once he knew it many doors would be open to him. Intimate contact with an Eastern culture would, in any case, enrich his poetry. To make her suggestion more palatable and as an additional incentive for sustained work during the winter months, she proposed to Rilke that he accompany her and her husband on a journey to Russia in the spring of 1899.

Rilke was overjoyed. The prospect of spending the coming months with his beloved Lou in the intimacy of his study delighted him. It would necessitate his moving to Schmargendorf, where she lived, and taking a room near her. This he did. It seemed a good omen that the name of the house was "Forest Peace." And it was a peaceful and productive time. Lou proved to be an exacting and capable teacher. Soon Rilke had mastered the elements of Russian and was able to read Dostoevsky in the original. He did not neglect his own work. He wrote poems and reviews for literary journals and worked on *The Last of Their Line,* a collection of prose tales.

Lou, too, continued her writing. She needed money for her trip to Russia. Between September of 1898 and February of 1899 she published no less than nine articles and reviews in such reputable journals as *Cosmopolis, Die Zukunft, Das Literarische Echo, Die Frau,* and *Pan.* She wrote on physical love, a theme that interested her more and more, on art, on the problems of the modern woman, and on Tolstoy. In addition she finished another book, *Children of Men,* which Cotta published in 1899. She was therefore well supplied with funds when, at the end of April, she set out with her husband and her young lover on that historic journey to Russia. Again one marvels at her courage in traveling together with a husband whose suicidal tendencies she knew and such an exuberant lover as Rilke. But again she seems to have managed the affair with consummate skill and there was no incident. Those among her friends who knew the relationship of the strange trio kept their misgivings to themselves. Their destination was Moscow, holy Moscow, the heart of Mother Russia, where they planned to spend the Easter holidays. Then they would visit Lou's relatives in St. Petersburg. They left Berlin on Tuesday, April 25, and after a short stopover in Warsaw, they arrived in Moscow on Maundy Thursday.

They could not have chosen a better time. The splendid pageantry of the rites of the Orthodox Church had transformed the town into one great temple of worship. Peasant pilgrims from far and wide crowded the churches, mingling the sounds of their chants with the booming voices of the church bells that reverberated across the massive walls of the Kremlin. The very atmosphere was charged with prayer and piety. The effect was overwhelming. Lou and Rilke, who were particularly susceptible to spiritual intensities, succumbed to it completely. Years later Rilke wrote Lou:

"I have experienced only one Easter. It was then, in that long, unusual, extremely exciting night when all the people crowded together and when in the darkness *Ivan Veliki* struck me, pealing, pealing. That was my Easter and I think it is enough for a whole life."

The religious spontaneity of the Russian people, their naïve and natural piety made a deep impression on Lou, too, although she did not experience the shock of recognition that Rilke felt. It was a remembrance of things past. The simple faith of these old men and women, to whom the figure of the risen Christ was a living reality, reminded her of her own faith as a child. To be sure, she had lost it and she knew that she could not recover it, but she knew also that she was back home at last. Russia was her country after all and these were her people. She had traveled far into the alien West with its secular way of life. Under Gillot's powerful influence she had turned her back on her Russian inheritance and, by cultivating her intellect, had tried to repress her impulses. Not very successfully, it is true. Her spontaneity was far greater than that of most of her contemporaries and was, in fact, the secret of her success both as a woman and as a writer. But she had been forced to dissemble it. In Moscow she found herself suddenly face to face with an almost elemental expression of feeling. Rilke's response to it made her understand that it is the mainspring of the creative spirit. Without it the intellect remains barren. Watching him, mute with awe, amidst the praying multitude of Russian mujiks during that long nightly Easter service, Lou sensed the vibrations in Rilke's soul that a few months later gave rise to the first prayers of the *Book of Hours.* Her husband's scientific detachment from all that went on around him seemed to her by comparison shallow and uninspired. She decided there and then to leave him behind the next time she went to Russia.

The week they spent in Moscow was memorable also in other respects. They met such prominent Russian artists and writers as Leonid Pasternak, the father of the poet Boris Pasternak, Prince Paul Troubetzkoy and Sofia Nikolaevna Schill. It was Pasternak who arranged their meeting with the grand old man of Russian letters, Tolstoy. The Count invited them to have tea with him in his study. They spent two hours in his company talking about the intellectual, social and political ferment in Russia. Lou noted that Tolstoy was not in sympathy with the efforts made by the Russian intelligentsia to enlighten the people. He felt that the Russian people did not need enlightenment as much as they needed love. All that was necessary was to tap the vast reservoir of their inner resources.

To Lou the matter was more complex. She thought that the childlike naïveté of the Russian people, their piety and warmth of heart, had to find some sort of accommodation with modern scientific thought and practices. The problem facing Russia was to effect a synthesis between Occidental knowledge and the needs of the heart. But is such a synthesis possible? Can reason be married to faith? The educated Russian embodied the whole tragedy of this conflict. He advocated progress because he wanted his people to emerge from their feudal past. At the same time he had the uneasy feeling that what he advocated was wrong, not because the Czar was opposed to it, but because his God did not and could not want it. For progress in secular knowledge inevitably leads to a decline in faith. The Bible was right: man's fall from grace began when he ate from the tree of knowledge.

Tolstoy did not seem to be much impressed with Lou's reasoning. What she called the piety of the Russian people he dismissed as superstition and he warned her not to be misled by it. Neither Rilke nor Andreas could easily follow this animated conversation carried on in Russian between Lou and Tolstoy, but they had a chance to observe the old man closely. Rilke was struck by the mixture of peasant shrewdness and urbanity in the Count's features. He felt overawed and ill-at-ease and was relieved when their visit came to an end. Before leaving he presented Tolstoy with a copy of his just-published *Two Tales of Prague*, which the Count accepted kindly, if somewhat absent-mindedly, and promptly forgot.

From Moscow the trio traveled to St. Petersburg where Lou introduced Rilke to her family and friends. Her home town was in the midst of preparations for the forthcoming celebrations of the centennial of the birth of Pushkin, a brilliant affair, which impressed on Rilke the veneration the Russians have for their poets. It was a truly national event. People from all walks of life paid homage to one of the great spokesmen of their race. With Lou's help Rilke gained some understanding of Pushkin's place in Russian literature. She told him that, after a period of decline following his death, his poetry was now universally admired, that he was considered one of the precursors of the Symbolist Movement and that his poem "The Prophet" had been Dostoevsky's favorite. But it was not only the educated Russian who read Pushkin. What moved Rilke was to hear illiterate peasants recite Pushkin's poems by heart. It reminded him of his own attempts to bring poetry to the people. Those attempts had failed because the poets in the West had become divorced from the people. But in Russia, where the people were closer to God, they were also closer to their poets. Rilke never forgot this experience for, as Miss Butler put it: "Russian songs sung by blind men and children, wandered like lost souls around him, touching his cheek and his hair, musical emanations from a people whose essential brotherhood, nearness, neighborhood were amongst the great experiences of his life."

It was Rilke's great good fortune that he was able to share Lou's love for the Russian people. But Lou was equally fortunate to

have Rilke at her side during this journey back home. His passionate surrender to all things Russian aroused her own enthusiasm and rejuvenated her. Seeing her native land through his eyes
gave her new and deeper insights and added to the joy of her
homecoming. It struck her almost as an act of poetic justice that
her return to Russia took place in the company of a man she loved
since, almost twenty years previously, it had been a man she
loved who had caused her to leave it.

As for Rilke, his happiness was complete. Lou, Russia and God:
to this trinity he now addressed his prayers, in their name he
celebrated the mystic union between eros and agape which found
expression in the superb poetry of the *Book of Hours.* Even Lou,
who had remained critical of much he wrote, was moved by the
mystic splendor of the following poem which, she says, he gave
her as a token of his love:

> Put out my eyes, and I can see you still;
> Slam my ears to, and I can hear you yet;
> and without any feet can go to you;
> and tongueless, I can conjure you at will.
> Break off my arms, I shall take hold of you,
> and grasp you with my heart as with a hand;
> arrest my heart, my brain will beat as true;
> and if you set this brain of mine afire,
> then on my blood I yet will carry you.

The most striking feature of this poem is the dramatic tension
that emanates from it. Line by line it grows until, at the very end,
it reaches both its climax and its denouement. There is triumph
and surrender in the climactic words "then on my blood I yet will
carry you." No ordinary lover speaks like this. The love expressed
in this poem transcends its object, plunges straight into God.
Here the human love partner has indeed become invisible. Only
God remains. No wonder Lou shuddered when Rilke gave it to
her. For the first time she wondered whether she was worthy of
his love.

But her more immediate concern was to continue, after their
return to Germany, with Rilke's Russian education, which had
begun so promisingly. Frieda von Bülow invited both of them to
spend the summer with her on the Bibersberg, an estate belonging to Princess von Meiningen, who had put it at Frieda's dis

posal. They accepted eagerly. They could hardly have found a better chance of being together undisturbed. Frieda was Lou's closest friend and understood her situation perfectly. Half mockingly, half seriously, she called Rilke Lou's "disciple" and Andreas the *"Loumann."* In a letter from St. Petersburg Rilke told Frieda how much he was looking forward to his visit and promised to make her a witness of his Russian discoveries.

As it turned out he was not completely faithful to his promise. At least, Frieda seems to have felt somewhat short-changed by her guests who spent most of their time together, all but oblivious of her presence.

"I have seen extremely little of Lou and Rainer in these six weeks," she complained in a letter to a friend. "After the extensive journey to Russia that they (including Loumann) undertook this spring, they gave themselves up heart and soul to the study of Russian and learned all day with a truly phenomenal industry; language, literature, history of art, world history, and the cultural history of Russia, as if they had to prepare for a terrible examination. And when we met during mealtimes they were so tired and exhausted that they had no strength left for any animated conversation."

But Frieda's loss was Lou and Rilke's gain. At last they were once more free to live as they pleased without any need for subterfuge and discretion. Frieda was a perfect hostess, asked no questions and left them alone. They studied hard, went for long walks and enjoyed each other's company. Their love was quieter now. Lou seems to have succeeded in holding her disciple to the task which they had jointly undertaken. But there were moments of rebellion when Rilke asserted his dominant role and bent her will to his bidding:

> I hardly know to choose from all the beauty
> which from your treasure richly reaches me.
> Sometimes your blond hair has a childlike sheen.
> Your strong will softens. It would seem
> that I direct it.
> And your kisses, now in cooler splendor,
> lie on both my eyes—tender, tender,
> as if asleep.
> Then I remember their tempestuous season,
> my pious child, my tender doe,

> when from afar I saw their longing rising
> upon your lips . . .

A letter from Lou's husband in Berlin with the news that her little dog Lottchen had fallen seriously ill hastened their departure from the Bibersberg. They returned to Berlin together about the middle of September. It was a sad homecoming for Lou. She was very fond of the dog and deeply grieved when, despite all the care she lavished on it, it died a few days later. Perhaps a feeling of remorse for having neglected Lottchen so long was mixed with her sorrow. She was an inveterate dog-lover and seldom without one. Indeed, her love for her dogs was as steadfast as that for her human friends was fickle.

For Rilke, the autumn of 1899 was a period of intense productivity. He had hardly arrived in Berlin when the flood of images that had risen in him as a result of his Russian experiences, foremost among them his mystic participation in the piety of the Russian people during the Easter service in Moscow, found release in the dark splendor of the poems of the *Book of Monkish Life*. Prayers he called them, and that is what they are, although the deity to whom they are addressed bears no resemblance to God as the orthodox Christian reveres Him. That God, Rilke felt, was dead, had become an empty symbol in the Sunday Service ritual of the West. To the Russian monk whose prayers he reports, there was something blasphemous in the way in which Western artists represented Him. Their efforts to limit the limitless One, to imprison Him in time and space, were deeply alien to the Russian concept of a growing God. It is this growing God, this unknown God of the future, whose coming Rilke heralds with a torrent of powerful and paradoxical metaphors. He is our neighbor, separated from us only by a thin wall which can break down at any moment; He is a little bird fallen out of its nest, a bearded peasant, the great dawn, red over the plains of eternity, the forest of contradictions. He is:

> . . . the deep epitome of things
> that keeps its being secret with locked lip
> and shows itself to others otherwise:
> to the ship, a haven—to the land, a ship.

Image after image crowds these fervent poems. A wealth of metric patterns and rhyme schemes keep them in constant mo-

tion. Enjambment, alliteration and assonance, used with great
effect, show what a skillful performer Rilke now was on the in-
strument of the German language. But what chiefly distinguishes
these poems is not so much their verbal virtuosity as the spiritual
intensity that emanates from them, the relentless probing and
searching for some ultimate reality.

Here we can detect Lou's influence. It was she who was obsessed with the problem of God's existence. Having lost faith in
Him as a child, she felt a painful void which all her life she
struggled to fill. No matter who was close to her at the moment
—whether Nietzsche in Tautenburg or Rilke in Moscow—sooner
or later her conversation would take a religious turn. In her writings, too, she returns again and again to the question of what con-
stitutes the phenomenon of religion. Her psychological probings,
her depth analyses, her philosophic speculations, were motivated
by an almost Kierkegaardian anxiety, which was bound to have a
profound impact on a precariously balanced personality such as
Rilke's.

The piety of the Russian peasants, the mystic chiaroscuro of
Russian icons, the thunderous sounds of the Kremlin bells, these
and countless other impressions provided the soil from which
these poems grew, but it was Lou's example that turned them
into prayers. It was the presence of the beloved woman that excited Rilke's imagination and caused him to embark on the almost blasphemous undertaking of creating a new God. Sensing
Lou's need—like Nietzsche before him—he responded to it by
concentrating his love exclusively on this one theme. And he
demonstrated again how closely related artistic, religious and
erotic exaltations are. It was therefore literally true when he said,
as he gave her these prayers, that they belonged to her. They are
a monument of their love.

Lou accepted them gratefully and kept them for years as her
private treasure. She cherished them both as a token of Rilke's
love and as manifestations of the mysterious workings of genius.
Once again she witnessed the transformation of human inade-
quacies into the pure achievement of art. The very forces that
made her fear for her young lover's sanity generated his genius as
a poet. It was a lesson that provided her with much food for
thought and sharpened her insights into those subconscious drives

that lie at the root of the creative process.

A turning point had come in her own life also. In Russia she had rediscovered her youth. For the first time she realized what she had missed by surrendering her youthful ardor to Gillot's tutelage and for the first time she felt really young. While Rilke moved inexorably forward into the solitude of the artist, where nobody could follow him, Lou moved backward in time to the point where she was at last able to love unencumbered by Gillot's invisible presence.

16

Tragic Guilt

THE DAWN OF THE TWENTIETH CENTURY FOUND LOU AND RILKE
still preoccupied with their Russian studies. Impatiently they
awaited the coming of spring, when they would once more set out
on an extensive journey to Russia, this time without Lou's husband. They planned to revisit Moscow and St. Petersburg, to explore the Ukraine and the Crimea, and to take a boat ride on the
Volga. With the aid of the Baedeker they mapped out a veritable
pilgrimage to all the holy places in Russia, including visits to
Kiev, Poltava, Saratov, Kazan and Nishni Novgorod.

Anticipating this long journey with Lou through her native
land, Rilke was stirred to an almost hectic activity. He approached
German editors and publishers with suggestions about articles on
Russian themes. He suggested that a special issue of *Ver Sacrum*
be dedicated to Russia, translated poems by Droshin, Lermontov,
and Fofanov, as well as Chekhov's play *The Sea Gull* (and may
have translated *Uncle Vanya*). While Lou was ill with a bout of
influenza he carried on a brisk correspondence with their Russian friends, imploring them to write him in Russian which, he
said, he could read easily now, and asking them to send him
Russian books.

With a single-mindedness bordering on mania, he plunged into
things Russian. He wore a Russian peasant blouse, had a Russian corner in his room in Schmargendorf, and spoke German
interspersed with Russian phrases. Russia, he insisted, was his

spiritual home. He hinted that he would settle there for good. Nor was this idea as farfetched as it sounds. Rilke knew very well that the ties that bound Lou to her husband could only be broken if she left Germany. He knew, too, that the thought of returning to her native land for good appealed to Lou. Perhaps he hoped that once they were in Russia together he could persuade her to remain there with him. And there were moments during their journey when Lou felt that she could not go back to Germany. According to her diary she toyed with the idea of informing her husband by telegram that she would remain in Russia.

However, weighty reasons made her decide against this step. One of them was the growing ambivalence of her feelings for Rilke. She was still very fond of him and could not help being moved by the ardor with which he espoused their common cause. Russia was her country but in less than a year Rilke had almost appropriated it. He had learned its language well enough to write Russian poetry. He was familiar with its history, its art, its customs, and professed a love for its people that few native-born Russians could equal. No prophet of Russia could have found a more devoted disciple than Lou had. But that was just it. The very intensity of Rilke's discipleship alarmed her. He tried to sweep her into an emotional whirlpool against which her mind rebelled. She felt there was something unhealthy in Rilke's complete surrender to an idealized Russia which, she suspected, was in reality his surrender to her. Once again his excessive enthusiasm disturbed her.

Her alarm grew when she noticed strange states of anxiety which Rilke began to suffer and during which he was almost paralyzed with fear. She tells that once during a walk he was suddenly fixed to the spot and could not take another step. With horror-stricken eyes he looked at an acacia tree in front of him as if it were a ghost. Her efforts to make him see that it was no different from any of the trees around it were in vain. Rilke was unable to walk past it. They had to turn around and go back the way they had come. Such incidents alarmed Lou. Rilke clung to her with the desperation of a drowning man, but no matter how much she loved him she was not willing to give up her life to take care of him. Her desire to regain her independence grew as Rilke became more and more dependent on her, until she reached the conclusion that it was necessary to end their affair. With a quiet finality she noted in her diary at the end of January: "Rainer must go."

She did not tell him so immediately, either because she was afraid of what an abrupt break might do to him, or because she herself was not yet ready for it. She may have hoped that during their Russian journey a less radical solution would present itself. In any case she was determined to go through with it. Whatever reservations she had toward Rilke, her love for her native country was so strong by now that it could not be denied. After twenty years abroad she felt the pangs of homesickness.

Their departure from Berlin, originally planned for April, had to be postponed several times, and it was not until May 7 that they finally left. As the year before, they traveled via Warsaw and arrived in Moscow on May 9. This time they spent three weeks there, a busy three weeks, visiting friends, churches and art galleries, attending concerts and plays, or walking through the numerous public gardens. They were again captivated by the charm of this ancient town, "a huge village, really, that has surrounded itself with the divine magnificence of the Kremlin." While Rilke was trying to recapture the spirit of that Easter night a year ago, Lou experienced the pure joy of homecoming. Here, among the sacred hills and churches of *Matuschka Moskua*, was her true home. Here she felt young again. Wherever their journey took them she vowed to return to Moscow. She left it with this resolution when they set out on their pilgrimage to Tolstoy's summer home at Yasnaya Polyana.

Their traveling companions were Leonid Pasternak, his wife and their son Boris. In his memoirs Boris Pasternak describes his impressions of Lou and Rilke on the train from Moscow to Tula. "On a warm summer morning of the year 1900 an express train leaves the Kursk station. Just before its departure somebody in a black Tyrolese cape steps to the window. A woman of tall stature is with him. She is probably his mother or his older sister. They talk animatedly with my father about something that occupies them all three. Occasionally, the woman addresses a few words in Russian to my mother. The stranger only talks German. Although I had a complete command of that language I had never heard it spoken like this. That is why, amidst all the people on the crowded platform between two sounds of the parting bell, the stranger seemed to me like a silhouette, like something imagined in the thicket of the unimagined."

In these few sentences Pasternak catches only one facet of Lou's relationship to Rilke: the mother-son aspect. What he did not see, what few people saw, was that Lou was also Rilke's wife.

As it turned out, their visit at Yasnaya Polyana proved something of an ordeal. They had decided to make it on the spur of the moment after learning from one of the elder Pasternak's friends on the train that Tolstoy had just moved to his summer home. They tried unsuccessfully to get in touch with him by telegram. When they reached Yasnaya Polyana, unexpected and unannounced, after a hectic cross-country journey by freight train and troika, they met with a reception that was anything but cordial. Tolstoy's eldest son opened the door, admitted Lou and, apparently not seeing Rilke, closed it abruptly in his face. Hesitating, Rilke followed after Lou and was introduced to Tolstoy who did not recognize him. A few minutes later the Count excused himself, leaving Lou and Rilke in the company of his son. They spent a few uneasy hours with him, first in a large ancestral hall decorated with family portraits, and later in the park. Upon their return to the house they met the Countess, occupied with putting books on a bookshelf. She took no notice of them at all and told them brusquely that the Count was ill. When they informed her that they had already seen him, she was taken aback, started throwing books on the floor and muttered something about having just moved in. Still hoping to see Tolstoy again, Lou and Rilke waited another anxious half hour in a small room adjoining the family drawing room, where a violent scene was now taking place: "Excited voices, a girl cried, the Count tried to console her, and in between the completely indifferent voice of the Countess. . . . Steps on the staircase, all doors are thrown open and the Count enters. Coldly and politely he asks you something, his eyes are not with us, only his distant glance meets me and the question: 'What do you do?' I forget what I answered. Maybe I said, 'I have written something.'"

As abruptly as he had entered, Tolstoy left again, making them wonder what they should do next. But before they could leave, he came in once more and asked them to accompany him on a walk through the park, his wife apparently having refused to ask them for lunch. He was obviously upset and paid little attention to his visitors. When Rilke told him that he was a poet, Tolstoy burst out in a tirade against poetry and advised Rilke to do something more useful. He spoke rapidly and forcefully, bending down to the ground from time to time to tear off forget-me-nots by the handful and squashing them against his face—a man in the grip of powerful emotions and quite oblivious of what went on around him.

Both Lou and Rilke have given idealized accounts of this visit which in reality was quite terrifying. Far from being the gentle, wise and understanding Russian peasant they described, Tolstoy was a tortured genius, self-centered and intolerant. His ideas on art and religion were diametrically opposed to theirs and had "no kind of attraction" for Rilke, as he later admitted. At the time, however, Rilke was so much under Lou's influence that he overlooked the unpleasant aspects of their visit. But he may have wondered in retrospect whether Tolstoy's brusque rejection of him as a poet was not symbolic of the whole journey. Its outcome, certainly, was quite different from what he had hoped. No such thoughts troubled Lou. Their visit to Tolstoy remained in her memory as the gateway to Russia.

From Yasnaya Polyana they traveled south to Kiev, the capital of the Ukraine and in many respects the rival of Moscow. The town and the surrounding countryside were in the full glory of spring. Flowering meadows made a festive ribbon along the banks of the Dnieper and acres of blossoming fruit trees scented the air. Added to this were the colorful garments of thousands of pilgrims who crowded the churches and monasteries of the holy city in celebration of Pentecost. Once again Lou and Rilke witnessed the religious fervor of the Russian people. They joined the solemn procession of candle-bearing peasants that wound its way through the dark corridors of the Pechevsky Monastery with its caves and catacombs, where the bodies of monks are buried and where hermits, interred in rude cells, used to spend their lives in eternal darkness for the glory of God.

Much impressed by the weird splendor of this scene Rilke wrote his mother that "even today you can walk for hours through these corridors (not higher than a medium-sized person and not wider than the span of his shoulders), past the cells in which the saints and miracle-performing monks in their holy frenzy used to live. Today there is in each cell a silver coffin, and the monk who once lived here a thousand years ago lies uncorrupted in the precious shrine, clothed in rich damask. Uninterruptedly, pilgrims from everywhere—from Siberia to the Caucasus—plough through the darkness and kiss the covered hands of the saints. This is the holiest monastery in the whole empire. Holding a candle in my hand, I have walked through all these corridors, once by myself and once in the midst of the praying throng. I have gained deep impressions from all this and intend to visit these strange catacombs again before I leave Kiev."

Again Rilke experienced an almost mystical exaltation, while Lou shuddered and longed to get back to the sun and the flowers outside. She had nothing in common with the God of these cave-dwellers. But there were other shrines she liked. The Cathedral of St. Sophia aroused her admiration. In loving detail she described its beautiful eleventh-century mosaics and frescoes, its blue and golden cupolas and its ancient altarpieces. The more she saw of them the greater became her love for the Russian icons. Unlike the pictures of saints in Western churches, the icon does not reveal the sacred person it depicts. Upon a golden background their dark-brown figures are almost unrecognizable, leaving it to the imagination of the beholder to think what he likes. "What he sees are merely questions, symbols, vessels for that which he pours into them. Between picture and icon there remains a difference in kind, not in degree only."

They spent two busy weeks in Kiev but decided that despite its beauty they did not really care for it. Rilke complained that the town was too Western, too cosmopolitan. And Lou voiced the typically Russian contempt for the Ukrainians. They were importunate and lacked the spontaneity of the Russians. Traveling by boat down the Dnieper, they made their way to Poltava, where they boarded the train for the long journey eastward to Saratov on the Volga.

Here began the second most memorable part of their journey: the boat ride on the Volga. They had been looking forward to it with great anticipation and they were not disappointed. For if Moscow is the heart of Russia, the Volga is its main artery. A broad and meandering river which at some places does not seem to have any banks at all and forms placid lakes dotted with islands that appear and disappear with the rhythm of the seasons, it winds its leisurely course for over two thousand miles from the Valdai Plateau to the Caspian Sea. Saratov, where Lou and Rilke first saw the great river, lies on the middle Volga in the region which occupies the western part of the central plateau of Russia. A broad, open landscape of meadows, fields and forests, it stretches as far as the eye can see and merges imperceptibly on the far horizon with the sky above.

Lou was charmed by it. She praised its wide and gentle aspect, its vast simplicity, its solitude. And Rilke felt that he had to re-think all dimensions. Everything was limitless: water, land and sky.

From the deck of the *Alexander Nevsky* they watched a peaceful procession of towns, villages and hamlets glide by quietly and dreamlike. Lou confided to her diary: "Here I would like to stay forever. Here, as so often, the Volga is not a river, it is as broad and comprehensive as the sea. But unlike the sea it is intimate and friendly." This combination of intimacy and grandeur seemed to her its peculiar charm. It caused her an almost physical pain to see it glide by. An inner voice told her that this Volga landscape was the landscape of her soul. Here is where she belonged. In a poem reminiscent of the love poem Rilke had addressed to her she expressed her love for it:

> Though you be far, I still will look at you.
> Though you be far, you are forever mine.
> You are the present that will never fade;
> You are my landscape harboring my heart.
> If I had never rested on your banks,
> I yet would know your open amplitude,
> And every wave and every dream would take
> me back to your enormous solitude.

Their boat ride lasted about a week—but "was it not years?" Lou wondered later. It took them past Samara, Kazan, Nishni Novgorod to Yaroslavl, where they disembarked. But when the dreaded moment of farewell came they could not tear themselves away. They decided to spend a few days in the small village of Kresta-Bogorodskoye. There they rented an *isba*, a typical

Russian peasant hut built by a newly married couple who had not moved in yet. For a few days they lived the life of Volga peasants, an experience which Lou ardently desired. Rilke, too, rejoiced at the thought of sharing a house with his beloved again. He remembered the little peasant house at Wolfratshausen, where they had spent the honeymoon of their love. Much had happened since then. He could not help feeling that Lou was no longer quite as intimate with him as before. Imperceptibly she seemed to withdraw more and more into herself. He noticed that even during their Volga boat ride she corresponded with the sister of the man in whom he may have sensed a rival. Perhaps it was the secret fear of losing Lou which prevented him from giving expression to his experiences during this journey. He certainly felt frustrated and worried about his inability to write. At Kazan he started a poem, but stopped abruptly because "it seemed wrong to express my inner joy, which was unrelated to anything else, in words that just then had lost their meaning in the face of the daily reality." The anguish of this cryptic sentence, which is followed by the bitter saying that he was glad his song had died, climaxes in the severe self-reproach: "I have ignored countless poems. I have passed over an entire spring, no wonder there is no real summer now. The whole future has found me closed. When I now open the door, the pathways are long and empty."

He had called Lou his future. Was it the change in her attitude toward him that made him mute with fear and caused the "daily losses"—poems he could not write—of the second Russian journey about which he complained so bitterly? Or was it something else—did he lack the means to express what he felt? Upon his return from Russia he blamed these "losses" on his immature eyes but he added significantly, "If I can learn from people, it is these people here [he is referring to the Worpswede circle of artists among whom he then lived] who are so much like a landscape that their closeness does not frighten me . . . And how they love me here." That was it. He felt he was losing Lou's love.

During the three days Rilke spent with Lou in the *isba* his fear that Lou's love for him was changing must have become a certainty. Why, if she still loved him as she had in Wolfratshausen, did she ask the peasant woman who prepared their straw mattress for the night to give them a second one? Lou writes that the woman could not understand it either. And how are we to interpret the cryptic entry in Lou's diary after the first night in the *isba:* "Splinters in my fingernails and in my nerves." Was this the night in which she told Rilke that she could no longer be his wife and that he must go?

The great crisis in their love did occur about this time. It left Rilke stunned and helpless and caused him to write Lou a "hateful letter" a few weeks later. It was not easy for Lou either. "I will not gloss over anything. Holding my head in my hands I often wrestled at that time with an understanding of myself. And I was deeply disconcerted when once, while leafing through an old tattered diary from a time when I had not yet much experience, I read the nakedly-honest sentence: I am faithful to memories forever. I shall never be faithful to men." This lapidary sentence which does more credit to Lou's honesty than her heart, sounds like an echo of Nietzsche's bitter comment that she was "unfaithful and sacrificed one man's friendship to the next."

Outwardly there was no change. After their three-day sojourn in the *isba* they continued their journey, apparently refreshed from this intimate contact with Russian peasant life. Lou found it hard to leave. She felt as if reborn in the presence of these simple people who treated her like one of their own. Sitting for hours around the steaming samovar, they told her the most intimate details of their lives, laughing uproariously when she failed to understand an allusion to a local character, or weeping unashamedly when they recounted a particularly tragic episode. Lou was fascinated by the quick change from humor to seriousness, by the profundity of their observations, and by their shrewd understanding of human nature. One old woman especially, the grandmother of the family, made a deep impression on her because she spoke "in the grand style of a chronicle and with an eye to eternity."

No doubt Rilke was also moved by these peasants whose lives were so much simpler and so much more elemental than his. But there is no indication that he wanted to stay with them. The heavy downpour that hastened their departure, transforming the whole countryside into a sea of mud, corresponded more adequately to his feelings. It must have come as a great relief to get away from the little hut which he had shared, and yet not shared, with his love. And however much he later praised the simplicity of life in a Russian village, he never again tried to live it. Indeed, Rilke's celebrated love of Russia was essentially an extension of his love for Lou. It was his emphatic response to her love for her native land. When the reality of his love for Lou faded, Russia faded with it, assumed an esoteric quality and the "unconvincing glamour of a never-never land."

From the Volga they journeyed back to Moscow, where they spent another fortnight sightseeing and exchanging impressions with their Russian friends who felt almost embarrassed by the praise of their country and its people which Lou and Rilke showered on them. When Rilke expressed the wish to pay a visit to the peasant-poet Droshin, whose work he admired, everybody saw to it that the visit took place under the most favorable circumstances. Droshin lived in the little village of Nizovka, in the province of Tver, a peasant among peasants. To make his humble abode worthy of his distinguished visitor, his landlord Nikolai Tolstoy, a distant relative of Count Leo Tolstoy, had it completely reconditioned. Sofia Schill, who was in charge of Lou and Rilke's traveling arrangements, wrote Droshin from Moscow that his visitors were prone to "idealize our Russian reality" and exhorted the peasant-poet to make them feel comfortable and at ease. Finally, Nikolai Tolstoy invited them to spend part of their time as his guests in his large manor house.

As a result of these elaborate precautions Rilke and Lou spent a delightful week, partly with the poet and partly with the Count, and returned to Moscow more convinced than ever that Russia was the country of their dreams. But this one little episode, harmless though it was, symbolized the self-delusion they indulged in during much of their journey. The Russia they saw was indeed the Russia of their dreams. For Lou it was a return to the dreams of her childhood, for Rilke it meant sharing the dreams of his beloved. The reality behind these dreams was quite different, and off and on Rilke caught glimpses of it. And when he found himself face to face with it, the shock was so great that he could hardly bear it.

Again, symbolically, it happened in St. Petersburg, Lou's home town. They went there because Lou wished to visit her relatives before returning to Germany. But when they arrived on the sixth of July, they discovered that Lou's family had left the city and gone to their summer home, Rongas, in Finland. Quickly making up her mind, Lou decided to join them there, leaving Rilke alone in St. Petersburg. Apparently she hardly said good-by to him, and left him for days without news of her arrival. He felt hurt and deserted. Was this the end of their love? How miserable it was to be left stranded in a little furnished room after her sudden departure, exposed to the almost hostile impressions of this foreign town. The more he brooded over the injustice of her treatment of him, the angrier he became, until in the end his long-repressed fears and his self-pity got the better of him and he wrote her the "hateful letter."

Lou tore it up. She had no patience with his childish temper tantrums and even less with his morbid self-reproaches. Her own life was just then replete with happiness. Here in the Finnish summer home of her childhood, surrounded as formerly by her family, her mother and her brothers, she experienced the climax of her homecoming. She remembered the summer, almost twenty years before, when she had left them with a rebellious heart, resolutely determined to free herself from all that love, tradition and custom demanded of her, and to make her own way in the world. This she had done. And now she returned, a mature woman, self-assured, a person in her own right and a well-known writer. There was no danger now of losing herself in daydreams. She had found herself and could wholeheartedly embrace all that she had rejected before, her family and her country. Everywhere, within the circle of her family and outside in the well-known landscape of forests and lakes, she heard the echo of voices from her childhood.

The only sad note in this joyful chorus was the absence of her father. He had long been dead, but she remembered him vividly now and a wave of gratitude for his love welled up in her heart. She felt that for the first time she really understood what he was like. He embodied all she had come to love in Russia, simplicity, human warmth, and greatness of soul. "Now," she confided to her Russian diary, "I would really have become his child."

Another figure of her past who now returned to Lou's memory was Gillot. He had made her what she was. He had forced her to find herself, but by so doing he had usurped the place of God in her heart. It had taken her many years to free herself from his tutelage. Now she could look on Gillot, too, with an untroubled mind. Humbly and with joyful wonder she felt her life swinging full-circle back to her beginnings. The long years of turmoil were over. The wanderer was home at last.

Rilke's bitter and reproachful letter sounded the only discordant note in the harmony of Lou's homecoming. It served as a sharp reminder that she was still involved in another life, a tortured and unhappy life, which made demands on her she could no longer grant. But she decided that the better part of wisdom was not to drive Rilke to despair by continued silence and she wrote him a letter in which she tried to convey to him a sense of her own happiness. "I am at home in happiness," she told him, "and wish that you could see me now."

Rilke's response was immediate: "I have your letter, your dear, dear letter, every word of which helps me and lifts me up like a wave, strong and rushing. It surrounds me as with gardens and bright skies overhead. It makes me happy and able to say what I have tried to say in vain in my last difficult letter: I long for you."

He said he felt ashamed of his last letter, the result of his solitude and inner confusion, which must have sounded strange to her "amidst the beauty that surrounds your life under these new conditions." And he reminded her of the young squirrels which he had kept on long chains in Italy as a child. "Perhaps it was wrong to impose my will on their nimble lives (when they were already grown up and did not need me any more), but it was also a little their intention to count on me in the future, for they often came running after me so that it seemed to me as if they wished for a chain." It was a pathetic little story and Lou shook her head when she read it. For she understood only too well what he meant by it. He felt like those squirrels and begged her to keep him on her chain. But this was precisely what she had no intention of doing.

"Come back to me, come back to me soon," was the refrain of this letter in which Rilke also complained about his solitary life in Petersburg. "You have no idea how long the days in Petersburg can be. And yet they don't contain much. Life is a continuous and aimless being-on-the-go here. You walk and walk and you drive and drive and wherever you arrive the first impression is always that of your own weariness." The town was against him, he would say later when he felt similarly dejected in Paris. But of course it was not the town. He suffered from an acute sense of failure. He realized that he had failed in his love and felt empty and frustrated. Longingly he looked back to the past when his loving heart had responded to the world around him with pure achievement. And he dreaded the future. Lou, on the other hand, radiated happiness when she rejoined him in St. Petersburg and did her best to cheer him up on the journey home. But she did not succeed. Rilke remained moody and withdrawn. He found it impossible to live close to her under these altered circumstances. He had to find a new circle of friends.

Hence, after their return to Germany at the end of August, Rilke did not stay in Berlin. He accepted an invitation from his artist friend Heinrich Vogler, who lived in the little village of Worpswede, near Bremen. Vogler introduced him to a group of dedicated young artists who had settled in this rather bleak moor-and-fen landscape so that they might work undisturbed by the distractions of city life. Rilke felt immediately at home among them and busied his heart with new friendships. He was especially attracted to two young girls: the fair-haired painter Paula Becker and her close friend, the dark, brown-eyed sculptress Clara Westhoff. Both of them took pity on the sad young poet and made him feel that life was worth living after all.

There were delightful Sunday-evening parties in Vogler's house that often lasted into the small hours of the morning, where Rilke found not only companionship and understanding but stimulating talk about art and life and religion, subjects that were of perennial interest to him. Both girls attended these parties and in turn invited Rilke to their studios and listened with rapt attention to his poetry readings. The diary Rilke kept during this time shows how quickly his spirits revived in their sympathtic company. He was still mourning the death of one love and already two new ones were in the offing. No wonder he felt that fate was more than chance. In Russia he had been unable to write anything, now his whole being was once more filled with song. In the presence of the two girls he recovered his faith in his poetic future. He decided on the spur of the moment to spend the autumn and winter with them and rented a little house in Worpswede.

But no sooner had he reached this decision than he abandoned
it as abruptly and returned once more to Schmargendorf and
Lou. Rilke's biographers have been at a loss to account for this
change in plans. Miss Butler wonders whether the rumor of
Paula Becker's engagement to Otto Modersohn had something to
do with it. And it is true that of the two girls, the blond painter
—Lou, too, was blond—had stirred Rilke's emotions more deeply
than Clara Westhoff. With her, and not with Clara, he had left his
notebook, which contained some of his dearest poems, when he
returned to Schmargendorf. Perhaps Rilke contemplated making
Paula the new custodian of his heart. If so, the news of her engagement must have come as a disappointment to him. Rilke himself told his friends that he could not remain in Worpswede because he had realized that his Russian studies made it imperative
that he be within easy reach of the facilities of a large city. But
that was surely not the main reason. He came closest to admitting
why he had given up the idea of making a home in Worpswede
when he wrote Paula: "Every home is like a mother, good and
warm. But I must still search for my mother, must I not?"

Lou had been a mother to him and more than a mother. He
could not tear himself away from her, try as he might. And she
may have encouraged him to remain in the sphere of her influence, offering him her friendship, if not her love, and reminding
him that he was wasting his time in Worpswede. He had devoted
much effort to his Russian studies and had progressed far. It
would be a pity to give them up merely because of their changed
relationship.

An undercurrent of sadness flowed through Rilke's letters to his
friends in Worpswede, when he told them that he would not return to them. "I am waiting," he wrote Paula, "I am waiting for
you and Clara Westhoff and Vogler and for Sunday and for our
songs. And nobody comes. And I know that nobody will come
and yet I wait. And I am almost afraid to wish for others to come
—Russians with whom I am supposed to work, and hardly anybody else." But although he now chafed under Lou's discipline
he kept on working. He read Russian books, wrote poetry, and
planned to write a series of prose tales, a novel trilogy, plays.
"Plans, but so weakly willed. What good is it making them day in

day out?"

He spent as much time with Lou as she would let him. At the end of November he wrote a Russian poem and gave it to her. He was still trying to rekindle her love. A few days later she invited him to meet Gerhart Hauptmann and they spent a beautiful evening together. But it was in vain. He could not adjust himself to the altered circumstances of their lives. To be near her who was the bridge to his future, and to feel her withdrawing more and more, paralyzed his faculties and filled him with melancholy. He recorded days of utter hopelessness, attacks of "asthma of the soul," in-between days that belonged neither to life nor to death, days that were ruled over by a sinister in-between God. And he wondered anxiously how many who are similarly afflicted with an in-between existence live and die in insane asylums.

Lou was appalled to see him succumb to such moods of depression and felt depressed herself. She knew the cause of his suffering, she had seen the same thing happen to Nietzsche when she broke with him, but she did not dare to face up to it. What Rilke needed—her love—she could no longer give him. But she still tried to console him by asking him to join her at various literary functions. Thus a few days before Christmas they watched the dress rehearsal of Hauptmann's new play, *Michael Kramer*, sitting alone together in the dark auditorium of the Deutsches Theater. But the end was rapidly approaching. "What I wish for in the coming year," Lou noted in her diary, "what I need, is stillness. I must be alone as I was four years ago."

Rilke, on the other hand, could not bear being alone now. Lou's withdrawal made it imperative that he find someone else, some other human anchor, or risk plunging into himself as into an empty well. He redoubled his correspondence with his friends in Worpswede, sent them books and implored them to visit him. "Please, dear friend," he wrote Paula Becker in January, "keep next Sunday free again for me. Very many Sundays in fact. Is that possible?" It was not possible because of Paula's forthcoming marriage to Otto Modersohn. So Rilke turned to her friend Clara Westhoff.

He had not been on quite such intimate terms with Clara as with Paula. On one occasion he had even refused Clara's request for a poem, something he rarely did. But Clara had gone out of her way to promote a friendship which meant a great deal to her. She had often written Rilke and had told him of her work. She had sent him presents—now a bunch of grapes, now a series of photographs of her sculptures. He had accepted her gifts and letters gratefully enough but without encouraging any closer ties. He had even warned her not to be disappointed if he failed to answer her letters because he was so deeply occupied with his work. And then, all of a sudden, in the middle of February, he declared his love to her and proposed marriage. This sudden decision puzzled and surprised Rilke's friends. But was it really so surprising? Was it not a human, a very human, reaction to his being rejected by Lou?

Lou was also surprised and even a little angry when she heard of Rilke's plans. She felt like a mother who resents her son's getting married. On the other hand, she realized that this was the decisive moment. It gave her the opportunity for the final break which she had long been contemplating. In a long letter with the heading "Last Appeal" she summed up the course of their love and cautioned Rilke against his proposed marriage.

Claiming the right to speak to him like a mother, she wrote that she was afraid he might suffer the fate of the Russian writer Garshin (who had committed suicide in a fit of depression) if he entered into any marital ties. The only way for him to find peace was through his work. She confessed that the violent changes in his moods, his exaltations alternating with depressions, had consumed her own nervous energy and that she had walked beside him mechanically, unable to give him any real warmth. "But then," she writes—and this is her most significant confession—"something else has happened, something almost like a tragic guilt toward you, the fact that in spite of our difference in age I have had to go on growing since Wolfratshausen, growing into that which I told you so happily when we said good-by— strange as it may sound—into my youth. For only now am I young, only now can I be what others are when they are eighteen: entirely myself. That is why your figure—so dear and so close in Wolfratshausen—gradually disappeared from my sight, like a single aspect in a large landscape, a wide Volga landscape, as it were, and the little hut was not yours. Without knowing it I obeyed the great plan of my life which smilingly and beyond all understanding and expectation held out a present to me. I accept it with great humility and now I know with prophetic clarity and I call out to you: Go the same way toward your dark God."

It was a moving letter but it failed in its purpose for it did not stop Rilke from marrying Clara. And yet Lou's forebodings were right: the marriage did not last. Rilke had to find peace in his work. In another sense, however, Lou was wrong. She was wrong in thinking that she could step out of Rilke's life entirely. This proved to be impossible. At every crisis in his life the poet turned to her for comfort and help. During those anxious weeks in the late fall of 1911, while he was waiting for a rebirth of his creative powers in the Castle of Duino, Rilke reflected once more on the course of their love. In a poem addressed to Lou he summed it up:

> As one will hold a handkerchief before
> accumulated breath—no, as one presses it
> against a wound from which in one spurt life's
> trying to escape, I held you to me, saw
> that you were red with me. Who can express
> what happened to us? We made up everything
> for which there'd been no time. I ripened rarely
> in every impulse of omitted youth,
> and you yourself, above my heart, beloved,
> entered upon a kind of wildest childhood.

To the very end of his life Rilke clung to Lou with passionate intensity. In December of 1926, as he lay dying in a Swiss sanatorium, half unconscious with pain, he implored his doctors to "ask Lou what is wrong with me. She is the only one who knows." She was, and she remained, his bridge to the future.

PART V

In Search of a Soul
1901-1937

17

Waiting for Freud

LOU ENTERED UPON THE FIFTH DECADE OF HER LIFE WITH THE radiance and vitality of a twenty-year-old girl. The discrepancy between her age and her incredibly youthful appearance was so great that her less fortunate contemporaries thought Lou must be in the possession of some magic formula of youth. Her husband's mysterious occupation with Oriental folk medicine left ample room for all sorts of speculation. To Lou herself, the fountain of youth was love. Love in all its manifestations: love of nature, love of the creature world, and love of the sexes.

Time had softened her features somewhat and she added a touch of femininity by wearing soft fur pieces, boas and capes, over her shoulders, and arranging her silver-blond hair in a loosely tied knot with wistful strands playing above her forehead. Her blue-gray dresses of raw silk emphasized the bright blueness of her eyes and revealed well-shaped breasts, a narrow waist and narrow hips. She was tall and walked with the rhythmic grace of long-legged women. Her physical beauty was matched, if not outshone, by the brightness of her spirit, her *joie de vivre*, her wit and her warm humanity. She had a contagious laughter without any trace of malice and was obviously at home in joy. And yet this warm-hearted, generous and highly intelligent woman passed during these years through one of the cruelest experiences of her life, an experience so painful that once again the thought of suicide crossed her mind.

After her break with Rilke in February, 1901, Lou spent the summer and autumn with Zemek in Saxon Switzerland and in Vienna. She had been in touch with him and his sister Broncia periodically during the three and a half years of her friendship with Rilke. But since she was very discreet in her personal relationships, it is quite possible that Zemek never knew that Lou and Rilke were lovers. At any event Zemek was at Lou's side when she needed him and she spent several enjoyable months in his company. Upon her return home to her husband in Berlin, the news of Paul Rée's death reached her. Suddenly she understood what a fateful role she had played in his life. She confided to Frieda von Bülow that Rée's death was the principal event of this late autumn:

"I could not get over it for weeks and for some rather terrifying reasons that I can only tell you orally. You probably know that he fell to his death in Celerina [Upper Engadine] where we used to spend our summers together and where he has been living alone for years, summer and winter. I have been reliving old letters and many things have become clear to me. The whole past has assumed a ghostlike present."

What she could tell Frieda only orally was her suspicion, amounting to certainty, that Rée's death was no accident, that he had killed himself because he could not forget her. For fourteen years he had borne his loss and now he could bear it no longer. His death filled Lou with a deep sense of remorse and she searched her heart in vain for the reasons why she had left him. Was this her curse, that she had to destroy the men who loved her? So intense was her grief that her body reacted to it by falling sick. She began to suffer from a strange heart disease resulting in fainting spells during which her pulse all but stopped. It was these spells that gave rise to the legend that Lou possessed the power of Indian fakirs, that she could make her heart stop. It was only a legend, of course, but her illness gave a physical reality to the major conflict in her life, the conflict between her impulsive heart and her imperative will. She never resolved it.

In her physical and mental distress she turned again to the man whose quiet fortitude had helped her in the past and whose love now offered her peace and fulfillment. Dr. Pineles, as she called him when he acted as her physician, or Zemek when they were husband and wife, realized that the cause of Lou's illness was nervous exhaustion. She had to learn to relax. She had been living too long on nervous energy and her body was finally rebelling against it. As one of Vienna's rising young internists, Pineles kept in close touch with neurology and knew the relationship between mental and physical exhaustion. He prescribed long bed rests, plenty of fresh country air, walks, and no books. Together they spent the summer of 1902 hiking in the Tyrol and in Carinthia, enjoying the magnificent mountain scenery, the wholesome food of Austrian village inns, and each other's company. The treatment was successful, so successful that Lou became pregnant.

What she had dreaded before now filled her with joy. So the circle of her strangely lived life would be completed after all. She would be a mother. In her letters to Zemek's sister Broncia, herself a young mother, Lou extolled the joys of motherhood: "How radiantly happy you must be now, you dear little mother," she wrote, "and how much I would give to be near you now just long enough to kiss you. . . . You must feel as if you had returned from a long journey full of marvelous adventures with the little miracle as booty in your arms."

And later, when Broncia had given birth to her second child, Sylvia, Lou wrote her: "I have had a very special love for Sylvia from the first glance into her sweet, sleepy little face, as if she were my own child. And perhaps she resembles those I might have had."

Well, now she was having one. With humble gratitude she watched her body's gradual changes. Life was stirring in her, she had conceived and she would give birth to a human life. It was wonderful. She was so blissfully happy, so filled with the warm vegetative contentment of the mother animal, that she completely forgot the unusual circumstances of her life. Zemek had taken her to Oberwaltersdorf, a small village in Lower Austria, where his sister Broncia was living with her husband and her two small children in a large, rambling country house surrounded by a parklike garden. Here Lou was to await her confinement. He would take care of the rest.

It seemed all so easy and natural in those warm spring and early summer days when life was ripening all around her. She could sit for hours by the window watching the apples grow round and sweet, wonderfully submerged in the warm current that flowed within and without. All so easy, so natural, so peaceful. But it was a deceptive peace and before long Lou would be driven out cruelly from her Austrian paradise. The ghost of a man who had died on her account rose up against her.

She herself may not have been aware of her anomalous situation in Oberwaltersdorf but others were. Broncia's husband was and so was her mother. Mrs. Pineles, a devout old lady brought up in the stern tradition of the Mosaic law, had been considerably disturbed for a long time by her son's illicit affair with a married woman. She loved Zemek and wished with all her heart that he would find happiness. But she was sure he could not find it with Lou. No matter what Lou's circumstances were, she was still a married woman and it was wrong for her to carry on as she did. It was not only socially wrong, old Mrs. Pineles found it morally reprehensible. If at first she had acquiesced in it, she had done so for her son's sake, but she resented his bringing Lou to live with them in Oberwaltersdorf. She resented being made a party to the affair. She could not understand why her daughter encouraged it. Broncia was a happily married woman. She should realize that Lou's behavior was an affront to her sex.

The climax of Mrs. Pineles' long-smoldering resentment came when she finally heard of Rée's death. This was too much for her. A woman who had caused a man's death was outside the pale as far as she was concerned. There was no room for Lou under her roof. She confronted her daughter with an ultimatum. Broncia was to tell Lou that she must leave Oberwaltersdorf within a week. At this point Zemek decided to go to Berlin, tell Andreas what had happened and ask for Lou's divorce. He wanted to marry her. It was the only way to reconcile his family and to protect Lou's and his own reputation. When he had suggested marriage in the past Lou had always insisted that her husband would not give her a divorce. But now things were different. Andreas would have to bow to a *fait accompli*. Not wanting to frighten Lou, Zemek did not tell her of his intention to see Andreas. He merely told her that he would have to take a short journey. But with a flash of intuition Lou knew where

he was going and what he was going to do. And this thought
terrified her. She knew her husband's fierce temper and she
feared for Zemek's life. All of a sudden her dreams of motherhood were shattered. As long as Andreas lived she could not
bear another man's child. Zemek pleaded with her, but she
remained adamant. The child must be taken from her.

We do not know what actually happened. According to one
story Lou lost her child accidentally when she fell underneath
an apple tree. But a surgical operation cannot be ruled out;
Zemek was certainly competent enough to perform it. The utter
secrecy that surrounds the whole affair, the fact that Lou does
not even mention Zemek's name in her memoirs, may point to
an illegal operation. Whatever happened, their situation was
desperate and for a time the Pineles family feared that it would
end tragically. When Lou and Zemek left Oberwaltersdorf to
go to Vienna and Dresden, a friend of the family was sent post-
haste after them. He was to stay close by them, try to comfort
them and see to it that they did not lose their heads. It is this
episode that Freud had in mind when, in writing his obituary
notice for Lou, he said that "the most moving event of her
feminine fate took place in Vienna."

The crisis passed but it left its mark on both Lou and Pineles.
It forced Pineles to accept the insolubility of Lou's bond to
Andreas and meant that he had to bury his hopes of making her
his legitimate wife, although he continued to live with her off
and on for a number of years. And it made Lou realize that
the joys of motherhood were not for her. With a trace of resignation she told Rilke the following year that she had renounced
motherhood. She had dedicated her life to other goals, although
she did not say what they were. She knew that she was not
an artist and that she found no real fulfillment in writing. One
had to learn the art of living, she thought, and that meant involvement in the lives of others. Perhaps that was where her
talents lay. She had tried to create fictional characters, puppets
fed on her own life's blood. But that had been a makeshift.
Life was far more interesting, wonderful and exciting than fiction.
She would turn more and more to study her own singular life
and the lives of people around her. It was more rewarding to
probe their problems and perhaps help solve them than to make

paper dolls.

The real turning point in Lou's life from a writer to a psychotherapist did not come until she met Freud in 1911. But during
the intervening years her literary activities gradually declined.
She still wrote a few books and an occasional article. Her interests, however, turned more and more to probing deeply the
people she came in contact with. What made them act as they
did? What forces pulled them up or tore them asunder? Such
questions had always fascinated her. Now she began to study
them seriously. She knew from her own experiences that sexual
love was one of the most powerful forces in the lives of men
and women. It had been the central theme of *In the Twilight
Zone,* a collection of short stories she published in 1902.

The book deals with such problems as a father's passionate
love for his young daughter, the infidelity of a newly married
husband who tells his shocked young wife: "Life is not what it
seems to you. Of course you cannot understand it. You still have
thousands of illusions and rightly so. But believe me, Lisotchka,
we are all poor sinners, poor sinners, nothing else." In the fourth
story, entitled "The Sister," love is the dark and mysterious power
that kills a young girl: "Where is Mascha? . . . What had a man
done to her Mascha? . . . Mascha had loved a man, that is why
Mascha is now dead."

Lou had felt the fateful force of love more than once and
she decided that it deserved to be studied without any false
shame or modesty. Upon the suggestion of Martin Buber, who
was then editor of a series of sociological studies, she wrote a
book on it. Entitled *Eroticism,* it appeared the year before she
met Freud, who confirmed many of her independently gained
insights.

Sexual love, Lou maintains, is first and foremost a physical
need like hunger or thirst and can be properly understood only
if it is seen as such. Rooted in the subsoil of our lives, we find
it associated even with the purely vegetative processes of our
bodies, such as dreams. It is an animalistic force pure and simple,
except that in man, the higher animal, the sex drive is combined
with a brain effect, causing nervous excitement: sex becomes
sensation. This leads to a romantic idealization of love and to
the desire that it be permanent. We demand eternal faithfulness

from those we love. In reality, however, all animal needs are quickly appeased and clamor for change. Requited love dies of satiation. Since all animal instincts are subject to the law of diminishing returns, repetition of the sexual act or its habitual performance deadens the stimuli and increases the need for new ones. It follows that "the natural love life in all its manifestations, and perhaps most of all in its highest forms, is based on the principle of infidelity."

Underlying the sex urge, Lou says, is the desire for total union. It can be seen most clearly in the reproduction of such unicellular animals as the amoeba, where the cell nuclei divide giving birth to new creatures. Procreation, birth, death and immortality are still one and the same process with them. The desire for total union is present in man also but, owing to the advanced state of differentiation of the human body, where the sex organs are reserved for procreation, physical love remains a partial union. And because it is partial it is often accompanied by a sense of shame. The non-participating organs intrude, as it were, like unwanted spectators. And yet the most powerful impulse at the height of sexual passion is the longing to merge completely with the love partner.

Total union means total surrender. Since this is impossible for man, he experiences, coincidental with the longing to merge with his love partner, a heightened sense of his own existence. His love partner becomes the match that kindles his own flames, releasing powerful creative forces within him. Hence, every love, even the most tragic, leaves a positive surplus. Not to have loved means not to have lived.

Sexual love, artistic creativity and religious fervor, Lou maintains, are but three different aspects of the same life force. For even religious fervor could not exist if we did not have a conviction that our highest dreams can rise from the most earthy soil. That is why the religious cults of many primitive peoples are expressions of their sexual customs. Every exaltation of the spirit leads to an exaltation of the body, and the more intense a spiritual love is, the stronger the longing for physical union. Symbolic of this threefold aspect of the life force is a woman's threefold function as mistress, mother and madonna.

The difference between erotic and artistic passion is that, in the former, the spiritual exaltations are secondary, the physical primary; with the latter the reverse is true. Hence, even during the creative exaltation of the artist, the germ plasma plays a role, as it does during the religious ecstasy of the saint.

Lou concludes from all this that we should realize that sexual love is both beautiful and dangerous. We should not expect it to last even when our hearts and minds long for permanence. We should not abuse it by mechanical manipulations, nor should we indulge in it with a bad conscience. We should use it as nature meant it to be used, as the great regenerative force of our lives. "If two people are entirely serious with this most transitory act, if they demand no loyalty from each other but are content with each other's happiness while it lasts, they live in a state of divine madness."

The distinction which Lou draws between the divine madness of sexual love and the quiet peace of conjugal happiness has often been drawn. It is one of the great themes of literature from Madame Bovary to Anna Karenina. As a rule it ends tragically. In real life, too, the conflict between marriage and love usually leads to tragic consequences, sometimes to death, more often to divorce. The point Lou tries to make, and she argues it very persuasively, is that there is room for both. We all need a life's partner, a husband or a wife, who is our refuge, our support, our helpmate, our brother and the guardian of our solitude. But we also need the rejuvenating power of love. Without it our lives become drab and frustrated. Love is the elixir of youth. When we are deprived of it, we decline.

Lou knew, of course, that her arguments for a marriage that permitted each partner the rejuvenating freedom of periodic love feasts were pretty fantastic. Not only because they run counter to the moral commandments of most religions, but because they conflict with the powerful and deeply rooted possessive instinct in man. How many wives would be willing to say what Lou said: she wished her husband would find a young and beautiful paramour? And how many husbands would let their wives depart every so often in the company of other men? Even if it is true that the "divine madness" of sexual love is only a dim memory in most marriages after they have lasted a few years, it is equally true that unrestricted sexual freedom would lead to social anarchy.

In fairness to Lou it must be remembered that her own marriage was not really a marriage at all and that her insistence on the ecstatic nature of love ruled out any casual affair. The cheap promiscuity depicted in many modern novels would have shocked her. Precisely because she conceived of love as an elemental force, she was equally opposed to the false modesty preached by her Victorian contemporaries and to the casual amours practiced by many emancipated women. She felt that because physical love touches the core of our being it must be treated as something precious and sacred.

Even so it still remains true that Lou's love life was unusual and fell outside the human norm. She lived and she loved dangerously. And the men she loved never got over it, even if she herself completely forgot them. Musing about his love affair with Lou in the perspective of almost half a century, a learned and chivalrous old gentleman said: "There was something terrifying about her embrace, elemental, archaic. Looking at you with her radiantly blue eyes she would say, 'The reception of the semen is for me the height of ecstasy.' And she had an insatiable appetite for it. When she was in love she was completely ruthless. It made no difference to her whether the man she loved had other ties. She merely laughed when one of her lovers confessed that he had moral scruples because he had vowed to remain faithful to his invalid wife. Such vows could not hold back the life force. It was stupid to make them. You might as well try to hold back the tides of the sea with moral adjuration. She was completely amoral and yet very pious, a vampire and a child. As far as men were concerned who wanted to love her she trusted her instincts entirely. Once when she had already checked in at a hotel and was going to spend the night with a friend, she suddenly felt it would not work. She left him abruptly, went to the station and took a room in a nearby town. But there she discovered that she was still in love with her friend. She remembered a letter he had written her which she carried in her purse. And to appease her longing for him she ate his letter. There was nothing sensational as she told this story. It seemed the most natural thing in the world to eat your lover's letter."

But again, how many men or women, no matter how passionately in love they are, would do that? What fascinated all men who knew Lou intimately was the elemental nature of her feminine passion coupled, as it was, with the virility of her almost masculine mind. In every case it proved a fatal fascination, for a man who had once been loved by Lou found no satisfaction in the arms of any other woman. Even Zemek, the Earthman, Lou's closest friend and husband except in name during these years, discovered this bitter truth.

If Lou had really wanted a divorce she probably could have had it, for at this time her housekeeper Marie gave birth to an illegitimate child and there cannot have been any doubt in Lou's mind that Andreas was the child's father. But she did not ask for a divorce. On the contrary, she seems to have accepted the little girl as if it were her own. It is, of course, possible that Lou did not want to involve her husband, who had just then been appointed to a chair in Oriental languages at the University of Göttingen, in any sort of scandal. Andreas was fifty-seven years old when he received this long-hoped-for appointment. It was probably his last chance to find the academic berth for which he was so well trained.

Besides, their move to Göttingen offered considerable advantages. After fifteen years of apartment-living they were at last able to afford their own house. They chose one on the outskirts of the town, a tall building precariously perched on the steep slope of the Hainberg with a magnificent view over the broad valley, the town below and the ridge of hills on the horizon. Lou moved into the upper story where she had a bedroom and a study leading to a large balcony. Her husband and Marie lived downstairs. They named it "Loufried," like the little peasant house in Wolfratshausen where Lou and Rilke had lived.

"It stands in a wide landscape," Lou wrote Rilke, "which it overlooks with its beech forests and long stretched ridge of hills, behind which, somewhere, the Harz mountains begin. In the valley at our feet lies the town. And we are surrounded by an old garden full of trees, an orchard and a vegetable plot. Even a poultry yard is not missing. Here I have become a peasant and my husband a professor."

The arrival of this strange couple in the fall of 1903 caused a sensation among the academic community of the small university town. Lou was far better known than her husband. Her friendship with Nietzsche made her an object of awe and curiosity, and there was considerable agitation among the faculty wives to meet the woman whose books had such a curious quality of arousing dormant feelings. To their disappointment they found Lou shy rather than provocative and entirely unwilling to participate in their social life. Andreas, too, kept himself strictly aloof from his colleagues and was hardly ever seen at the university.

Theirs was certainly a strange ménage. There were rumors that they did not have a common bedroom, that they lived on separate floors and that their housekeeper had taken over the functions of housewife. It was all most unusual. And what was the reason for Lou's frequent absences? Almost every spring she left Göttingen. She was seen traveling in the company of other men. In the secrecy of their hearts these solid mothers and wives of deans and university professors rather envied Lou's freedom. One of them finally took her courage into both her hands and asked Lou point-blank what she was doing on her travels.

"I suppose, Frau Professor," she said with a meaningful glance, "every spring you get that special restlessness, that feeling . . . you know what I mean?"

"I do, I do indeed," replied Lou, looking straight at her questioner with her smiling blue eyes, "but alas, Frau Geheimrat, I get this special feeling all the time, not only in the spring."

It was impossible to get close to Lou, and after a few years of trying, Göttingen gave up. They felt that there was something very odd about the people in the house on the Hainberg, but they did not quite understand what it was so they left them alone. This is exactly what Lou and Andreas wished. They knew that their lives did not fit into any social pattern and, being nonconformists, they were not willing to change them to please the good people of Göttingen.

Lou's traveling companion during these years was Zemek. Since he was her doctor, she may have felt that she could be seen with him without causing too much tongue-wagging. But those who knew her intimately, like Rilke, guessed at their relationship. It is certainly significant that in the first letter Rilke wrote Lou after their break he requested that she let him have Pineles' address. We do not know if she granted him this request. Something like a comedy of errors between Lou and Pineles on the one hand and Rilke on the other occurred in the following years. In May, 1904, Lou and Zemek were in Venice and Rilke was in Rome. He felt terribly depressed and longed for a reunion with Lou. But she only sent him a postcard. Breathlessly Rilke replied:

"You were so near. I felt all the time that you would come to Italy. When one day I saw your postcard, your handwriting and the Italian stamp, I hoped much for a moment, too much . . ." In August that same year Lou and Zemek passed through Copenhagen on a journey to Norway. Again Lou sent Rilke a postcard. The poet was at that time in Sweden but when he received Lou's card he immediately traveled to Copenhagen and went straight to Lou's hotel where he discovered that Lou had been registered with Pineles but had already left. Again Rilke was dismayed and left word that if she should pass through Copenhagen on her return journey she should telegraph him. He would once more make the trip from Sweden to meet her. But Lou did not send Rilke a telegram. Instead, in a letter from St. Petersburg, she apologized for her postcard and said it had been stupid of her to send it. Rilke's pleas for a personal meeting became increasingly more desperate, but Lou discreetly rejected them. It was not until the middle of 1905 that she permitted him to visit her in Göttingen.

Sometimes with women friends, sometimes with Zemek, Lou continued her extensive travels that led her from Norway to Spain and from France to the Balkans. She frequently visited her family in Russia, or her large circle of friends in Berlin, which now included Eugen Diederichs, Max Reinhardt, Walter Rathenau, and Käthe Kollwitz. When she passed through Vienna she was in the habit of sending her luggage straight from the station to Zemek's apartment. But the latter found it more and more difficult to play the part which Lou had assigned to him. He disliked being kept in the background and treated as a sort of convenience. He still loved her and wanted to marry her. But it was useless. Lou would not hear of it. So he decided to end the affair himself although he knew it would break his heart.

When, once again, Lou's luggage arrived, he had it sent to a hotel.

A few years later, while she was working with Freud in Vienna, Lou saw Zemek now and again, but he was not much more than a memory. She had found other friends and other interests. Zemek sought forgetfulness in his work. He became a great physician, a respected member of the medical faculty of the University of Vienna, and was idolized by his fellow workers, his assistants, and his patients. He never married. Of the many women who offered to share their lives with him, none appealed to him as much as Lou had. For over a quarter of a century until his death in 1936, he carried her picture in his heart. Only his family knew the cause of his sadness.

18

Exorcising Devils

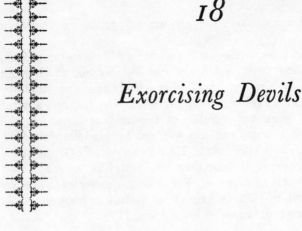

MIRRORS—IT STARTED WITH MIRRORS—THE BIRTH OF MAN'S SELF-consciousness and his realization that he had been cut off from *Magna Mater,* the great Earth Mother, and hence from the source of life. In the Greek legend the shock of recognizing his own identity caused the death of the beautiful youth Narcissus. He fell in love with himself and drowned as he tried to embrace his own reflection in the water.

According to Freud a powerful narcissistic trait is present in all men. It is the germinal point of our ego-ideal and lies at the root of autoeroticism. Lou had pondered the problem of self-love even before she met Freud. In her book *Eroticism,* as well as in an earlier article, "Thoughts on Physical Love," she had treated it as one of the two conflicting emotions that are aroused during the sexual act—the other being the longing for self-surrender. Her psychoanalytical studies and the experience of her own life provided additional insights into this dual aspect of man's subconscious drives. Indeed, her major contribution to psychoanalysis is her insistence that the narcissistic phenomenon properly understood always includes both self-love and self-surrender. For "one must remember that the Narcissus of the legend does not stand in front of an artificial mirror but before one of nature. Perhaps he does not only see himself reflected in the water but, in addition to himself, everything else as well, otherwise would he have stayed? Would he not have fled in horror? Does not his face express melancholy as well as enchant-ment?" Enchantment because he was delighted with his own image, melancholy because he had suddenly become aware of his separate existence, aware that he was no longer an integral part of earth, water and air.

This basic duality of our subconscious is a recurrent theme in Lou's writings and runs through her life like a leitmotif. She was both strongly self-centered and recklessly generous. As a result, at times she lived almost like a recluse, like the "Pope in the Vatican," and at others she all but threw herself away. There was something elemental in her response to any given situation. Being uncompromisingly true to herself she was in-capable of being true to anyone else. Loyalty for loyalty's sake was alien to her. She would have called it self-betrayal.

On the occasion of her fiftieth birthday Lou was asked to write a brief autobiographical sketch. Entitled "In the Mirror," it appeared in the October, 1911, issue of the *Literary Echo*. She begins as always by recalling the fantasy world of her child-hood, pointing out how it conflicted with the real world around her. And she tells the episode of her being called a liar by her young cousin who was startled when she heard Lou's fabulous account of what had happened to them on their walk. But did Lou tell a lie? She did not think so. To her the story was true. Evidently, the world in which she lived was different from that of her cousin although it was inhabited, just like her cousin's world, by real people, people she met at home or observed in the street. She merely penetrated their everyday lives, imagined what they had been like as children or what the future held in store for them. She followed them inwardly as far as she could until they were completely incorporated into her own scheme of things.

"While they passed by me unsuspectingly, men, women, chil-dren and old people, their lives had already been determined and they possessed all at once their own past youth and their future fate, their ancestors or their grandchildren. . . . And if I had died of the measles as a child, I would probably have had the uneasy feeling that I was responsible for countless destinies. That is why I began to write, to make signs by which life be-comes conscious of itself. It remained a makeshift."

Soon after Lou had written these words, she met Freud and learned from him that through the art of analysis she could gain insights into those subconscious forces of life which she had tried to express as a writer. They met halfway, as it were, coming from opposite directions. Freud, the rationalist, descending into the depth of the subconscious, and Lou struggling to ascend into the realm of conscious relationships.

"Only by following you," she confessed later to Freud, "did I understand that what has become conscious represents the meaning and value of unconscious drives."

By a curious twist of fate the man who introduced Lou to Freud, the Swedish psychotherapist Poul Bjerre, soon fell into disgrace with the Freudian school and lost Lou, whom he loved, to one of Freud's closest disciples. In her memoirs Lou does not mention Bjerre any more than Pineles. And it almost looks as though, by repressing their names from her memory, she wants to eliminate these two men from her life. She may have had good reasons for doing that but she would be the first to admit that an act of repression always indicates that something important lies behind it.

Lou met Bjerre at the home of a distant relative of his, the Swedish writer Ellen Key, who was one of Rilke's earliest friends and admirers. She had known Ellen for years and visited her often. Bjerre was married and fifteen years younger than Lou, but like most men he seems to have succumbed to her charms at first sight. They quickly became lovers and for a brief period they were passionately happy. Almost at the end of his life, reflecting on his affair with Lou with the calm detachment of a wise old man who has suffered much and learned much, Bjerre gave this account of her:

"One noticed at once that Lou was an extraordinary woman. She had the gift of entering completely into the mind of the man she loved. Her enormous concentration fanned, as it were, her partner's intellectual fire. I have never met anyone else in my long life who understood me so quickly, so well, and so completely, as Lou did. In addition, there was the almost startling frankness of her expression. She discussed her most intimate and private affairs with the greatest nonchalance. I remember I was shocked when she told me of Rée's suicide. 'Don't you have any pangs of conscience?' I asked her. But she merely laughed and said that conscience was a sign of weakness. I realize that this may have been bravado, but she did seem unconcerned about the consequences of her actions and was in this respect more like a force of nature than a human being. Her unusually strong will liked to triumph over men. She could be very passionate, but only momentarily so, and with a strangely cold passion. I think Nietzsche was right when he said that Lou was a thoroughly evil woman. Evil, however, in the Goethean sense: evil that produces good. She hurt me much but she also gave me much. When I met her I was working on the foundations of my psychotherapy which is based, in contrast to Freud's, on the principle of synthesis. In my talks with Lou things became clear to me that I might not have found by myself. Like a catalyst she activated my thought processes. She may have destroyed lives and marriages but her presence was exciting. One felt the spark of genius in her. One grew in her presence.

"Our relationship lasted almost two years and was very close in the beginning. We lived and traveled together. She first visited her mother in St. Petersburg and joined me later in Helsingfors where I was giving a series of lectures. She wrote me from Berlin, from Petersburg and from Göttingen. But when I met her again in Munich in 1913 she was completely changed. She had turned away from me and had gone over to Freud. And there was, of course, young Tausk who was head over heels in love with her and who later killed himself. In Munich Lou told me that she had burned my letters and asked me to do likewise. She did not want to have any of her letters around. I promised to do that and I kept my promise. At that time I was hurt and no longer interested in her. But today I am sorry. For the fascinating aspect of her letters was that they completely reflected her personality. They were the letters of a passionate woman who was, at the same time, a scholar and philosopher. I remember that she had started to learn Swedish because she wanted to read my books in the original. What she said about the Swedish language was extraordinarily interesting, even from the philological point of view. She had a great gift for languages. In fact, she combined an unusual intuition with an unusual intellect. A very rare combination. The former trait seemed to me Russian, the latter Western.

"She told me that she had been pregnant once but that she could not, or did not want to, become a mother. There may have been deeper reasons, however, for her refusal to accept motherhood. To become a mother means to give something away from one's own person to the child. A woman who becomes a mother sacrifices herself in a certain sense to her child. But that was precisely what Lou could not do. She could never, not even during the most passionate embrace, and then she was by no means cold, give herself completely. She always talked about it but she could not do it. Intellectually she could merge into her partner but not humanly. Perhaps this was the real tragedy in Lou's life. She longed for deliverance from her strong personality but did not find it. In the deepest meaning of the word, Lou was the unredeemed woman."

In fairness to Lou it should be added that she, too, thought that Bjerre was unredeemed and unfree. She knew that he had vowed to remain faithful to his invalid wife and that he suffered from his infidelity. She thought this showed his lack of inner freedom. "Like a typical compulsion neurotic, he was bound by thousands of fixations and reproaches. He needed a halo. To atone for his love he had to be his wife's nurse."

Mutual recriminations of this kind are, of course, a sign of mutual disillusionment. While they were in love they saw each other in quite a different light. To young Bjerre, Lou was inspiration personified, the mother of his yet unborn thoughts, the mistress of his youthful passion. And for a brief moment Lou was carried away by her lover's ardor. His ideas fascinated her because they touched on problems with which she had been struggling herself. When Bjerre suggested that she accompany him to the third psychoanalytical congress in Weimar, she accepted eagerly. Once again love turned the wheel of fate. It was Gillot's love that helped her find herself; through Rée's love she gained her independence; and now Bjerre's love led her to Freud. In each case her lover acted as a catalytic agent and was discarded as soon as the new relationship had been established.

The Weimar Congress of the International Psychoanalytical Association got under way on September 21, 1911. It was attended by some fifty-five members and guests from many parts of the world. In contrast to other such meetings it took place in a relaxed and friendly atmosphere. The president of the Association was the Swiss Carl Jung, but Freud, its undisputed head, presided over the congress with benign authority. He was then in his mid-fifties and in the prime of his life. A gentle and soft-spoken man, he was surrounded by an aura of dignity and old-world charm. He was of medium height, not heavily built but with that inclination toward rotundity that is characteristic of the scholar. His face sported a greying mustache and was framed by a well-trimmed beard. It was a distinguished face, animated by the dark and restless eyes of the explorer who had trained himself to see through the mirage of the world. According to his mood, Freud's eyes could be stern and sad or sparkle with quick flashes of humor. By temperament he was "a *conquistador*—an adventurer, if you want to translate the word—with the curiosity, the boldness, and the tenacity that belong to that type of being."

Lou was introduced to Freud by Bjerre at the beginning of the Weimar Congress. She remembers that Freud laughed at her "vehemently expressed desire to study psychoanalysis." She was only five years younger than he, but she acted like a child who had just seen a wonderful new toy and wanted to possess it. Her eagerness seemed a bit naïve. For no man knew better than Freud how devious the ways of the subconscious are and the patient labor that is necessary to uncover it. It had taken him half his life to reach his conclusions, and here Lou was, eager to appropriate them in a brief course of studies. No wonder he was amused and asked her with a twinkle in his eyes if she perhaps mistook him for Santa Claus. But Freud's irony did not deter Lou and gradually his amusement gave way to wonder. What a strange woman she was! He had heard that Lou was a writer and knew of her close association with Nietzsche. Surely Nietzsche's fate must have taught her how complex the human psyche is. But as she stood before him, vital and radiant, she seemed a living contradiction of any tragic world view. She was obviously a thoughtful woman; indeed, listening to Lou talk, Freud was struck by the profundity of her remarks. There was no doubt about her intellectual brilliance. Even during their first meeting Freud felt that Lou understood him perfectly. Why then, in the face of all the evidence to the contrary, did she persist in her "blithe optimism"? This question puzzled Freud and continued to puzzle him in the many years of their friendship.

Nietzsche's name was often mentioned in informal discussions during the Weimar Congress. It was generally known that Nietzsche's sister, Elizabeth, lived in the town and was the energetic head of the Nietzsche Archives which she had founded. Lou, of course, carefully avoided her great antagonist. And it must have amused her when she heard that two of Freud's closest collaborators paid a visit to Elizabeth and told her that her famous brother had anticipated many of Freud's findings. Knowing Elizabeth's virulent anti-Semitism, Lou could see her squirm at the thought that her brother's name was coupled with Freud's. The "Faithful Llama" was furious when she heard that Lou was in town. That Russian adventuress had given her enough trouble in the past. She had publicly challenged her, Elizabeth's, right to be the sole authoritative interpreter of Nietzsche's philosophy. Was she now going to drag her brother's name into the psychoanalytic mud? Elizabeth felt infuriated that she could do nothing about it. For better or worse Lou was the living link between Nietzsche and Freud.

What Lou learned in Weimar made such an impression on her that she decided to make a serious study of psychoanalysis. Working partly on her own and partly with Bjerre, she quickly mastered Freud's major concepts. But the deeper she entered into the complexities of the new science the more she felt that she would have to spend some time working with Freud himself.

"Since I was permitted to attend the Weimar Congress last autumn," she wrote him, "I have not been able to leave psychoanalysis alone, and the deeper I penetrate into it the more it fascinates me. I have only one wish: to come to Vienna for a few months. May I then address myself to you, attend your lectures and obtain permission to join your Wednesday-evening seminars? My only reason for coming to Vienna is my wish to devote myself entirely to this matter."

Freud graciously granted her request, saying he felt that it was a "favorable omen" that she had attended the Weimar Congress. He would happily share with her the few aspects of psychoanalysis that could be communicated to a layman. Thus encouraged, Lou went to Vienna at the end of October, 1912, accompanied by her young friend Ellen Delp, and spent half a year there. It was a period of concentrated work, of long, often heated, discussions, and of many heart-to-heart talks with the founder of the new movement.

The relationship between Lou and Freud which had begun so auspiciously grew in intensity as the years passed and remained untroubled by major disagreements. This is the more remarkable since both Freud and Lou had strong convictions that were by no means always identical, and since neither of them found it easy to compromise intellectual positions for the sake of friendship. When Lou joined Freud the latter was embroiled in a number of very disagreeable feuds with former followers. He had already parted company with his erstwhile collaborator Alfred Adler, and was in the midst of a bitter controversy with another prominent member of his inner circle, Wilhelm Stekel. Worst of all, the threat of apostasy of his Swiss favorite, C. G. Jung, which had been hanging over Freud for some time, became acute just then and caused him a great deal of personal unhappiness.

Unwittingly Lou was drawn into the Freud-Adler conflict because she had expressed a desire to attend Adler's lectures as well as Freud's. Since all relations between the two men and their adherents had been broken off, something Lou did not know, her request must have seemed rather naïve. But both sides tacitly agreed to make an exception in her case and to admit her to their meetings provided she kept strictly to herself whatever transpired in either group. Right from the beginning Lou was thus introduced to one of the less pleasant aspects of psychoanalysis: the violent personality clashes of its practitioners, their claims and counterclaims and their often vituperative attacks on each other.

For a short time Lou submitted to this quasi-schizophrenic position but she soon stopped attending Adler's lectures and cast in her lot with Freud. This early experience may be the reason for her strongly worded defense of Freud in her later psychoanalytical writings. She begins almost every article with a reference to Freud's detractors. What alienated Lou from Adler was his insistence that organic defects are the cause of psychic disturbances. She thought that psychoanalytically nothing was gained by trying to discover physical reasons for every inferiority complex. Adler's ironic rejection of Freud's libido theory—"the sexual flourish that is supposed to be the essence of things"—widened the rift between him and Lou. For Lou shared Freud's conviction that sexual drives in the widest understanding are the prime movers of human actions, and indeed, of life itself. And finally Lou resented Adler's personal criticism of Freud. It seemed to her petty and unjust. For she admired Freud's unflinching honesty in exploring those hidden and often repulsive aspects of the soul that the conscious mind tries to repress. She knew that at heart Freud was a rationalist who would have been far happier if he had not been forced to acknowledge the vast power of irrational forces that shape our destinies. She knew, too, that the clash between Freud's rationalistic predilection and his growing insight into the power of the subconscious lay at the root of his pessimism. He saw no hope for a world controlled by the irrational drives, fears and frustrations of men.

With her it was otherwise. Having a different focus, she saw in the subconscious the source of life, the great reservoir of all creative activity, and she approached it with awe and wonder. The gift that psychoanalysis offered her was "the radiant expansion of her own being" by enabling her to grope closer to the roots that link it to the totality of life. She felt that the "hidden river-god of the blood" and the God of her childish dreams formed the great circle that encompasses life. Humbly she accepted the fact that man's highest aspirations and his most earthy needs rise from the same source. When she expressed herself in such terms Freud remarked dryly that she apparently saw in psychoanalysis a kind of magic key that opened the gate to the most wonderful world. And she agreed happily. For with her psychoanalysis was not a means to solve inner conflicts but a way to gain deeper insights. There had been no disharmony between her subconscious drives and her conscious acts. To be sure, the unresolved tensions between her impulsive heart and her strong will had caused unhappiness to her as well as to others, but the major conflicts in her life had resulted because by following her drives she had violated social conventions and taboos. Now Freud taught her that the restraints imposed upon the individual by society tend to stunt his growth by compelling him to repress his drives. This knowledge made her see how fortunate she had been in her own life, and how right in refusing to bow to the dictates of society. If she had any doubts left on that score she lost them completely now.

Lou's entrance into the Freudian circle was hailed as a "favorable omen" not only by the master himself—who admitted that he became so attached to her that seeing her seat empty during his lectures upset him—but by most of his followers as well. They felt that Lou's presence and that of her beautiful young friend Ellen added a touch of feminine warmth to their often rather dreary discussions. Most of the time Lou listened quietly, sometimes taking notes, sometimes knitting, but always paying close attention to what was being said. She was quite unperturbed by the most startling presentations of neurotic behavior or by the emphasis placed on sex. Once, while she was knitting, somebody pointed to her and said humorously that Lou seemed to enjoy herself by indulging in continuous coitus as symbolized by the movement of her knitting needles. She just smiled and kept on knitting.

The contrast between Lou's happy temperament and Freud's gloomy world view led to some rather amusing episodes. One day, for example, Freud told her that he had just come across Nietzsche's "Prayer to Life" and thought it was atrocious. It was beyond him how a philosopher could write such grandiloquent nonsense as:

> Millennia to be, to think, to live!
> Hold me in both your arms with might and main!
> If you have no more happiness to give:
> Give me your pain.

"No, no," Freud said, "I could not go along with that. A good head cold would cure me of all such wishes!" Little did he know that he was not making fun of Nietzsche and that the perpetrator of this nonsense was sitting right in front of him. Perhaps Lou told him. In any case she was far too fond of him to be hurt by his irony and she probably joined in his laughter.

That she was able to laugh at herself, that she bore no malice and was devoid of any vanity concerning her own person or her literary achievements, were traits in Lou's character that Freud admired. Most of his collaborators were terribly ambitious and serious young men, easily hurt, who faced him with the rebellious spirit of sons who feel that their father is in the way. No matter how justified their feelings were—and there is no doubt that

Freud presided over his school like an Old Testament patriarch—
it was a welcome relief to find someone who refused to be drawn
into their eternal family squabbles. Doubly so if this someone
was a radiant woman, experienced and mature, whose well-
trained mind could easily follow his most subtle arguments. True,
Freud could not share Lou's optimism, and when she exclaimed
that no matter what, "Life was magnificent," he wondered
whether she had understood anything at all of what he had been
trying to tell her. But then she would always surprise him with
amazing insights gained by some sort of intuitive synthesis that
went far beyond the limits of his own analytical method. Summing
up their differences, Freud said that, while he was writing prose,
Lou was "the poet of psychoanalysis." On this basis of mutual
respect they entered upon a friendship that lasted to the end of
their lives, for the better part of a quarter of a century. In all
these years Lou was one of Freud's most devoted interpreters.

It was inevitable that in the course of Lou's six months' stay
in Vienna, during which she learned the art of analysis which
she would soon practice herself, she would form close personal
ties to one or the other of the young men around Freud. Inevitable: because age had increased rather than diminished her
sex appeal and particularly inevitable in a climate where sex
was the constant topic of conversation. When a man and a
woman who share the same intellectual curiosity, and spend hours
talking on a subject that is bound to arouse their emotions, find
that they are also physically attracted to each other, the result
is not hard to foresee. Long before Lou had met Freud she had
written that many ways lead from intellectual excitement to
physical love and the experiences of her life had borne her out.
Now she found herself once again in such a situation. It was no
secret that Bjerre was Lou's lover when she joined Freud in
Weimar, but Bjerre was not in Vienna and was not very highly
regarded by Freud in any case. Hence it was reasonable to assume
that sooner or later somebody else would claim his place. Apparently quite a few did. Even young Baron von Gebsattel, the
"Benjamin" of the group, found Lou's charms irresistible, although
she was more than twice his age. Rumor has it that he hurt Lou
much when, during an intimate hour, he asked her point-blank
how old she was. The man who finally won Lou's love was one

of the most gifted of Freud's younger disciples, Dr. Victor Tausk.

Tausk, then thirty-five years old—sixteen years younger than Lou—a tall and handsome man, possessed to a high degree that quality which women find fascinating and dangerous. Even Lou's young friend Ellen Delp was badly tempted by him and might have succumbed if Lou, who had designs of her own on Tausk, had not intervened. Tausk had invited Ellen, who was an actress, to his rooms for a private reading of the Gretchen scenes in *Faust*. But shortly before the appointed time for the rendezvous, Lou told her friend that Tausk had asked her to be excused—he was otherwise occupied. Apparently this was not true. Tausk waited for Ellen and asked her later why she had not come. When Lou's emotions were involved she could be ruthless.

Although Tausk was a great favorite with women, he was a profoundly unhappy man. The brief history of his life reads like an obstacle race which he could not hope to win and which in the end he gave up in despair. He was a Croatian, had studied law and had become a judge. Bitter personal experiences forced him to give up his profession soon after he started it. He took up journalism and worked for a time in Berlin and Vienna. There he came in contact with Freud and decided to devote his life to psychoanalysis. Like many others, Tausk was undoubtedly attracted to the new science because he hoped it would help him find the key to the riddle of his own life. Handicapped by an appalling domestic situation—he was unhappily married and the father of two boys—and by a chronic lack of money, he had taken up the study of medicine and was preparing himself for his final examinations when he met Lou.

Tausk was one of Freud's discussion leaders whose sessions Lou attended regularly. She liked the way he presented Freud's ideas, only occasionally did she think he followed the master too slavishly, and sometimes she disagreed with his conclusions. He was clearly the most outstanding of the discussion leaders but Lou noticed that Freud was much more critical of him than of the others. Apparently Freud thought that Tausk was too impetuous, too prone to venture forth into regions that had not yet been thoroughly explored. But this was precisely what appealed to Lou. She sensed a primitive power in Tausk, the "beast of prey" as Freud called it, a power which Tausk repressed by

forcing himself to think analytically. Lou noticed the struggle
between these conflicting tendencies and hoped that her love
would help ease it. "I felt from the beginning that it was precisely
this struggle that moved me so deeply: the struggle of the human
animal. Brother animal. You."

And what love could do, Lou's love did. For a time Tausk was
at peace with himself. They worked and they played together.
They talked about philosophy, a subject that was frowned upon
by Freud. Tausk showed Lou an essay he had written on Spinoza
which she read with great interest. Since Spinoza was the only
philosopher to whom she had had an inner relation even as a
young girl, she was delighted to discover that he was the
philosopher of psychoanalysis. She was so much impressed with
Tausk's philosophical acumen that she advised him to express
himself more often in that idiom which seemed natural to him,
even at the risk of displeasing Freud. Sometimes they deserted
their studies and, like students cutting a class, enjoyed themselves secretly by going to the movies, those early silent movies
one remembers with a certain smiling nostalgia. Lou, too, smiled
as she reflected on it later. But she did not share the intellectual's
contempt for this "Cinderella among the arts."

"Even if it is only superficial entertainment, it enriches our
senses with a wealth of pictures, forms and impressions." She
predicted that the movies would have a great future in a world
where the increasing monotony of work caused such inner fatigue
that the more demanding forms of art could no longer satisfy the
needs of the majority. And she did not feel sorry for those stolen
half hours she spent with Tausk at the Urania Cinema in Vienna.
It was fun and she enjoyed herself. As for Tausk he felt more
relaxed than ever. For the first time in his life he had met a
woman who was willing to share in both the serious and light-
hearted aspects of his temperament—a woman with a brilliant
mind, a wonderful body and the gift of making him feel at home
with himself.

One wonders what direction Tausk's life would have taken if
Lou had been able to stay with him. As it was, the fact that she
favored him convinced Freud that there must be more to Tausk
than he thought, and he admitted privately that, but for Lou, he
would have dropped Tausk because he considered him a threat

to the future of psychoanalysis. But Lou could not stay with
Tausk, as she may have made clear to him in a long conversation
they had about unfaithfulness. Tausk called the capacity of some
women to enter into many intellectual relationships with men
"sublimated polyandry." But Lou objected that women who are
unfaithful do not necessarily leave one man for the next. They
are often merely compelled to return to themselves. Their unfaithfulness is not betrayal. "A woman," she said, "is like a tree
longing for the lightning that splits it, and yet also like a tree
that wants to grow." Therefore she had only the choice of
remaining a "split tree," the so-called better half of a man—and
it was beyond Lou how any half could be better—or of starting
a new growth after each stroke of lightning, the choice between
sacrificing her wholeness or becoming unfaithful. Love was an
elemental passion; the attempt to conserve it was as unrealistic
as it would be to conserve a tempest. Each tempest blows itself
out, that is the nature of tempests. And so with love. The more
passionate a love the shorter its duration. People can remain faithful to each other only if their elemental passions are not involved.
There are crimes of passion but a passionate marriage is a contradiction in terms.

Tausk, who was passionately in love with Lou, listened to her
arguments with mixed emotions. His mind told him that she was
right and yet he could not help but feel that "all love wants
eternity, wants deep, profound eternity." When Lou terminated
the brief affair and returned to Göttingen, Tausk threw himself
into his work with a desperate fury. He passed his examinations,
became a neurologist and, during the war, the chief physician in a
field hospital. Returning to Vienna after the war, depressed by
the horrors he had witnessed, he tried to re-establish his medical
practice under the most difficult circumstances, got engaged and
was about to be remarried. But a week before his marriage despair
overwhelmed him and he killed himself. Rumor has it that he
died a particularly gruesome death by first castrating himself. He
was forty-two years old. When she heard of his death Lou wrote
Freud: "Poor Tausk. I loved him. I thought I knew him and yet I
would never have thought of suicide. . . . I imagine his death
was that of a violent and yet, at the same time, a suffering man."

The outbreak of the war and the brutalities committed in its course by civilized men in both camps seemed to confirm Freud's most pessimistic assessment of human nature. How thin the veneer of civilization was and how powerful the self-destructive forces in man! "Where is your optimism now?" he asked Lou. And Lou found it hard to answer. The war had a special dimension of horror for her: it cut her off from her family in Russia and involved in mortal combat the country she loved and where she was born with the country where she made her home. She could not share the patriotic feelings of her German countrymen —how could she rejoice over the victories they won at the beginning of the war over her Russian brothers?—nor could she wish them harm. It was a fratricidal war, literally speaking, as far as Lou was concerned and it left her numb with horror.

"I can scarcely express in words what causes me such anguish," she wrote Rilke in September, 1914, "but, you know, it is this: that the war resembles a doll in our understanding. The other day I read that an enemy uniform, complete with all its trappings, had been hung up in front of a locomotive like a dangling dummy; and, involuntarily, I thought: this is the image, the symbol." The enemy dummy was the visual representation of their self-hatred. But, alas, instead of being content to vent it on such a lifeless thing as a dummy they start shooting into live bodies, unaware of the monstrous deception, just as if during maneuvers live ammunition had been issued by mistake. That was what horrified her: the uncanny unreality of the war, its vampire-like sucking of blood to appease man's self-destructive urge. But there was no escaping it because "we are all and always murderers of our own selves and of each other. That is perhaps unavoidable but because of it our guilt is terribly universal and our only means of redemption is to accept it as such, to feel the universality of our guilt. . . . When I had understood this I realized with astonishment that for this reason I would have fought too, if I had been a man, and if I had borne sons I would have sent my sons to war."

Lou's use of the word "guilt" is significant here because in the first article she contributed to Freud's journal, *Imago*, about a year before the war, she had said that she had an "inborn prejudice against all consciousness of guilt." Now she accepted it as an inevitable condition of human existence, but she still refused to submit to despair. The horrors of the war and her growing insight into the dark abysses of the soul caused her to give more muted expression of her joy of life. It increased her feeling of compassion for her fellow men and broadened her sympathies. Purely theoretical discussions of psychological themes or literary attempts to present them in fictional form no longer satisfied her. She wanted to alleviate, as best she could, the anguish and suffering of the human animal. Although she had no formal training in medicine, she had spent most of her adult life in the company of doctors from whom she had learned much and she had a native ability for the art of healing. With Freud's encouragement she took up the profession of psychotherapy.

The war and the postwar chaos brought about a sharp increase in mental disorders of all kinds and a demand for psychiatric help that could not be met by traditional means. Freud's long struggle for professional recognition now entered a new phase. Many of his formerly skeptical colleagues wanted to know more about his method of curing the mentally sick, and requests for teaching analysis multiplied. Since he and his followers could not fill them all he sometimes suggested Lou instead. Thus she spent half a year in Königsberg analyzing five doctors of a mental hospital as well as a number of their patients. It was exhausting work. Freud warned her that ten hours of psychoanalysis a day was too much and might harm her. But she persisted. She found her work fascinating and if she felt tired at the end of the day she also felt amply rewarded by the confidence her patients had in her. One of the doctors she analyzed then has given the following account of Lou's psychoanalytical work:

"I confess that the way Lou analyzed me left a deep impression on me and has been a great help to me all my life. Since then I have been much less inclined to be shocked by the actions of others. For if you have once faced your own 'inner scoundrel' —and we all have him—you are far less ready to be morally outraged by the behavior of your fellow men. That is the great value of such analyses: they make you humble.

"For the rest, I had the impression that Lou was more interested in the psychological than in the medical aspects of psychoanalysis. And after all: every life is a novel. For a writer, such as Lou was originally, nothing can be more interesting than to descend into the lives of others. Those are living novels. I gained the impression that Lou found it much more rewarding to participate in the lives of others than to write novels of her own. I can understand this very well. Being a physician I hardly read novels now. Why should I? I hear and see things every day that no writer could possibly imagine. For life surpasses art by far. I suppose that Lou turned to psychoanalysis because it enabled her to penetrate into the deepest secrets of life in her fellow men.

"She had a very quiet way of speaking and a great gift of inspiring confidence. I am still a little surprised today how much I told her then. But I had always the feeling that she not only understood everything but forgave everything. I have never again experienced such a feeling of conciliatory kindness, or if you like, compassion, as I did with her.

"We usually sat opposite each other in semi-darkness. Mostly I talked and Lou listened. She was a great listener. But sometimes she would tell me stories of her life. I remember one in particular. 'Once,' she said, 'I was sitting in a train with Rilke and we amused ourselves by playing the game of free association. You say a word and your partner answers with any word that comes to his mind. We did this for quite a while. And suddenly I understood the reasons why Rilke wanted to write his military school novel and I told him so. I explained to him the nature of the subconscious forces that were urging him to write because they had been repressed while he was at school. He laughed at first, then he looked serious and said that now he did not have to write the novel at all. I had taken it off his soul. This shocked me and I suddenly realized the danger of psychoanalysis for the creative artist. To interfere here means to destroy. That is why I later always advised Rilke against having himself analyzed. For while a successful analysis might free an artist from the devils that beset him, it would also drive away the angels that help him create. A germ-free soul is a sterile soul.' As I listened to Lou's story I understood why she was so interested in the relationship between the creative process and depth analysis. It was a theme to which she gave considerable thought, although she knew intuitively that for the artist the work of art—and not analysis—is the road to salvation."

Her work in Königsberg, exhausting though it was, gave Lou a great deal of personal satisfaction. But this was not always the case. Once she received a call from the head of a sanatorium near Munich who asked her to assist him in the treatment of his patients, mostly women in various stages of mental distress. The work sounded interesting and the terms attractive. Lou accepted and agreed to spend some time there as a resident psychotherapist. But much to the surprise of her nephew, Franz Schönberner, who was then the editor of *Simplizissimus,* she returned to Munich abruptly a few days later and said that she could not go on working because the head of the sanatorium had rid himself so successfully of all his inhibitions that he was in the habit of sleeping with his women patients. Although not easily shocked, Lou felt that such behavior violated professional ethics.

Göttingen was not a good location for a practitioner of Freud's art. A small town, it had all the prejudices of a small town and looked askance at the goings-on in the house on the Hainberg. But Freud continued to refer patients to Lou and others found their way to her on their own. She treated all types of the mentally sick from minor cases of hysteria to seriously disturbed neurotics. Quietly sitting in her chair and listening to the stories her patients told her, she seemed to be lost in thought and absentminded. Actually her mind was hard at work to detect the revealing incidents in every story, the significant phrase or word that would provide the key to the problem. Nothing could deter her from this alert pursuit, not even the threat of bodily harm. Once during a session, one of her women patients, who suffered from an acute anxiety neurosis that led to occasional outbreaks of violence, suddenly seized a long, pointed paper knife that had been lying on the table and threatened Lou with it. Lou leapt up from her chair and, dancing around the table, which she tried to keep between herself and the raging woman, kept on repeating to herself: "Listen now! Listen to what she is saying." She expected, and rightly so, that the vituperative language of the woman, who was foaming at the mouth, would reveal the key to the nature of her illness. Such dramatic incidents were rare, however. Most of the time nothing interrupted the stillness of Lou's study except the voices of her patients, who felt encouraged by her understanding sympathy to transfer their problems to her. Just as she, as a child, had, in the stillness of the night, transferred her problems to a kind and forgiving God.

In addition to her psychotherapeutic work Lou still found time for some writing, mostly, though not exclusively, on psychoanalytical subjects. She contributed articles to Freud's journal, *Imago*, on such topics as anal eroticism, narcissism, early religiosity, femininity. She wrote reviews and articles on Russian themes for the *Literary Echo*, and she published a number of books. Some like *The House* and *Rodinka*, she had written almost two decades earlier; others, like *Three Letters to a Boy* and *The Hour without God and Other Stories*, she wrote during and after the war. Into this period also falls her most unusual piece of writing, a verse-play in seven scenes, entitled *The Devil and His Grandmother*.

In colorful language that does not shun four-letter words, the play treats the devil's return to God. God is life, justice, perfection, but His birthplace is the great Earth Womb, Lou called it "the devil's grandmother." And the devil himself is God's eldest son. Another wanderer, he has left God and has set himself up against God like a dark mirror reflecting the primordial oneness of God and Satan. But now there is no more need for the devil because:

> God has long since become just
> and long since man, straying from God,
> has made his own hell.

Bored with his work among the dead and secretly in love with life, the devil, a seduced seducer like Mephistopheles in Goethe's *Faust*, decides to die just as his younger brother, Christ, did and return to God, although he knows that:

> Nobody will mourn for me
> as millennia have mourned my brother
> who died on the Cross.

The meaning of this strange parable in which religious and psychoanalytical elements are grotesquely mixed is that love conquers death. Even the outcast is reborn in love. Once again Lou treats a theme that occupied her all her life: the regenerative force of love. But a new dimension has been added. The poetic form emphasizes the power of the subconscious, and the introduction of a movie scenario in one of the scenes, a bold and expressionistic device, lends dramatic power to the action. Artistically

The Devil and His Grandmother is Lou's most successful work. It shows that her preoccupation with psychoanalysis did not weaken her creative faculties.

But in spite of the satisfaction she derived from her work, her life at the end of the war and in the period following was not easy. The Russian revolution caused her a great deal of personal anxiety. She knew that the lives of her brothers and their families were in danger. And she tried in vain to help them. In her distress she even turned to one of her former suitors. But the letter she sent to Georg Ledebour, who was now a member of the Reichstag, was returned to her unopened. He could not forgive her for having rejected him more than twenty-five years previously.

What the Bolsheviks did to the social ideals of the Russian people, which Lou shared, seemed to her a monstrous betrayal. And yet she continued to hope. For "who can decide about ultimate values? But life, tremendous life, goes on in this continuously dying and continuously reborn country, where during the famine little children ran away from the Volga villages so that they would not be eaten alive." To be sure there was suffering and starvation in Europe too, and "if one would not die of old age," Lou sighed, "one would die of sadness," but of all the peoples in the world the Russians were drinking the bitterest cup. Their martyrdom, she thought, sanctified them and prepared them for the leading role they were destined to play in the world of tomorrow. Like Spengler, Lou believed that the days of the West were numbered. Spiritually the West was dead. It had no faith left, not even faith in its own future.

Once again her health declined. As a result of a serious attack of influenza at the end of the war, she temporarily lost nearly all her hair and had to wear a lace bonnet like a little old lady. For the first time in her life she felt that she was getting old. She had never worried about her age before and she did not seriously worry now. In a sense she felt ageless. But after passing her sixtieth birthday she admitted that she had crossed a great divide, although she still insisted that she would never enter the "change of life."

Money worries too made themselves felt once more during the German inflation in the early twenties. Lou needed money for her starving relatives in Russia and for the upkeep of her house, now badly in need of repairs. In this predicament Freud came to the rescue by sending her generous sums, sharing with her his newly earned wealth, as he put it. He also invited her to spend some time in Vienna with him as his guest. This she did and her visit strengthened their already cordial friendship. Freud now addressed her as "dearest Lou" and shared with her his most private thoughts, such as his feelings for his daughter Anna and his bitter disappointment when Otto Rank, whom he had treated like a son, deserted him.

Freud, too, was getting old and the fortitude with which he bore his painful illness moved Lou deeply. She remembers their last meeting in Berlin in the autumn of 1928. It was a glorious autumn. The colors in the park of Tegel, where they went for long walks, were particularly brilliant that year. Red, blue and purple pansies were in full bloom, row upon row of them. Freud presented Lou with a bunch. His illness made it hard for him to talk, but they reminisced for hours about their first meeting in 1911 and all the years they had known each other. Suddenly Lou asked Freud whether he still remembered her "Prayer to Life," the poem which he thought Nietzsche had written. Freud smiled and said he did. "And then something happened," she writes, "that I did not understand myself, but no power in the world could have stopped me: my trembling lips in revolt against his fate and martyrdom, burst out: 'You have done what I, in my youthful enthusiasm, only raved about.'" Startled by her own words, Lou burst into tears. Freud did not answer. "I only felt his arms around me."

On the occasion of Freud's seventy-fifth birthday, in 1931, Lou paid public tribute to her friend and his work in her book *My Gratitude to Freud*. In his acknowledgment, Freud, equally generous, called Lou's book "a genuine synthesis . . . from which one could expect that the bundle of nerves, sinews and arteries into which the analytical knife had transformed the body, could be retransformed into a living organism." This was unusual praise for the usually critical founder of psychoanalysis. The fact that his beloved daughter Anna had become a close friend of Lou's and was one of her great admirers no doubt contributed to Freud's own high regard for Lou. Next to Anna he felt that Lou was closest to him now. Indeed, he once said that she was "superior to us all." As a token of his esteem he gave her one of the five rings he had made for his most trusted friends.

Lou had every reason, then, to feel satisfied with her work as a psychotherapist. After she had weathered the difficult postwar years, her circumstances improved again and her life flowed on in a quiet rhythm. Even her husband, largely ignored until now, began to play a more important role. It started when in the late twenties he visited her in a Göttingen hospital where she was recovering from a serious operation. After living together—and yet separate—for almost half a century they suddenly confronted each other in a hospital room. Andreas, now in his mid-eighties, was still vigorous and not an old man but, as Lou said, a temperament. Lou herself nearing seventy was not old either; her face merely showed that the passage of time had matured rather than aged her. At first they did not know what to say to each other. They felt like two people who had met again, unexpectedly, after a long and difficult journey. But there was not much need for talking. Had they not both reached, following their separate paths, the most difficult goal that life has to offer: maturity without disenchantment? Quietly they looked at each other, barely able to suppress a subtle smile as they remembered the obstacles they had had to overcome before reaching this high plateau of peace and serenity.

But fate soon intervened once again and their conjugal happiness did not last. One day, quite suddenly, not long after they had finally met again, Andreas died. Lou was left alone in her house on the Hainberg. Not quite alone it is true, for Mariechen and her husband lived with her and took care of her physical needs. But she felt more and more isolated in a world that was once more drifting into chaos. The open world of her youth and of her most active years had died with the war. It was no longer easy to travel to Petersburg, Paris or Rome. Hostile guards greeted the stranger at every border. Europe was in the throes of vast, irrational forces that would presently engulf it in another murderous conflict. And the long night of Stalin's dictatorship was settling over Russia.

"I often think with envy of those who have died in the last few years without experiencing all this," Rilke had written to Lou at the outbreak of the first World War. But Rilke, too, was dead

now and spared the horrors that she had to face. And yet, and
yet: there must be no retreat from life. One must not lose faith
in it even in the midst of a manmade hell.

In this spirit Lou watched the devil's cauldron boil and bubble
in Germany until it overflowed, spewing forth Hitler. She knew
what the Nazis thought of Freud and all his works and, having
just paid public tribute to him, she knew what might be in store
for her. She knew the implacable hatred which Elizabeth Nietzsche, who was still alive and who, like the mythical dragon of the
Nibelungs, guarded her brother's hoard, harbored against her.
It was no secret to her either that the Nazis twisted Nietzsche's
thoughts to fit their aims and that they called her a "Finnish
Jewess." Should she risk their wrath and remain in the Third
Reich? Or should she follow the example of many of her friends
and go into exile? Perhaps she never seriously thought of leaving.
After all, she was old and sick and where could she go? But
perhaps, too, she felt that it would be out of character for her to
flee. She had never done that in her life. So she stayed and
watched and waited.

19

The Sibyl of the Hainberg

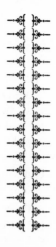

FROM THE BALCONY OF HER HOUSE ON THE HAINBERG HIGH ABOVE Göttingen, between heaven and earth as it were, where Lou spent the last years of her life, she watched the gathering storm. She was not afraid. For she knew, as she gazed into the shimmering land below, that no matter what men did to each other, the great rhythm of life went on undisturbed. Every day the sun rose behind the beech woods and set in glowing splendor beyond the western hills. Every spring the trees in her garden burst into bloom and the songbirds, which she so lovingly cared for, returned from the south. Every year nature was reborn, ripened and died. And man, too, died and was reborn. Her faith in this elemental law of life remained unshaken. It had carried her safely across the many vicissitudes of her own life and would safely carry her beyond it. Of this she was certain. "There will be arms outstretched to receive me," she said as she talked about death during one of the numerous illnesses that plagued her now.

She suffered from diabetes and from cancer of the breast and had to have one of her breasts removed. When it was decided that this operation was necessary she quietly left her house, without telling even her closest friends where she was going. She informed them only after she returned from the hospital of what had happened. She disliked the idea of people feeling sorry for her. As long as her mind remained active, there was no need to be alarmed about the natural decline of the body. Placing some padding beneath her silk dress to offset her lost breast, she said with a quizzical smile to the friend of her old age: "Nietzsche was right after all. Now I do have a false breast."

Although she lived quietly and withdrawn, she was not cut off from the world. She still saw an occasional patient, kept up her correspondence, and still received letters from total strangers. People who had read her books turned to her for advice. Her early novel *Ruth*, especially, which depicts the Héloïse-Abelard episode of her youthful love for Gillot, found avid readers among young girls. They would write and tell her how much her book had meant to them and how well they understood the feelings of her heroine. Sometimes they would ask if they could come and see her. She did not always encourage personal meetings, but when she felt that it was not idle curiosity but a real human need that moved her correspondents, she received them generously. Her friendship with Ellen Delp started that way and so did others.

The young daughter of a well-known Göttingen professor, braving the opprobrium of her family who called Lou the "witch of the Hainberg," paid secret visits to her when she found out that Lou was the author of *Ruth*. She was struck by the candor with which Lou answered all her questions, even the most intimate ones.

"She told me everything, absolutely everything. It was as if she stood naked before me without the slightest hint of embarrassment. She even let me take the Gillot letters home with me and I read them secretly in my room at night. Although she was so much older than I, I never had the feeling that I was talking with an old woman. She was more like an elder sister to me and shared everything with me as sisters do. She told me of the men she had traveled and lived with and that she always knew instinctively how far she could go. I was young and came from a totally different world, a closed world compared with the open world in which Lou lived. I admired her greatly and she changed the course of my life. Whether for good or bad, I cannot say. She was such a strong personality. What was right for her was not necessarily right for others."

But it was not only young girls in the turmoil of adolescence who sought Lou's advice. She was approached by mature men and women who saw in her one of the leading exponents of Freudianism in Germany. One of them was Viktor von Weizsäcker, the founder of medical anthropology. He turned to Lou during a critical period of his life:

"I must still mention one woman to whose acquaintance I owe my encounter with psychoanalysis: Lou Andreas-Salomé. Around Christmas time in 1931 I came across her book *My Gratitude to Freud* which she had written on the occasion of Freud's seventy-fifth birthday. It made such an impression on me that I wrote a letter to the unknown woman which led to a correspondence and to a visit to her; a visit that proved a great help to me at that time of anxiety I have mentioned above. Lou was then seventy years old and quietly carried on in Göttingen a psychoanalytical practice, living the mysterious life of a sibyl in the realm of the spirit. It is well known that when she was a young girl Nietzsche loved and wanted to marry her. Her book on him has remained one of the best presentations of his life and work. She was very close to Rilke, too, for many years. And she wrote a good book on him. Finally she gained Freud's friendship. Her letters to me showed an unequaled sagacity. She must have known from the beginning with whom she had to deal and what lay at the root of my anxiety. Perhaps she could not help me, but she loved the spirit and was at home in the world of solitude. It was a great relief to me to notice even in her book on Freud that because of her own originality she was entirely free of psychoanalytical dogmatism. She proved that what is true of a doctrine can be translated into other languages. I was very much moved by her femininity and her natural warmth and, though it was perhaps no mistake, it was certainly a loss that our interchange, so lively in the beginning, later ceased. She had fulfilled her mission with me and I could not offer her anything she might need in her advanced age.

"The extraordinary woman was still blond and she moved with the supple movements of a young tree. She was less monumental than Gertrud Bäumer or Ricarda Huch, but she was endowed with a graceful, searching or groping empathy and she lacked the too strongly masculine predominance of the female intellectual. My respect for Freud and my admiration for his work never needed any affirmation. But the effect of psychoanalysis resembles somewhat that of an inexorably choking noose. You cannot become involved in it without crying for help as it were, or at least without constantly wrestling with it. In Lou Andreas-Salomé I met the rare case of somebody who, having understood this new science profoundly, had yet remained herself. I have never again, either before or afterwards, met it as convincingly as with her."

As Lou pondered the meaning of her life in these twilight hours, a sense of gratitude welled up in her heart. She now saw that there was a grand design underlying the apparently erratic and contradictory course she had followed from her childhood in Russia to this retreat on the Hainberg. And like Lynceus, the keeper of the tower in Goethe's *Faust*, she saw in all things "the grace without end." In a world of mass-produced mediocrity she had succeeded in preserving her separate identity. For better or worse she had not succumbed to the forces of social or moral standardization. She had remained true to herself. This fact seemed to her of sufficient importance to warrant a public confession. Not that she thought her life had been exemplary and could be a model for others to follow, nor because she wanted to exhibit her innermost secrets to the gaze of the curious in the manner of Rousseau, but simply by presenting her life as a phenomenon in the spirit of Luther's: "Here I stand. I can do no other. God help me."

Lebensrückblick she called this, the last book she wrote. It is an autobiography, a review of her life, or, in her own words: *The Ground-Plan of Some Reminiscences*. It is a strange book and not easy to read because it is written in a very involved style, a style which often, instead of revealing, seems to conceal her thoughts. And yet it is a fascinating book, wholly unlike most memoirs in that it does not follow a chronological development. Time is irrelevant, Lou seems to say. What she does is to present a number of basic experiences, such as her experience of God, her experience of love, her experience of Russia and her experience of Freud. Like spokes of a wheel, all these experiences are anchored in a central hub, the core experience of Lou's life: her almost mystical concern with, and insight into, the "unity of being."

"Just now," she says, "we were everything, undivided and indivisible from us some form of life existed, then we were forced into birth and became a mere particle of the whole." Hence, our earliest memory is the shock of having been torn off from the source of life and thrust into an indifferent universe. At first we find shelter in the warmth of paternal love and seek to bridge the gap between our original wholeness and our divided present in the fantasy world of our childhood, where everything is still interchangeable: animals and trees and dolls and people. If we are religiously inclined we call this all-encompassing force God, and have as free and natural a relation to Him as we have to our parents. This was her own case. God was not an idea implanted on her from the outside. He was her own creation, the link between her and the rest of the world. An all-knowing, all-forgiving and all-powerful father. When He suddenly disappeared, when the gap was torn open between her imagined wholeness and the reality of her separate existence—she mentions the startling impact of mirrors on her youthful mind—she was at first disconsolate and mourned Him like a lost paradise. Her efforts to find an intellectual substitute for the God of her childhood failed, and since it would have been hypocritical to pretend that she had found Him, she left the Church, never to return. But the effect of her awareness of the godlessness of the universe was not despair. Quite the reverse. It filled her with a deep compassion for all the creature world, for were they not all forced to live without His sheltering presence? Were they not all cut adrift amid indifferent stars? She developed a deep and abiding reverence for life, all life, and a great longing to get as close to the roots of it as she could. Her intellectual concerns as a writer and as an analyst were directed to that end, and so were her personal relationships.

What the mystic calls "union with God" Lou called "unity of being," and while the former tries to attain it through prayer and meditation, she sought it in love. The desire for "total union" was the propelling force of her love life. Her reverence for life made her the intimate of flowers and animals. The goal of her intellectual curiosity was to penetrate the phenomenal world. The feeling that she was indissolubly joined to all that exists in an "immense community of fate" had a controlling influence on the course of her life. It was responsible for both her audacity and her humility. For if you feel that you are nothing but an infinitesimal wavelet in the limitless sea of life, your pride gives way to submission; at the same time it fills you with a sense of daring for, no matter what you do, you know that you are borne up by the great surge of life which nothing, not even death, can destroy. It was this feeling that made Lou choose as her life's motto: "Dare everything—need nothing."

Her personal needs had never been extravagant and were modest indeed during her declining years. She no longer traveled, spent most of her time in her house, her garden, or in solitary walks in the woods, and ate her frugal vegetarian meals alone in her room. She had never taken part in the social life of Göttingen and the fragile link that had connected her with the university while her husband lived had been cut by his death. She was really alone now, a recluse and an outsider. She was almost a stranger in her own house, for with the people who lived on the ground floor, Mariechen and her husband, she had nothing in common.

As she worked on her memoirs the question of what would become of her literary estate, her books, her manuscripts, her letters, began to trouble her. There were Nietzsche's letters, for example, much sought after by friend and foe. She had jealously guarded them all these years, either in her bank safe or by depositing them with her nephew in Munich who, being the editor of *Simplizissimus*, seemed the most logical heir to her estate. But Hitler's rise to power had driven Schönberner into exile and there was nobody to advise her what to do with Nietzsche's letters. Would it be wise to have them published now that Nietzsche had become the patron saint of the Third Reich? She knew that Hitler had paid a personal visit to her arch-enemy, Elizabeth. Would it not draw unwelcome attention to herself if she permitted publication of Nietzsche's letters and of that famous Lucerne photo which showed the "Aryan" philosopher pulling a cart with a "Finnish Jewess" in it? For a long time she hesitated, and when she finally handed both letters and photograph to the young Nietzsche scholar, Erich Podach, she did so perhaps because she feared that unless they were published they might be destroyed after her death. She knew that Elizabeth Nietzsche, who had done everything in her power to discredit her during her lifetime, would not hesitate to destroy her brother's letters if they fell into her hands.

And what was to become of her voluminous correspondence

with Rilke? Should it revert to the poet's daughter Ruth, who, in collaboration with her husband, Dr. Carl Sieber, had established the Rilke Archives in Weimar? Lou did not cherish this thought either. She knew that her book on Rilke had not found favor with Rilke's relatives. They objected particularly to her statement that on his deathbed Rilke had said: "Ah, but the hells!" in which some Rilke commentators had seen a refutation of the poet's faith in life. In their eagerness to correct this impression and to present Rilke as an affirmer and "yea-sayer," Ruth and her husband forced Lou to make a public disavowal of what she had said in her book. On March 8, 1936, there appeared in the Nazi literary journal *Deutsche Zukunft* the following announcement:

Rilke did not use this expression at all but, as Frau Andreas writes us, it crept into her book "because it is connected with many memories of our conversations." It has nothing to do with a last word or anything like it. In order to prevent further misuse of this expression we wish to state this emphatically.

Little did Ruth or Dr. Sieber know that Lou had in her possession a letter, the last letter Rilke wrote her as he lay dying in Switzerland, which contains the identical phrase. For the sake of peace and because she did not want to become involved in yet another controversy, Lou submitted to this forced disavowal. But she was determined that Rilke's letters must not fall into the hands of his relatives.

At this final juncture of her life fate once more came to the rescue in the guise of two young men—young, that is, compared to her—who came seeking her help and who stayed to provide solace for her old age. Both of them are still alive. It is therefore premature to write a comprehensive account of their role in Lou's life. But it would be a serious omission to ignore them entirely. Their coming put the final touches on a pattern that had started with Lou's childhood, when she was the only girl in a company of brothers, and that had been repeated in various combinations all through her life.

One of her visitors, Josef König, at present a professor of philosophy at the University of Göttingen, need only receive brief mention. His visits gave Lou a chance to discuss those topics that had always interested her: the concept of Being, the problem of knowledge, the condition of man. Philosophical speculation had

been more than a pastime with her. It had been her lifelong occupation. And as she listened to this young man's account of the
trends in modern philosophy, the efforts to put man's individual
existence, rather than any rational system, into the center of
thought, she must have remembered Nietzsche and their impassioned talks, or Rée and his tragic fate, or her own early interest in Kierkegaard. There were new names now, Jaspers and
Heidegger, but they said nothing new to her. When they stressed
that anguish was the only means for man to attain an insight into
his authentic existence, she understood them perfectly. Had she
not been close to Nietzsche and Rilke, and had she not herself
experienced the anguish of creative insight? She agreed with
Jaspers that during such fleeting moments man senses the background of Being from which everything springs. Smilingly she
realized that she had lived what these modern philosophers
taught. In her book on Freud she had written:

"Human life—indeed all life—is poetry. We live it unconsciously
day by day, piece by piece, but in its inviolable wholeness it lives
us."

Nothing more need be said.

Deeper and more complex was Lou's relationship with Ernst
Pfeiffer, the closest friend of her old age. Pfeiffer, quiet and retiring, was in his early forties when, in 1933, he began to pay
regular visits to Lou. He was living in Göttingen to finish his
studies which had been interrupted by the first World War. A
product of that generation which has been called "lost," Pfeiffer
found it particularly difficult to adjust himself to life in postwar
Germany. He had been a Prussian officer, had served his country
with courage and distinction in the war, had been wounded
several times and was bitterly disillusioned by Germany's defeat.
Like Ernst Jünger, he belonged to those German idealists and
patriots who felt betrayed when the Weimar Republic was proclaimed. The myth that the German army had been "stabbed-in-
the-back" was not purely a Nazi invention. Many Germans who
never became Nazis believed it.

Seeking solace in the past for a present in which he felt ill at
ease, Pfeiffer chose as his literary hero the tragic Prussian playwright, Heinrich von Kleist, who had committed suicide in
despair over his country's defeat by Napoleon. Again Pfeiffer was

ot the only one who felt that there was a close historic parallel between the times in which Kleist had lived and his own. Many disillusioned Germans shared his views and revered Kleist as a martyr in the cause of their German fatherland. Neglected and forgotten for the better part of a hundred years, Kleist at long last found his rightful place in German literature. But even so, not many Germans would agree with Pfeiffer who holds that Kleist is the greatest writer Germany has produced, greater even than Goethe. Such a judgment shows personal affinity rather than critical perception. Pfeiffer's interest in Kleist probably reflects a personal need. Kleist expressed what Pfeiffer feels deeply: an ardent Prussian patriotism—"into the dust with all the foes of Brandenburg"—a deep sense of injustice suffered, an almost pathological confusion of feelings.

A man so constituted must have watched the rise of the Nazi movement with mixed emotions. On the one hand, he could not help but be moved by the rebirth of patriotism, especially among Germany's youth, which was so marked in the early thirties. On the other, he must surely have wondered about the aims of those who made use of it. Torn between acceptance and rejection of the new force in German life, Pfeiffer found it increasingly difficult to continue his studies. In the end, feeling perhaps that he needed help—he himself says that he had a friend who was mentally disturbed—Pfeiffer made his way up to the Hainberg. He was received with open arms.

Lou sensed at once that here was a human being lost in the confusion and turmoil of a world that offered him no place. She taught him how to relax, made him lie on her couch and encouraged him to tell her the story of his life. "She was such a quiet listener that I sometimes thought she had fallen asleep. But when I stopped and waited, her gentle voice, coming as from far away, said: 'Go on.'"

In these sessions that were carried on in the semi-darkness of her study, Lou may not have subjected Pfeiffer to a formal analysis, but she helped forge a link between herself and Pfeiffer very similar to that which is often established between the analyst and his patient. Transfer took place. By relating his life to Lou, Pfeiffer became more and more dependent on her. She gave him what he had been seeking in vain until he met her: a goal and a purpose in life.

A friendship of this kind is, of course, never a one-way street. If Pfeiffer needed Lou, she also needed him. Repaying his frankness with an equal frankness of her own, she told him the story of her life, read him chapters from her memoirs, asked him to edit them and, two and a half years before her death, made him a spontaneous present of her entire literary estate. It was a generous gesture but quite in keeping with her personality. She knew that nobody would take more loving care of her letters and manuscripts than this friend of her old age. She knew that he loved her and that he would continue to love her even after her death. And she was not mistaken.

During the last months of her life, when she was rapidly growing weaker as a result of uremic poisoning, Pfeiffer visited her almost daily. Like a faithful paladin he sat by her bedside, ministered to her needs and read to her from her memoirs. Sometimes she would interrupt him quietly and say: "Yes, that is how I would say it today, too." Once she looked up suddenly and said in a surprised tone of voice: "I have really done nothing but work all my life, work . . . why?" And then toward the end, her eyes closed and, as if talking to herself, she murmured: "If I let my thoughts roam I find no one. The best, after all, is death."

She died in her sleep in the evening of January 5, 1937. Only König and Pfeiffer accompanied her on her last journey from Göttingen to the crematorium in Hannover. She had asked that her ashes be scattered in her garden. That would have been a fitting finale to a life dedicated to the proposition that we return to the roots in the end. But it was not to be. A German law forbids the scattering of human ashes. They have to be preserved in an urn and interred in consecrated ground. This was done. The urn with Lou's ashes was buried in her husband's grave in the municipal cemetery of Göttingen. No memorial marks the spot. By a final twist of fate Lou was bound to Andreas even in death.

Appendices

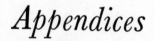

I

The Writings of Lou Andreas-Salomé

Books

1. *Im Kampf um Gott* (A Struggle for God) by Henri Lou, Leipzig-Berlin: W. Friedrich, 1885.

2. *Hendrik Ibsens Frauengestalten* (Women Characters in Ibsen), Jena: Eugen Diederichs, 1892.

3. *Friedrich Nietzsche in seinen Werken* (Frederick Nietzsche in His Works), Wien: Carl Conegen, 1894.

4. *Ruth,* Stuttgart: Cotta, 1895.

5. *Aus fremder Seele* (From a Troubled Soul), Stuttgart: Cotta, 1896.

6. *Fenitschka. Eine Ausschweifung* (Fenitschka. A Debauch), Stuttgart: Cotta, 1898.

7. *Menschenkinder* (Children of Men), Stuttgart-Berlin: Cotta, 1899.

8. *Ma* (Mom), Stuttgart-Berlin: Cotta, 1901.

9. *Im Zwischenland* (In the Twilight Zone), Stuttgart-Berlin: Cotta, 1902.

10. *Die Erotik* (Eroticism), Frankfurt/Main: Rütten & Loening, 1910.

11. *Drei Briefe an einen Knaben* (Three Letters to a Boy), Leipzig: Kurt Wolf, 1917.

12. *Das Haus* (The House), Berlin: Ullstein, 1919.

13. *Die Stunde ohne Gott, und andere Kindergeschichten* (The Hour Without God), Jena: Eugen Diederichs, 1922.

14. *Der Teufel und seine Grossmutter* (The Devil and His Grandmother), Jena: Eugen Diederichs, 1922.

15. *Rodinka*, Jena: Eugen Diederichs, 1923.

16. *Rainer Maria Rilke*, Leipzig: Insel, 1928.

17. *Mein Dank an Freud* (My Gratitude to Freud), Wien: Internationaler Psychoanalytischer Verlag, 1931.

18. *Lebensrückblick* (Memoirs), ed. Ernst Pfeiffer, Zurich: Max Niehans; Wiesbaden: Insel, 1951.

19. *Rainer Maria Rilke-Lou Andreas-Salomé Briefwechsel* (Rilke-Salomé Correspondence), ed. Ernst Pfeiffer, Zurich: Max Niehans; Wiesbaden: Insel, 1952.

20. *In der Schule bei Freud* (In Freud's School), ed. Ernst Pfeiffer, Zurich: Max Niehans, 1958.

Articles

1. "Die Wildente I," *Freie Bühne*, September 10, 1890.

2. "Die Wildente II," *ibid.*, September 17, 1890.

3. "Friedrich Nietzsche," *Vossische Zeitung*, Sonntag No. 2–4, 1891.

4. "Ein holländisches Urteil über moderne deutsche Dramen" (Sudermann und Holz), *Freie Bühne*, June 3, 1891.

5. "Ein holländisches Urteil über moderne deutsche Dramen" (Holz und Hauptmann), *ibid.*, June 10, 1891.

6. "Der Realismus in der Religion I," *ibid.*, October 14, 1891.

7. "Der Realismus in der Religion II," *ibid.*, October 21, 1891.

8. "Der Realismus in der Religion III," *ibid.*, November 4, 1891.

9. "Gottesschöpfung," *ibid.*, February, 1892.

10. "Zum Bilde Friedrich Nietzsches," *ibid.*, March, 1892.

11. "Zum Bilde Friedrich Nietzsches II," *ibid.*, May, 1892.

12. "Ein Apokalyptiker (Die Wiederkunftslehre Friedrich Nietzsches)," *Magazin für Literatur*, October, 1892.

13. "E. Mariot" (Emilia Mataja), Vossische Zeitung, Sonntag No. 31–34, 1892.

14. "C. Schubin" (Lola Kirchner), *ibid.*, Sonntag No. 2–3, 1892.

15. "Harnak und das Apostolikum," *Freie Bühne*, Vol. 3, 1892.

16. "Ideal und Askese," *Zeitgeist*, Berlin No. 20, 1893.

17. "Ibsen, Strindberg, Sudermann," *Freie Bühne*, Vol. 4, 1893.

18. "Die Duse," *ibid.*

19. "Hanna Jager, Ein Nachwort," *ibid.*

20. "Der Talisman," *ibid.*

21. "Ein Frühlingstraum," *ibid.*

22. "Hartlebens Erziehung zur Ehe," *ibid.*

23. "Hannele," *ibid.*

24. "Von der Bestie zu Gott," *Neue Deutsche Rundschau*, Vol. 5, 1894.

25. "Probleme des Islam," *Vossische Zeitung*, Sonntag No. 29–30, 1894.

26. "Vom Ursprung des Christentums," *ibid.*, No. 51, 1895.

27. "Winterlaub," *Die Frau*, April, 1895.

28. "Ricarda Huch: Erinnerungen von Ludolf Urslen dem Jüngern," *ibid.*, October, 1895.

29. "Kampfruf," *ibid.*, February, 1896.

30. "Jesus der Jude," *Neue Deutsche Rundschau*, Vol. 7, 1896.

31. "Skandinavische Literatur," *Cosmopolis*, Vol. 4, 1896.

32. "Abteilung: Innere Männer," *ibid.*, Vol. 5, 1897.

33. "Russische Dichtung und Kultur I," *ibid.*, August, 1897.

34. "Russische Dichtung und Kultur II," *ibid.*, September, 1897.

35. "Aus der Geschichte Gottes," *Neue Deutsche Rundschau*, December, 1897.

36. "Die russischen Heiligenbilder und ihr Dichter," *Vossische Zeitung*, Sonntag No. 2, 1898.

37. "Leo Tolstoi, unser Zeitgenosse," *Neue Deutsche Rundschau*, November, 1898.

38. "Russische Philosophie und semitischer Geist," *Die Zeit*, January 15, 1898.

39. "Religion und Kultur," *ibid.*, April 2, 1898.

40. "Vom religiösen Affekt," *Die Zukunft*, April 23, 1898.

41. "Missbrauchte Frauenkraft," *Die Frau*, June, 1898.

42. "Mädchenreigen," *Cosmopolis*, September, 1898.

43. "Physische Liebe," *Die Zukunft*, October 29, 1898.

44. "Adine Gemberg: Der dritte Bruder," *Das Literarische Echo*, November 1, 1898.

45. "S. Hochstetter: Sehnsucht, Schönheit, Dämmerung," *ibid.*, November 15, 1898.

46. "Thomas P. Krag: Die eherne Schlange," *ibid.*, January 1, 1899.

47. "Ein Wiedersehen," *Die Frau*, February, 1899.

48. "Grundformen der Kunst," *Pan*, February, 1899.

49. "Ketzereien gegen die moderne Frau," *Die Zukunft*, February 11, 1899.

50. "Vom Kunstaffekt," *ibid.*, May, 1899.

51. "Erleben," *Die Zeit*, August 19, 1899.

52. "Der Mensch als Weib (Ein Bild im Umriss)," *Neue Deutsche Rundschau*, Vol. 10, 1899.

53. "Ellen Key Essais," *Das Literarische Echo*, October 1, 1899.

54. "Friedrich Nietzsche i hans Voerker," *Samtiden*, November–December, 1899.

55. "Russische Geschichten," *Die Zeit*, December 9, 1899.

56. "Zurück ans All," *Die Romanwelt*, Vol. 1, 1899.

57. "Zurück ans All," *ibid.*, Vol. 2.

58. "Zurück ans All," *ibid.*, Vol. 3.

59. "Der Egoismus in der Religion," (in Arthur Dix, *Der Egoismus*, 385 ff.) 1899.

60. "Wilhelm Bölsche: Vom Bazillus zum Affenmenschen," *Das Literarische Echo*, January 15, 1900.

61. "Die Schwester," *Die Romanwelt*, October 27, 1900.

62. "Gedanken über das Liebesproblem," *Neue Deutsche Rundschau*, Vol. 11, 1900.

63. "Zur Würdigung des 'Michael Kramer,'" *Der Lotse,* Hamburg, Vol. 1, 1901.

64. "Alter und Ewigkeit," *Die Zukunft,* October 26, 1901.

65. "An den Kaiser," *Die Gesellschaft,* June, 1901.

66. "Der Graf von Charolais," *Die Zukunft,* Vol. 50, 1905.

67. "Das Glashüttenmännchen," *ibid.,* Vol. 54, 1906.

68. "Frühlingserwachen," *ibid.,* Vol. 58, 1907.

69. "Vier Kammerspiele," *Die Schaubühne,* February 20, 27 & March 5, 1908.

70. "Lebende Dichtung," *Die Zukunft,* February 22, 1908.

71. "Die Russen," *Die Schaubühne,* September 23, 1909.

72. "Der Lebensbund," *Die Neue Generation,* October, 1910.

73. "Das Kindlein von Erika Rhenisch," *Das Literarische Echo,* September 15, 1911.

74. "Im Spiegel," *ibid.,* October 15, 1911.

75. "Eine Nacht," *Geistiges Leben,* May, 1912.

76. "Marie Luise Enkendorff: Realität und Gesetzlichkeit im Geschlechtsleben," *Das Literarische Echo,* September 1, 1912.

77. "Elisabeth Siewert," *ibid.,* September 15, 1912.

78. "Von Paul zu Pedro," *Die Neue Generation,* October, 1912.

79. "Vom Kunstaffekt," *Deutsche Monatsschrift für Russen,* July, 1912.

80. "Aus dem Briefwechsel Leo Tolstois," *Das Literarische Echo,* October, 1913.

81. "Vom frühen Gottesdienst," *Imago,* Vol. II, No. 5, 1913.

82. "Zum Typus Weib," *ibid.,* Vol. III, No. 1, 1914.

83. "Kind und Kunst," *Das Literarische Echo,* October 1, 1914.

84. "Seelchen, eine Weihnachtsgeschichte," *Velhagen und Klasings Monatshefte,* Vol. 28, 1914.

85. "Seelchen, eine Ostergeschichte," *ibid.*

86. "Das Bündnis zwischen Tor und Ur," *ibid.*

87. "Zum Bilde Strindbergs," *Das Literarische Echo,* March 1, 1915.

88. "Bericht über einen Weihnachstmann," *Velhagen und Klasings Monatshefte,* Vol. 29, 1915.

89. "Anal und Sexual," *Imago*, Vol. IV, No. 5, 1915.

90. "Angela Langer," *Das Literarische Echo*, Vol. 19, 1916.

91. "Expression," *ibid.*, April 1, 1917.

92. "Psychosexualität," *Zeitschrift für Sexualwissenschaft*, April–June, 1917.

93. "Luzifer: Eine Phantasie über Ricarda Huchs Buch 'Luthers Glaube,'" *Die Neue Generation*, May, 1917.

94. "Nadja Strassers Russin," *Die Neue Rundschau*, August, 1917.

95. "Die Psychosexualität," *Das Literarische Echo*, September 1, 1917.

96. "Karl Nötzel's Tolstoi," *ibid.*, August 1, 1918.

97. "Dichterischer Ausdruck," *ibid.*, December 15, 1918.

98. "Der russische Intelligent," *Die Neue Rundschau*, January, 1919.

99. "Leopold von Wiese: Strindberg," *Das Literarische Echo*, March 1, 1919.

100. "Des Dichters Erleben," *Die Neue Rundschau*, March, 1919.

101. "Der geistliche Russe," *Der Neue Merkur*, November, 1919.

102. "Agnes Hennigsen," *Das Literarische Echo*, January 15, 1920.

103. "Nikolaus Leskow: Die Kleriserei," *ibid.*, April 15, 1920.

104. "Isolde Kurz: Im Traumland," *ibid.*, May 15, 1920.

105. "Unser Anteil an Dostoevski und Tolstoi," *Vossische Zeitung*, July 23, 1920.

106. "Kurt Engelbrecht: Dieckmanns Denkwürdigkeiten und Erinnerungsbücherei, Vol. I, Die Liebe," *Das Literarische Echo*, August 1, 1920.

107. "Tagebuch eines halbwüchsigen Mädchens," *ibid.*, September 1, 1920.

108. "Waldemar Bonsels," *ibid.*, October 1, 1920.

109. "Michael Saltykow-Schtschedrin: Satiren," *ibid.*, November 1, 1920.

110. "Gustav Landauer: Der werdende Mensch," *ibid.*, December 1, 1921.

111. "Russische Romantik," *Romantik*, Vol. 5/6, 1921.

112. "Narzissmus als Doppelrichtung," *Imago*, Vol. VII, No. 4, 1921.

113. "Die Geschwister," *Deutsche Rundschau,* Vol. 189, 1921.

114. "Tendenz und Form russischer Dichtung," *Das Literarische Echo,* January 1, 1922.

115. "Eros," *Faust,* Berlin, Vol. 1, 1923.

116. "Zum 6. Mai 1926 (Freuds 70. Geburtstag)," *Almanach des psychoanalytischen Verlegers,* Wien, 1927.

117. "Was daraus folgt, dass man nicht die Frau geworden ist, die den Vater totgeschlagen hat," *ibid.,* 1928.

118. "Rilke und Russland," *Russische Blätter,* No. I, October, 1928.

119. "Der Kranke hat immer recht," *Almanach des psychoanalytischen Verlegers,* Wien, 1933.

Unpublished MSS

1. *Die Russlandreise* (A Russian Diary), 1900.

2. *Der Stiefvater,* a play in three acts, 1925–1930.

3. *Die Tarnkappe,* a fairytale play, (no date).

4. *Jutta,* a novel begun 1921.

II

Notes

The source of quotations based on information obtained through personal interviews is not given.

Preface

Page

4   wherever Lou went   Dieter Bassermann, Review of LAS *Lebensrückblick*, *Neue Schweizer Rundschau*, May, 1952; 55.

4   she walks through life   Helene Klingenberg, *Lou Andreas-Salomé*, *Deutsche Monatsschrift für Russland*, 1912; 237.

Chapter 1 *The Salomés of St. Petersburg*

27	sons and grandsons	Rilke-Salomé Correspondence, 240.
32	I remember	LAS, *Lebensrückblick*, 59.
32	Nitschewó	*ibid.*, 59.
34	you see	*ibid.*, 53.
34	now I am	*ibid.*, 52.
34	the most accomplished	*ibid.*, 52.
35	aroused the maddest passions	*ibid.*, 53.
36	she was a gentle	*ibid.*, 75.

Chapter 2 *Between Day and Dream*

39	in my memory	*ibid.*, 54.
39	disturbed	*ibid.*, 14.
42	we stared at each other	*ibid.*, 75.
42	it was hardly possible	*ibid.*, 76.
43	life will treat you	*ibid.*, 68.
43	have you ever seen	LAS, *Im Zwischenland*, 51.

Page

44	others regarded it	Leroy-Beaulieu, *The Empire of the Tsars and the Russians*, Part I, "The Country and Its Inhabitants," New York: Putnam, 1905; 212.
45	what other country	*ibid.*, 212.
45	this frequent cohabitation	*ibid.*, note, 211.
46	why is it	LAS, *Rodinka*, 218.
46	Europe has no mysteries	Gertrud Bäumer, *Gestalt und Wandel, Frauenbildnisse*, Berlin-Grunewald: F. H. Herbig, 1939; 484.

Chapter 3 *God and Gillot*

49	in our German home	LAS, *Rodinka*, 18.
49	oh, yes, there was	LAS, *Lebensrückblick*, 288.
52	now my solitude	*ibid.*, 289.
52	a living being	*ibid.*, 32.
54	slightly ill-humored	*ibid.*, 35.
55	I am surprised	*ibid.*, 289 f.
56	to do anything wrong	*ibid.*, 289.
57	my persistent childlikeness	*ibid.*, 33.
58	as they sat together	LAS, *Ruth*, 167.
58	slowly Ruth	*ibid.*, 326.
59	what did she matter	*ibid.*, 328.
59	a voluptuous harlot	*ibid.*, 230.
60	Zurich in Switzerland	Leroy-Beaulieu, *op. cit.*, 220.
61	fear not	LAS, *Lebensrückblick*, 291.

Chapter 4 *From St. Petersburg to Rome via Zurich*

66	your daughter	*ibid.*, 312.
68	assuredly, a friend	*ibid.*, 47.
69	Russia	*Memoirs of Malwida von Meysenbug: Rebel in Bombazine*, New York: Norton, 1936; 159.
71	a little woman	*ibid.*, Foreword.
72	the atom of carbon	*ibid.*, 177.
72	away from the great	*ibid.*, 178.
72	it is long since	Erich Podach, *Friedrich Nietzsche und Lou Salomé: Ihre Begegnung 1882*, Zurich: Max Niehans, 1937; 135.
73	it happened in Rome	LAS, *Lebensrückblick*, 93.
74	I have often observed	*ibid.*, 301.
74	our ideas of good	Paul Rée, *Philosophie* (Nachgelassenes Werk), Berlin: Carl Duncker, 1903; 11.
74	our body is nothing	*ibid.*, 130.
77	imagine my pained	Podach, *Nietzsche und Salomé, op. cit.*, 135 f.

Chapter 5 *Sowing the Wind*

84	into the small	Stefan Zweig, *Baumeister der Welt*, Wien, Leipzig, Zurich: Herbert Reichner, 1936; 332.
86	greet this young Russian	Friedrich Nietzsche, *Werke in 3 Bänden*, ed. Karl Schlechta, Munich: Hanser, 1956; III, 1179.

Page

88   spoke Columbus   Friedrich Nietzsche, *Werke*, Taschen-ausgabe, Leipzig: Kröner, 1922; VI, 410.

89   this Messina   *Nietzsche's Briefwechsel mit Overbeck*, Leipzig: Insel, 1916; 171.

89   while beauty in my face   Nietzsche, *The Joyful Wisdom* ("La Gaya Scienza"), trans. Thomas Common, Edinburgh & London: T. N. Foulis, 1910; 362.

89   here I lie   Nietzsche, *Werke, op. cit.*, VI, 381.
90   but perhaps   *Friedrich Nietzsche's Briefe an Peter Gast*, Leipzig: Insel, 1924; 91.

90   nobody   LAS, *Lebensrückblick*, 305.
91   what in the devil's   *ibid.*, 96.
92   from which stars   *ibid.*, 99.
93   the first strong   LAS, *Friedrich Nietzsche in seinen Werken*, 11 f.

94   my dear sister   *Friedrich Nietzsche's Briefe an Mutter und Schwester*, Leipzig: Insel, 1926; 308 f.

Chapter 6 *The Mystery of Monte Sacro*

99   it seems that I offended   LAS, *Lebensrückblick*, 100.
99   whether I kissed   *ibid.*, 308.
100   I owe to you   *ibid.*, 307.
100   the Lou of Orta   *Nietzsche Archiv*, N. V, 8; 35.
103   I have suffered   A. Baeumler, ed. *Nietzsche in seinen Briefen und Berichten der Zeitgenossen*, Leipzig: Kröner, 1932; 268.

Chapter 7 *The Tautenburg Idyll*

105   I was too excited   C. A. Bernoulli, *Franz Overbeck und Friedrich Nietzsche: Eine Freundschaft*, Jena: Diederichs, 1908; I; 337.

106   it has been a strange   Nietzsche an Gast, *op. cit.*, 87.
107   I am genuinely happy   Podach, *Nietzsche und Salomé, op. cit.*, 137.

107   as firmly as anything   Baeumler, *op. cit.*, 263 f.
108   you cannot possibly   Podach, *Nietzsche und Salomé, op. cit.*, 138.

109   as regards my sister   *Nietzsche's Briefwechsel mit Overbeck, op. cit.*, 173.

109   my dear friend   Schlechta, *op. cit.*, III; 1182.
110   Now, my dear friend   Baeumler, *op. cit.*, 267 f.
111   that poem   Nietzsche an Gast, *op. cit.*, 89
112   and, indeed   E. Newman, *The Life of Richard Wagner*, New York: Knopf, 1946, Vol. IV; 612.

117   don't get the idea   Erich Podach, *Neue Deutsche Rundschau*, April, 1958; 364 f.

119   Nietzsche, on the whole   Podach, *Nietzsche und Salomé, op. cit.*, 141 f.

121   if somebody had listened   *ibid.*, 144.

Page

121	are we really close	*ibid.*, 144 f.
122	one day a bird	Nietzsche an Gast, *op. cit.*, 93.
122	I have had to pass	*ibid.*, 94.
122	Lou is staying	*ibid.*, 95.
123	the basically religious	Podach, *Nietzsche und Salomé, op. cit.*, 144.
124	while no road leads	LAS, *Im Kampf um Gott*, 130.
125	all love is tragic	*ibid.*, 176.

Chapter 8   *Reunion and Farewell*

127	for the rest	Schlechta, *op. cit.*, III; 1188.
127	the weeks in	Nietzsche's Briefwechsel mit Overbeck, *op. cit.*, 175 f.
129	that would be only one	Schlechta, *op. cit.*, III; 1189.
129	I have never had	Nietzsche's Briefwechsel mit Overbeck, *op. cit.*, 178.
129	Ah, my friend	Nietzsche an Gast, *op. cit.*, 99.
131	for intellect	Baeumler, *op. cit.*, 268.
131	a span of time	LAS, *Im Kampf um Gott*, 88.
133	just as Christian	LAS, *Lebensrückblick*, 315 f.
133	courage	Josef Hofmiller, "Nietzsche," *Süddeutsche Monatshefte*, II, November, 1931; 104.

Chapter 9   *The Birth of Zarathustra*

134	Lou's health	Nietzsche's Briefwechsel mit Overbeck, *op. cit.*, 178.
135	if only I could	*ibid.*, 184.
135	poisonous vermin	*Nietzsche Archiv*, N. VI, I; 59 f.
136	please don't write	*ibid.*, 80.
136	I do not reproach	*ibid.*, 83 f, 86.
136	watch out	*ibid.*, 106 f.
136	I have not created	*ibid.*, M. III, 3; 18 f.
136	farewell, my dear	*ibid.*, N. VI, 1; 120.
137	my dears, Lou and Rée	Schlechta, *op. cit.*, III; 1196.
137	dying a painful death	Nietzsche's Briefwechsel mit Overbeck, *op. cit.*, 185.
138	either he marries	Podach, *Nietzsche und Salomé, op. cit.*, 73.
138	it was during	LAS, *Lebensrückblick*, 318.
138	every other man	Podach, *Nietzsche und Salomé, op. cit.*, 157.
141	pregnancy	*ibid.*, 151.
142	in spite of	Bernoulli, *op. cit.*, I; 338.
142	for some time	Hofmiller, *op. cit.*, 107.
142	you may say what	*ibid.*, 104.
144	I have endured	Bernoulli, *op. cit.*, I; 339.
145	my sister is	*ibid.*, 341.
145	it is he who	Podach, *Nietzsche und Salomé, op. cit.*, 87.
146	since this affair	Nietzsche's Briefe an Mutter und Schwester, *op. cit.*, 325.
146	it is released in us	LAS, *Im Kampf um Gott*, 306.

Chapter 10   *"Brother" Rée*
Page

154	I must confess	LAS, *Lebensrückblick*, 326.
159	I lost God	LAS, *Im Kampf um Gott*, 23.
159	could there be	*ibid.*, 28.
159	the highest means	*ibid.*, 307.
161	breaking out	*ibid.*, 62.
161	passions that	*ibid.*, 77.
161	you must know	*ibid.*, 83.
162	not I seduced	*ibid.*, 138.
162	into the loneliest	*ibid.*, 140.
162	the Christian	*ibid.*, 151.
163	she does not want	*ibid.*, 247.
163	Lord Jesus	*ibid.*, 286.
163	death would mean	*ibid.*, 303.
163	the grave is not	*ibid.*, 308.
163	I have found no peace	*ibid.*, 313.
165	the matter itself	Bernoulli, *op. cit.*, II; 97.
165	all men are equal	Rée, *Philosophie*, *op. cit.*, 195.
166	he left late	LAS, *Lebensrückblick*, 114 f.
167	I found myself	*ibid.*, 115.

Chapter 11   *Andreas*

171	a work of such clarity	H. Lommel, *Erinnerungen an Friedrich Carl Andreas und Lou Andreas-Salomé*, 7 (unpubl.).
172	resembling	LAS, *Lebensrückblick*, 248.
174	later it often	*ibid.*, 260.
175	I could not stop	*ibid.*, 268.
177	in his bright study	Lommel, *op. cit.*, 3.

Chapter 12   *The Road to Freedom*

180	once upon a time	LAS, *Hendrik Ibsens Frauengestalten*, 3.
182	for understanding and love	*ibid.*, 135.
182	in both cases	*ibid.*, 141.
183	two people equally	LAS, *Lebensrückblick*, 260.
184	once in a moving hour	*ibid.*, 268.
185	resurrection	Ernst Seiffarth, *Freie Bühne*, Vol. 2, 1891; 165 f.
186	excessive emphasis	Theodor Heuss, *Lou Andreas-Salomé*, *Der Kunstwart*, January, 1908; 12.
187	those types	LAS, "Vom Kunstaffekt," *Die Zukunft*, Vol. 27, May, 1899; 396.
187	you must let me	LAS, *Lebensrückblick*, 333.
189	as a student	LAS, "Ein holländisches Urteil über moderne deutsche Dramen," *Freie Bühne*, Vol. 2, 1891; 671.

Chapter 13   *The Emancipation of the Flesh*

| 192 | a woman does not | Ilonka Schmidt Mackey, *Lou Salomé*, Paris: Librairie A. G. Nizet, 1956; 180. |
| 195 | the good blessed bread | LAS, *Fenitschka*, 40. |

Page

195	how often	*ibid.,* 45.
195	our lives depend	*ibid.,* 102.
196	I watched	*ibid.,* 103.
196	a giant	LAS, *Lebensrückblick,* 128.
196	or was it	LAS, *Lebensrückblick,* 129.
198	certainly	LAS, "Ketzereien gegen die moderne Frau," *Die Zukunft,* Vol. 26, February, 1899; 237 f.
198	the insane fascination	LAS, *Das Haus,* 80.
198	wasting her most	LAS, *Lebensrückblick,* 344.
199	psychologically most	*ibid.,* 345.
199	extreme readiness	Helene Klingenberg, *op. cit.,* 237.

Chapter 14 *My Sister, My Spouse*

206	the gigantic force	Rilke-Salomé Correspondence, 9.
206	I felt like one	*ibid.,* 9 f.
206	for if one owes	*ibid.,* 10.
207	famous Lou	*ibid.,* 508.
207	with a few roses	*ibid.,* 12.
208	I was your wife	LAS, *Lebensrückblick,* 173.
209	dreams seem to me	Rainer Maria Rilke, *Erste Gedichte,* Leipzig, Insel, 1928; 57.
210	I felt it then	Rilke-Salomé Correspondence, 119.
211	even at the last	LAS, *Jesus der Jude,* 349 f.
212	amidst the triumphant	*ibid.,* 351.
212	I have many reasons	RMR, *Sämtliche Werke,* Wiesbaden: Insel, 1959, III; 790.
212	unfortunately I have	Rilke-Salomé Correspondence, 258.
213	perhaps the visions	*ibid.,* 300.
213	in tone	*ibid.,* 301.
214	the waxen God	RMR, *Sämtliche Werke, op. cit.,* III; 146.
214	I have looked	Rilke-Salomé Correspondence, 14.
215	then I do not see	*ibid.,* 21.
215	I want to be you	*ibid.,* 23.
216	with gentle blessing	LAS, *Lebensrückblick,* 176.
217	the land is bright	RMR, *Sämtliche Werke, op. cit.,* III; 177.

Chapter 15 *God in Russia*

221	when we have children	*ibid.,* 591.
222	whether I am already	RMR, *Tagebücher aus der Frühzeit,* Leipzig: Insel, 1942; 18.
222	but once you have	*ibid.,* 26.
222	believe me, beloved	RMR, *Sämtliche Werke, op. cit.,* III; 617.
222	maidens are like	*ibid.,* I; 172.
222	let something happen	*ibid.,* I; 243.
223	today a mother	RMR, *Tagebücher aus der Frühzeit, op. cit.,* 74.
223	the artist's effort	*ibid.,* 118.
223	a woman's way	*ibid.,* 119.
223	after a few days	*ibid.,* 87.
224	there is no anxiety	*ibid.,* 87.
224	even now	*ibid.,* 89.

Page
224   no, and I was   *ibid.*, 91.
224   I am ashamed   *ibid.*, 91.
224   a glow-worm   *ibid.*, 92.
224   I wish very much   *ibid.*, 114.
225   you magnificent one   *ibid.*, 117.
225   I did not want   *ibid.*, 136.
225   I felt so miserable   *ibid.*, 137.
225   be always ahead of me   *ibid.*, 138 f.
227   I have experienced   Rilke-Salomé Correspondence, 139 f.
229   Russian songs   E. M. Butler, *Rainer Maria Rilke*,
                                 Cambridge, England: Cambridge Uni-
                                 versity Press, 1941; 95.

230   put out my eyes   RMR, *Sämtliche Werke, op. cit.*, I;
                                 313 (trans. B. Deutsch, *Poems from
                                 the Book of Hours*, New York: New
                                 Directions, 1941; 39).

231   I have seen   RMR, *Briefe und Tagebücher aus der
                                 Frühzeit*, Leipzig: Insel, 1933; 420.
231   I hardly know   RMR, *Sämtliche Werke, op. cit.*, III;
                                 660.
232   the deep epitome   *ibid.*, I; 327 (Deutsch, *op. cit.*, 37).

Chapter 16   *Tragic Guilt*

237   on a warm summer   Boris Pasternak, *Gedichte. Erzählun-
                                 gen. Sicheres Geleit*, Frankfurt:
                                 Fischer, 1959; 117.
238   excited voices   RMR, *Tagebücher aus der Frühzeit,
                                 op. cit.*, 282.
239   even today   Sophie Brutzer, *Rilkes Russische
                                 Reisen*, Stallupönen: Klutke, 1934;
                                 140 f.
241   though you be far   LAS, *Lebensrückblick*, 90.
242   it seemed wrong   RMR, *Tagebücher aus der Frühzeit,
                                 op. cit.*, 233 f.
242   I have ignored   *ibid.*, 234.
242   if I can learn   *ibid.*, 315.
243   I will not gloss over   LAS, *Lebensrückblick*, 183 f.
246   I have your letter   Rilke-Salomé Correspondence, 37.
246   perhaps it was wrong   *ibid.*, 38 f.
246   come back to me   *ibid.*, 39.
246   you have no idea   *ibid.*, 39.
248   every home is   RMR, *Briefe und Tagebücher aus der
                                 Frühzeit, op. cit.*, 54.
248   I am waiting   *ibid.*, 266.
249   please, dear friend   *ibid.*, 93.
250   but then   Rilke-Salomé Correspondence, 42
251   as one will hold   RMR, *Sämtliche Werke, op. cit.*, II;
                                 39 (trans. J. B. Leishman, *RMR
                                 Poems 1906–26*, London: The Ho-
                                 garth Press, 1957; 127).

Chapter 17   *Waiting for Freud*

256   I could not get over it   LAS, *Lebensrückblick*, 331 f.
257   how radiantly happy   LAS to Broncia (Pineles) Koller

Page

		Schmargendorff, November 22, 1896 (unpubl.).
257	I have had	*ibid.*, November, 1898 (unpubl.).
259	the most moving event	LAS, *In der Schule bei Freud*, 286.
260	life is not	LAS, *Im Zwischenland*, 249.
260	where is Mascha	*ibid.*, 328, 331.
261	the natural love life	LAS, *Die Erotik*, 14.
262	if two people are	*ibid.*, 59.
264	it stands	Rilke-Salomé Correspondence, 118.
266	you were so near	*ibid.*, 175.

Chapter 18   *Exorcising Devils*

268	one must remember	LAS, *Narzissmus als Doppelrichtung*, 366.
269	while they passed by	LAS, *Im Spiegel*, 87 f.
270	only by following you	LAS, *Mein Dank an Freud*, 109.
272	like a typical	LAS, *In der Schule bei Freud*, 149 f.
273	a conquistador	Ernest Jones, *The Life and Work of Sigmund Freud*, ed. and abridged by Lionel Trilling and Steven Marcus, New York: Basic Books, 1961; 227.
274	since I was permitted	LAS, *In der Schule bei Freud*, 11.
275	the sexual flourish	*ibid.*, 14.
277	no, no, Freud said	*ibid.*, 261.
280	I felt from the beginning	*ibid.*, 189.
280	even if it is only	*ibid.*, 103.
281	a woman in love	*ibid.*, 133.
281	poor Tausk	*ibid.*, 232.
282	I can scarcely express	Rilke-Salomé Correspondence, 377.
282	we are all	*ibid.*, 379.
286	God has long since	LAS, *Der Teufel und seine Grossmutter*, 44.
287	who can decide	Rilke-Salomé Correspondence, 484.
288	and then something	LAS, *Lebensrückblick*, 213.
288	a genuine synthesis	LAS, *Lebensrückblick*, 360.
289	I often think	Rilke-Salomé Correspondence, 368 f.

Chapter 19   *The Sybil of the Hainberg*

293	I must still mention	Viktor von Weizsäcker, *Natur und Geist: Erinnerungen eines Arztes*, Göttingen: Vandenhoeck & Ruprecht, 1955; 186.
294	just now	LAS, *Lebensrückblick*, 9.
298	human life	LAS, *Mein Dank an Freud*, 14.
300	yes, that is how I would say it	LAS, *Lebensrückblick*, 386.

Index

498%